CORPORATE PLANNING

CORPORATE PLANNING
A Systems View

Lloyd R. Amey

PRAEGER

New York
Westport, Connecticut
London

Library of Congress Cataloging-in-Publication Data

Amey, Lloyd R.
   Corporate planning.

   "Praeger special studies. Praeger scientific."
   Bibliography: p.
   Includes index.
   1. Corporate planning.   I. Title.
HD30.28.A44   1986   658.4′ 012   86-8110
ISBN 0-275-92077-1 (alk. paper)

Library of Congress Catalog Card Number: 86-8110
ISBN: 0-275-92077-1

First published in 1986

Praeger Publishers, 521 Fifth Avenue, New York, NY 10175
A division of Greenwood Press, Inc.

Printed in the United States of America

♾™

The paper used in this book complies with the Permanent
Paper Standard issued by the National Information Standards
Organization (Z39.48-1984).

10 9 8 7 6 5 4 3 2 1

Preface

The study of organizations, and of how people behave in organizations, has responded very unevenly to the advent of systems thinking. While many organization theorists and some social psychologists and sociologists now view organizations as open systems, this has not been the case in other related disciplines. In accounting, and to a lesser extent economics, organizations (whether private or governmental enterprises or economies) continue to be discussed in a closed-systems framework, which is entirely inappropriate. The terms *open system* and *closed system* are defined in Chapter 1 and in the Appendix at the end of the book.

This book represents a step toward redressing that situation by looking at organizational planning within an open-systems framework. Although the main focus is on planning by private business enterprises, much of the discussion carries over, with little modification, to public enterprises and national economies.

The main message is that conventional planning, which in many quarters has come to be held in disrepute, is bound to fail more often than not because of its essentially closed-system basis. Viewing organizations as open systems is likely to lead to better planning, which is not to say that such planning is a guarantee against failure. Indeed, from an open-systems viewpoint it is hard to see how planning can be dispensed with; it assumes the role of a crucial management function, carrying the main burden of continuously adapting the organization to its changing environment. Failure to adapt effectively puts the organization's survival in jeopardy.

This message is not new, having been espoused most insistently by Russell Ackoff. What is new about this book is (1) an attempt to formalize these ideas in a systems model of the firm and to describe the role of planning in terms of this model; (2) to explain fairly precisely the meaning of *system* and what is to be gained by following a systems approach; and (3) to examine carefully all of the main arguments advanced against planning.

The book is intended particularly for students of accounting in MBA programs. It is hoped that it will also be of interest to professional accountants working in industry. Most MBA programs, in North America at least, offer a second-level management accounting course on control. As narrowly viewed in accounting, *control* means financial control, and this is usually exercised in relation to a plan (budget). So planning and control in this sense are interrelated. Yet in these courses there is, characteristically, precious little discussion of planning. If planning in practice is often a dis-

v

mal failure, where does that leave control and performance evaluation? Some discussion of planning at a more fundamental level in accounting courses therefore seems to be called for, unless we should agree that control be exercised in relation to something other than a plan, or even to dispense with planning altogether.

While the book proposes a systems approach to planning, no previous knowledge of systems is assumed. Such prerequisites as are required of readers (introductory-level microeconomic theory, calculus, matrix algebra, and elementary set theory) are possessed by MBA students. The sections containing mathematics are a small part of the whole, and may be skipped by other readers without loss of continuity.

An overview of the contents should begin by pointing out that at the beginning of Chapter 1 the reader is strongly urged to read a lengthy and somewhat abstract Appendix at the end of the book on systems and the systems approach. It is realized that this is expecting the reader to take a lot on trust, but it is believed that the payoff will justify the effort, and not only for the immediate purposes of this book. The material contained in this Appendix should also influence students' thinking about the other elements of management accounting: decision making, control, and performance evaluation. The subtitle of the book is *A Systems View,* and an open system perspective is central to the argument throughout. The Appendix makes the work self-contained in this respect, and should persuade the reader of the gain in explanatory power afforded by following a (open) systems approach. Since firms and business planning are being viewed in a framework entirely different from that to which accounting students are accustomed, a superficial discussion of systems simply will not do.

Chapters 1 through 5 contain a review of existing work on planning. Chapter 1 seeks to establish the case for planning on systems grounds: namely, that a business enterprise is an open system that must adapt in order to survive. Planning along systems lines is seen as the main instrument for adapting the firm. Other subsidiary reasons why it may be necessary to plan are briefly discussed.

Chapter 2 contrasts the conventional "how to get there" planning with the new "where should we go?" planning, noting what the latter entails for the design of the firm's information system and organizational structure. Chapter 3 looks at the hierarchy of aims that business planning should seek to fulfill, ranging from basic purposes through missions to long-range objectives and short-range goals. It discusses how conflicts may arise over aims, whether they need to be resolved, and if so how. Chapter 4 considers planning and plans along several different dimensions. The new (systemic) planning is shown as having, in addition to the usual strategic and tactical levels, a third level variously called *normative planning* or the premises on which the other two levels are based. Other dimensions of planning or plans discussed in this chapter include duration, flexibility, frequency, and whether plans are static or dynamic.

Chapter 5 asks whether it is useful to model the planning process, and proceeds to review a number of planning models that have one characteristic in common, namely that they are all in some degree nonsystemic. This review is prefaced by a discussion of what "cost" should mean in different types of planning models. The principle of classification adopted in reviewing existing types of planning models was their scope, the size of the decision space to which they refer. What are referred to as "global" models span the entire decision space of normative, strategic, and tactical levels of planning or at least the last two, while "partial" models relate only to tactical planning or to some even narrower decision space. The disproportionate treatment of input-output analysis may strike the reader as ill-advised, particularly as this is rarely used by North American firms as a planning tool. The justification for doing so is that this model has frequently been featured in the accounting literature. The chapter ends by examining the implicit or explicit systems logic underlying conventional accounting budget models, exposing the weakness of current practice from a systems point of view.

The remaining chapters, 6 through 8, represent the main claim to an original contribution. Chapter 6, the key chapter in this section, formalizes a number of ideas about business behavior from a systems viewpoint by adumbrating a systems model of the firm and describing the role of the new systemic planning in terms of this model. This is the first known attempt to develop a theory of the firm regarded as an open system. Some of the ideas contained in the model were found to link up with earlier work by Herbert A. Simon.

The objective of the firm regarded as an open system is taken to be long-term survival through continuous adaptation, the firm's survival prospects being measured in terms of a probability. Planning within this framework becomes a dynamic process that must bear the brunt of selectively adapting the firm to its environment for long-term survival. To be operational the systems model, and with it systemic planning, awaits a means of making the objective of long-term survival formally well defined. Under this objective organizational structure emerges as a key variable, and an appendix to the chapter examines the only known formal attempt at answering the question: What characteristics would the organization structure offering the greatest probability of long-term survival possess?

Following this largely unqualified espousal of the necessity of adopting a systems approach to planning, Chapters 7 and 8 look at the other side of the coin, seeking to redress the balance by trying to refute the case in the spirit of scientific inquiry.

For the intended audience, *Chapter 7 may be omitted without losing the thread of the discussion on planning.* The question raised here is whether a systems approach is always appropriate, provided that the subject of discourse is a system. The main aspects of systems—interrelatedness of parts, and system structure as defined in the Appendix on systems— are seen as calling for a holistic approach, which is the very antithesis of piecemeal problem solving. One discipline, economics, was examined to see the relative use it makes of these two modes of problem solving. In the whole of economics there are only two cases, general equilibrium analysis and welfare economics, where the economy is treated holistically and at the same time in sufficient detail to permit analysis of the behavior of its parts. Do these two branches of economics follow a systems approach? In its fullest development the general equilibrium model was found to be less than fully equivalent to a systems approach. In the even more abstract welfare economics, however, two cases were identified where a systems approach is redundant and a piecemeal approach is valid.

The final chapter catalogues the main criticisms of planning and attempts to answer them. Many of these criticisms are directed at conventional planning and hence may be dismissed if we believe conventional planning is misconceived. Arguments calling for more serious consideration are that planning is futile because large organizations (including firms) are too complex to be understood; that planning is useless because the world has become too uncertain; and that the benefits of planning, in particular systemic planning, may not justify the costs. These arguments are carefully examined. The last cannot be answered because the evidence is not yet in.

My indebtedness to other scholars is considerable, as the references will attest. The main influencers were Russell L. Ackoff, Stafford Beer, George A. Steiner, the late Ludwig von Bertalanffy, the late W. Ross Ashby, Walter Buckley, Jay Forrester, Herbert A. Simon, Richard M. Cyert, James G. March, Fred E. Emery, and Mario Bunge. To all of them I gratefully acknowledge my indebtedness and of course absolve them from responsibility for any errors of interpretation. I also thank my colleague G. Alex Whitmore for his help in formalizing the systems model of the firm.

My one-time research assistant Robert Blohm read many of the chapters in draft and made some useful suggestions, and Miss Louise Galley typed several drafts of the entire manuscript. To them I express my thanks.

Contents

List of Tables and Figures

TABLES

FIGURES

1
The Need for Planning

Planning has been described as the designing of a desired future and of effective ways of bringing it about. It can also be described as anticipatory decision making, a process of deciding what to do, when and how to do it, in advance of the time when decisions have to be taken (Ackoff 1970: 1–2). Plans are thus decisions that are subject to possible revision; decisions are plans not subject to replanning. This book is concerned with planning the activities of corporate enterprises, although much of the discussion is equally applicable to public enterprises.

The underlying philosophy of the book is that planning cannot be fully understood unless it is approached from a systems point of view. (The same applies, in fact, to performance evaluation and control.) This point of view is followed throughout the book. Consequently it is essential that readers have a clear understanding of what is meant by "system" and the "systems approach," know something about system properties, various system classifications, and how different kinds of systems differ in their typical behavior patterns. Even more important, they should have an understanding of *why* the systems approach is being used, especially as most books that employ it do not give readers a good understanding of why it is useful to think in terms of systems, particularly when studying human and organizational phenomena. An appendix on systems and the systems approach has therefore been provided that makes the text self-contained in this respect and which, it is hoped, will convince the reader of the gain in explanatory power afforded by the systems approach. *This appendix should be read before proceeding with Chapter 1,* and referred back to as necessary.

It will suffice to include in the record at this point a few unsubstantiated statements, which will give the flavor of the systems approach, but which are not to be taken as a substitute for reading the Appendix:

1

Most of the things we deal with in our everyday lives are systems (e.g., machines, people, and social organizations, including corporate enterprises).

Every science studies systems of some kind, natural or artificial. Until 30 to 40 years ago each species of system was studied separately. It then began to be noticed that there are some concepts and structural principles that seem to hold for systems of many kinds, and some modeling strategies (e.g., the state-space approach) that seem to work universally. Systems theory (or systemics) refers to the set of theories or ideas that focus on the structural characteristics of systems, and can therefore cross the largely artificial barriers between disciplines.

The systems approach represents an addition to, not a substitute for, the traditional scientific method. Instead of trying to explain the behavior of some whole solely by studying the behavior of its parts, it is now recognized that the whole, if it is a system, is capable of behaviors that none of the parts can exhibit. It has certain "emergent properties." Everything is part of some system, and every system except the universe, the totality of systems, part of some larger system. The systems approach augments the traditional method of science by the complementary use of synthesis and analysis. We need to understand not only how the parts of a thing are arranged, and their relation to the whole, but also the orientation of the whole to a larger whole or wholes. From this combination of synthesis and analysis comes the power of the systems approach.

A corporation is one form of social organization, and hence a system. It is in fact a sociotechnical system, set up to carry out certain transformations on a set of inputs (materials, energy, information) to yield other things that are more desired, and hence have enhanced value. This set of transformations we call production, or the technical system. The firm is also a social system in that the transformations require the interaction of individuals and groups; and the social system of the corporation interacts with other individuals and groups. Moreover, it is a purposeful system, a functional entity that selects its goals as well as the means of achieving them. It displays choice of both means and ends. The system as a whole displays will.[1] Unlike a human being, its parts (e.g., departments, divisions, functions) will also display wills of their own. Firms, then, are organizations that are defined as purposeful groups whose parts are also purposeful groups that perform different functions.

Our aim in this chapter is to inquire why such systems need to plan their future activities. That they need to do so is not altogether self-evident.

For example, they could simply take decisions, and rely on rapid feedback of outcomes to inform them of the "correctness" of their decisions. Over time a certain amount of organizational learning might take place, leading to a higher proportion of "correct" decisions. We shall also look at the state of the art of corporate planning and ask whether, in view of the nature of the corporation as a system, this activity is justified, and whether it is approached in the right way.

UNCERTAINTY AND CHANGE

One reason why a corporation needs to plan stems from the fact that it is an open system,[2] exposed to all the vagaries of an environment. A firm is subject to more or less continuous disturbances from within and from its environment. The latter consists principally of other organizations and their activities. In the midst of this constantly changing scene, a firm directs its efforts toward producing one or more future states, which are desired and which are not expected to occur automatically. Planning tries to reveal and clarify future opportunities and threats, and prepare for them in advance. Obversely, it tries to avoid incorrect actions and missed opportunities. Thus, as Ackoff notes (1970: 4), planning always has both a pessimistic and an optimistic orientation. It seeks to accentuate the positive and eliminate or reduce the negative influences on the system. In order to do this the firm must first forecast the future. The future cannot be known with certainty, and usually the uncertainties increase with the length of the planning horizon and an increasing rate of change of the environment.

Uncertainty is the ultimate reason why firms are established in the first place (Coase 1937), as we will now explain. Exchange transactions on the market and the direction of production by management within a firm are alternative methods of coordinating production. The distinguishing mark of the firm is that it supersedes the price mechanism. The firm becomes larger as additional transactions, which could be exchange transactions coordinated by the price system, are organized within the firm by management. Now there is a cost in using the price system, namely in discovering what the relevant prices are. In fact no type of market ever completely eliminates these contract costs; they are the cost of uncertainty. But formation of a firm results in avoidance of some of this uncertainty. This is because a business is set up only if the owners have expectations that this form of investment will prove to be more to their advantage, after taking risk differentials into account, than other forms or other courses of action.

Once a firm is created, uncertainty continues to be a fact of life. All firms face an uncertain future. Imperfectly competitive firms are uncertain about the present as well as the future, while in all decentralized firms there is uncertainty between the parts, each of which possesses a different body of knowledge.[3] As we shall see in Chapter 3, there are different planning philosophies and objectives. For all of these philosophies and objectives, however, one reason why firms need to plan, although not the most important, is that they face an uncertain and frequently changing future. As Ackoff notes (1970:4), if the firm believed that the natural course of events would bring about its desired future there would be no need to plan.

There is a counter-argument, however. As indicated at the outset, uncertainty is sometimes cited as a reason for *not* planning: a firm may minimize the need for predicting uncertain future events by substituting feedback data for expectations—acting "blind," and learning from past mistakes. This assumes that it is always possible to identify the faulty expectation from among the numerous factors contributing to the decision outcome. More important, however, it is only consistent with a planning philosophy that seeks to avoid the undesirable rather than to attain the desirable. It is what Ackoff (1974: 24) calls a reactivist philosophy. As such, we regard it as a rather limited outlook, as we will show in Chapter 3. Firms should try to avoid uncertainty wherever possible; but uncertainty avoidance does not eliminate the need for planning. The two things are not antithetical. The need for planning goes much deeper; in fact it goes right to the heart of the conception of the firm as a complex open system, as we will see below.

THE SYSTEMS RATIONALE FOR PLANNING

The essential rationale for planning derives from the definition of "system." Ackoff (1970: 2–4) describes this with admirable clarity. The fact that the firm is a system, and a highly complex one at that—level eight on Boulding's nine-point scale of complexity (see reference in Appendix: Systems and the Systems Approach)—means that we are faced with a large set of interrelated decisions concerning the firm's future operations. This set of decisions is so large, and contains so many interdependencies, that the planning stage is the only stage at which it can be tackled, the only opportunity to pull everything together by taking into account the firm's system properties. (Recall from the Appendix that an aggregate of independent components is a whole, but not all wholes are systems, that is, integrated, unitary wholes.) Planning is an attempt to deal simultaneously with a system of problems. Even so we can hope to solve the planning problem only approximately, whether it is tackled as a whole sequentially by top management or done separately at different levels of a multilevel enterprise and an attempt made simultaneously to integrate all these separate plans.

Integration, Coordination, and Orientation to the Environment

We begin by distinguishing two terms. By *integration* is meant the cohesion or systemicity of a system. There are degrees of integration: some systems are more tightly knit than others. The degree of integration of a system depends on the strength of the binding relations (inner couplings) between the system's components relative to the environmental forces tending to disintegrate it. If the inner couplings are strong and "positive" (mutually supportive), the degree of integration is high for given environmental forces. If they are "negative" (repulsive), there is no integration at all. To remain a viable system, some minimum degree of integration is necessary. Some of the inner couplings may be "positive" and some "negative," in which case the degree of integration depends on which is uppermost. If a system has subsystems, not just components, integration of the subsystems competes with that of the overall system. In this case the systems designer (or the management of the firm if the system already exists) must try to strike a balance. It would be wrong to maximize the cohesion of each subsystem, for then it would become self-sufficient instead of serving the corporate goals. The more cohesive each subsystem is, the less cohesive is the total system. It would be equally wrong to minimize the cohesion of each subsystem because the latter would then become unstable. Some medium degree of cohesion satisfies the needs of the subsystems and of the system as a whole (Bunge and Garcia-Sucre 1976). Planning seeks to change the system's environment so as to enhance tendencies toward cohesion in the system and to check those toward disintegration. If the integration of a system fails, the system undergoes *structural* breakdown.

Coordination concerns the harmony of relations between system components, or of functions, which results in functional maintenance, and the continuance of some processes.[4] There can be integration without coordination, but not conversely. Planning aims at establishing "functional unity," a condition in which all parts of the system work together with a certain degree of harmony or internal consistency, and without producing persistent conflicts that cannot be resolved, regulated, or tolerated. When coordination fails, the system undergoes *functional* breakdown. Coordination may require the intervention of a control system, because one way in which functions are coordinated is through feedback. But there are other methods of coordination that do not require a control system.

Applying these ideas to planning, recall that a firm is a purposeful system, some of whose interrelated parts are also purposeful systems. It is also of course an open system, exposed to an environment that is sometimes turbulent and never entirely static. It faces a system of problems. It must ensure that its components or subsystems cohere at least minimally, otherwise the system will disintegrate. As indicated in the Appendix, survival entails coordinating those activities that are related, and not coordinating unrelated activities (i.e., integrating *components* and coordinating related *activities*). Planning is the principal means available for integrating system components and one of the means of coordinating their behavior. If, as they commonly will be, these components are also purposeful systems, we must ensure that subsystem goals and behavior are congruent with system goals.

This is not quite the whole picture. In addition to seeing that the system's inner couplings are appropriate to avoid instability and to work toward system goals, planning should not overlook the system's *orientation to the environment,* the external couplings of system components to the environment. (We also see in the Appendix that some system components may be linked indirectly, through the environment.) The most effective plans are plans that constantly match, selectively, the firm's orientation to the state of its environment (selectively, because not all parts of the environment influence the system's behavior significantly). They will include provision for the organizational structure and internal working arrangements most likely to bring this about.

Most complex organizations, corporations included, have a multilevel organizational structure. Each level must be planned for, and planning at each level must be integrated with planning at every other level. We refer to this again in the beginning of Chapter 4. That the organization is a system also means that planning must be coordinated: All aspects and functions of the enterprise should be planned for interdependently. As Ackoff observes (1974: 29), "In planning, breadth is more important than depth and interactions are more important than actions."

Planning is needed, then, because a system must be appropriately integrated and coordinated. Integration and coordination are needed for survival and growth. Without them the firm might break up. Comprehensive planning helps to tie together the interrelated parts in the pursuit of system goals, provide a framework for decision making throughout the firm, and prevent the piecemeal taking of interrelated decisions. It provides the only opportunity for appropriately orienting the system as a whole to its environment.

Adaptation and Learning

A system is described as *adaptive* if, when there is a change in its environment and/or internal state that reduces its efficiency in pursuing one or more of its goals, it reacts or responds by changing its own state and/or that of its environment so as to increase its efficiency with respect to that goal or goals (Ackoff 1971: 668). If the system over time becomes more efficient at doing this it is called a *learning* system. *Adaptation is essential if an open system is to survive*; successful long-run adaptation can be assured only if the system's state of orientation is always selectively adapted to match the state of its rapidly changing environment. To do this the system must be able to monitor, discriminate among, and take selective action upon changes in its environment. Organizational learning takes place if the system has the capacity to improve this behavior over time toward some ultimate goal or goals.

The characteristics a firm must possess if it is to adapt and learn effectively have been identified by Ackoff (1974: ch. 2 and appendix). Its controlling subsystem, that is, management, must be able to identify problems, plan and make decisions, control decisions once made, and obtain the information required to perform each of these functions.

Implicit in these remarks are the facts that a firm is an open system (it must be open to entropy transfer in order to survive; a closed system may, within limits, be capable of adapting reactively, but not actively) and a purposeful one (the system rather than the environment determines the goals to be pursued as well as the means of attaining those goals); also that a control system exists to aid in the process of adaptation (i.e., an open system adapts reactively in response to feedbacks, as well as actively). By "adapting actively" is meant that the system is capable of selectively matching its state to the state of the environment autonomously, not in response to an outside stimulus. This is by virtue of the spontaneous interactions between system components (the system dynamics) described in the Appendix.

Frequency of Plans

Because both the composition and structure of the firm and its environment are changing constantly, plans are more or less outdated the moment they are made. Planning therefore needs to be an ongoing activity if the firm is to benefit by it, that is, to adapt and learn effectively. The problems of open systems "do not stay solved," as Ackoff aptly puts it (1974: 31); they must continually be re-solved, and their solutions need to be controlled. In Beer's words (in Jantsch 1969):

> Corporate planning becomes a machine for sequentially aborting incompetent plans. Planning is essential if the enterprise is not to be randomly perturbed by the interplay of future events. But, paradoxically, the next most important feature of corporate management is the organizational capability to abort the plans on a continuing basis. . . . Adaptation is the crux of planning, . . . the continuous adaptation of the enterprise towards continuing survival. . . . this planning process which sequentially aborts its actual plans . . . is found in organizational structure, because this structure alone is that which adapts.

Participation in Planning

A related point is that planning should be participative. As Ackoff again notes (1974: 28), the principal benefits of planning are not derived from consuming its product, but from engaging in the production. In other words, what is important is the process (planning), not the product (plans). Everyone who can be affected by planning should be afforded an opportunity to participate in it. They should be provided with the information, instructions, and motivation to enable them to plan effectively.

Conclusion

An open system must adapt or cease to exist. The better it becomes at adapting the longer it will survive. Hence the whole existence and "success" (level of performance) of the system is tied up with its capacity to adapt and learn. Throughout this book, and especially in the beginning of Chapter 3, we will therefore have a continuing interest in these processes. Adaptation may occur in various ways and at different levels within the firm. We merely note here that it is only at the planning stage that adaptation of the firm as a whole can be contemplated and attempted. All other adaptations are partial. Only planning spans the two essential orientations, of parts to system and system to environment. Consequently the need for planning on a more or less continuous basis is compelling on these grounds. For the present we can think of adaptation occurring through plan revision and through the responses to feedback of deviations between observed results and the expectations incorporated in the plan. Other methods will be mentioned later. As stated earlier, planning reveals and clarifies future opportunities and threats—forewarned is forearmed. Business history is filled with cases of failures that could have been prevented if the future had been planned; railroads are a notable example. Less common but no less spectacular are cases of success through foreseeing and grasping opportunities, which is not to say that a firm might not sometimes fail in spite of planning.

PLANNING REGARDED AS ANTICIPATORY CONTROL

As an extension of the remarks in the preceding sections (together with the fact that in order to adapt, open systems must remain flexible in all respects at all times), a further reason why planning is needed can be seen by regarding planning as a form of anticipatory control. To show how this arises it is necessary to consider various types of adaptive mechanisms employing feed processes,[5] and to note their properties, advantages, and limitations. The following classification of such mechanisms will be convenient for our purposes (Rosen 1975). It will be assumed throughout that the control objective is to ensure adaptation of the controlled system as a whole, that this involves confining the state of the controlled system to a particular set of acceptable states, and that the most stringent test of adaptability is survival of the system.

A Classification of Adaptive Mechanisms Involving Feed Processes

Type I: Feedback Control

This type of control, consisting of two subsystems, the controlled system and the controller, operates on an error signal that can be regarded as the result of randomness in the environment. The controller observes the controlled system only, not the environment. While this is the most familiar type of adaptive mechanism, it can malfunction for a number of reasons: because the acceptable states are incorrectly defined for adaptation (the controlled system is kept at an incorrect level of the controlled [state] variable), because of an inappropriate choice of control variables, or of the coupling of the controller to the controlled system, because of an inaccurate sensing of the state of the controlled system by the controller, or because the time delay in operating the feedback loop is excessive for the kind of environment in which the controlled system operates. With a hierarchy of feedback loops this delay may become intolerable, because the state of the controlled system is deteriorating, perhaps irreversibly. If the environment is changing very rapidly, feedback control systems will track the effects of the fluctuations and may never bring the system under control. Moreover, a feedback control that operates on the effects of only one or a few aspects of the environment can be "fooled." For example, a thermostat designed to keep water from boiling (i.e., one that monitors water temperature) will fail if the pressure of the water is lowered (Rosen 1975).

Type II: Feedforward Control

This type of system embodies, in addition to the controlled system and the controller, a model of the environment. The controller has direct access to the environment, and can monitor an environmental variable, w, whose current value is thought to correlate with some future value of the state of the controlled system, v. In type II control we will assume that w represents a single environmental variable. The correlation between $w(t)$ and $v(t + \tau)$ is built into the controller, which can then modify the control variables in accordance with the current values of w and v to maintain some function of v constant. So type II control introduces two new features: a model of the environment, and prediction (or choice of some future desired state of the controlled system). Unlike type I, this kind of control operates on regularities in the environment, as represented by the correlation between w and v, rather than on randomness of the environment. Not being tied to an error signal, feedforward control is more direct and timely than feedback control. Nevertheless, type II controls can also malfunction: because the model of the environment (the correlation between w and v) is inaccurate or even spurious, because of poor sensory mechanisms (monitoring devices), or because the controller selects inappropriate responses to be made by the controlled system.

Type III Control: Feedback Control with Memory

This type of system keeps a record of its past experience, and can make a memory trace of this experience to alter its present behavior. For these behavior modifications to be adaptive, of course, some improvement in the performance of the control (and hence of the controlled system) must

result. Type III removes some of the limitations of type I but is still subject
to time delays (which may be even greater), and the addition of memory
does not compensate for the lack of direct access to the environment.

Type IV Control: Feedforward with Memory

This kind of control can modify its models of the environment on the
basis of past experience, that is, modify the correlation between the current
values of w and future values of v. In order to do so, however, it must employ an error signal, the deviation of a predicted or desired state of w from
some past state of w, to modify its model of the environment. Hence type
IV becomes subject to the limitations of all feedback systems. At the same
time this type of control offers considerably greater adaptive power than the
previous three types. Most of the "adaptive control systems" referred to in
mathematics, engineering, and in the literatures on artificial intelligence
and self-organization fall in this class, as well as all the learning and condi-
tioning behaviors exhibited by the higher organisms (Rosen 1975).

Type V Control: Universal Adaptive System
(feedforward with memory and multiple sensors)

Unlike type II, this class of control is not limited to monitoring a single
environmental variable, but has unlimited access to the environment. It can
establish many correlations between elements of the vectors w and v, and in
principle function effectively in any environment. Its effectiveness is constrained only by the limitations of feedbacks in modifying its model of the
environment. Human beings, regarded individually, are said to approach
this class of adaptability.

The foregoing classification of adaptive mechanisms is arranged in increasing order of flexibility of performance; that is, feedforward
mechanisms are in many respects superior to feedback mechanisms; control systems equipped with memory are better than those without; systems
capable of monitoring multiple aspects of the environment are better than
those with few sensors. Only type V mechanisms are capable of modifying
and extending their couplings with the environment *and* with the controlled
system, but against this they may be subject to intolerable lag effects.

Based on this discussion, Rosen concludes that the inherent limitations of feedback loops (the delay in operating the loop, and the ease with
which such systems can be "fooled," mainly because they do not monitor
the environment directly) make them unsatisfactory as the *sole* adaptive

mechanisms available to ensure survival. Anticipatory mechanisms (types II, IV, and V) are superior, with class V the most effective of all, *providing* human organizations can develop sensors that are as effective as those evolved by some members of the animal kingdom and human beings over hundreds or thousands of years.

The reasons for this lengthy digression on adaptive mechanisms was to point out that there is a sense in which planning can be regarded as anticipatory control. Based mainly on biological systems, Rosen says that adaptation cannot be brought about solely by error-activated controls; it requires anticipatory controls as well. He asserts that it is particularly in the area of anticipatory control that our social adaptations are singularly defective. Arguing by analogy from *motivated* biological behavior is valid, provided the two sets of behavior have enough in common for the explanation of one to provide at least a partial explanation of the other, and provided also that we make the necessary modifications required by the increased complexity of organizations compared with organisms. Our argument that planning, regarded as anticipatory control, is necessary to increase a business system's chances of adapting and surviving is only presumptive, therefore, until the necessary modifications (if any) are made and tested.

Incidentally, the discussion of this section provides substantiation of the point made in Chapter 4 ("Should planning budgets and control budgets be formally distinct?") that planning budgets and control budgets should be formally separated. A model of the control budget comprises the controlled system and the controller, whereas a model of the planning budget *should* include a model of the environment also. The two systems are therefore quite different, and it is unlikely that either model will successfully serve both functions.

MEASUREMENT OF PERFORMANCE

The performance of a business can be thought of in several different ways. In the present context we will focus on two of these. In the financial sense, a firm is a success if it is able to maintain a state of solvency. Failure in this sense implies that the business is unable to meet certain claims on it as they fall due, and has become involved in certain legal consequences. Note that success or failure in this sense refers only to past results. In the economic sense, on the other hand, the success or failure of a firm is judged in relation to its expectations: a firm is considered a failure if the returns realized on its invested capital fall short of the highest returns that were expected to be available elsewhere, after allowing for differences in risk. It is a failure in the sense that, had this state of affairs been foreseen, the firm would not have been brought into being. The economic success of an ongoing firm would be measured in relation to its expected earnings for the period.

In practice we could measure a firm's performance in many ways: in relation to its own results in a past period, or in relation to the current results of other firms. Accounting practice usually follows economics in measuring performance in relation to a plan, articulated in the short-term operating budgets and master budget. There are good reasons for adopting an internal rather than an external standard. The firm itself possesses more information on the activities that are organized within it than the market does, or than other firms do, since every firm differs in some respects from every other. It is therefore in a better position to say what its capabilities are than is any other source. Of course what the performance measure that emerges from this comparison really means will depend on the level of achievement expressed in the plan, as we shall see in Chapter 3. In addition, the actual performance elicited will not be unaffected by the level of the planning targets, unless there are separate budgets for planning and control (see Chapter 4, "Should planning budgets . . ."). But we can safely assume that plans of some kind are needed in order to measure the firm's performance, its demonstrated ability to adapt. For the present we will assume that these plans are more or less continuously revised. Later, in Chapter 6, we will see what form a performance measure may ultimately take when the firm is regarded as an open system. It turns out that "performance," like "adaptation," is an ambiguous term.

BEHAVIORAL ASPECTS: MOTIVATION

Planning, as we have seen, is anticipatory decision making.[6] Spanning the whole set of decisions expected to be necessary over a certain interval of time, and their interrelations, it seeks to establish ends, means, and the resources required to implement the plan (Ackoff 1974: 29–30).

Now under the economic arrangements found in market economies people are under no compulsion to conform to a plan; they must be motivated to do so. Motivation, in either its intrinsic or extrinsic forms, may be injected into the system in various ways. But the locus of motivation in the management process is still very much an open question. One way is to build motivation into the plan, in the form of performance targets. Participative planning may also help to motivate people to carry out the plan effectively. These forms of intrinsic motivation are unlikely, however, to be fully effective on their own. Other things, such as organization structure, the management system, and incentives will usually need to be considered. As Ackoff observes (in Jantsch 1969: 495), "[There is a] need for planners to design new social institutions and organizations and to redesign old ones so that they become more responsive to their environment and the needs of those they serve."

Indeed, the ramifications of the motivation question are particularly far-reaching, leading us ultimately to consider the explicitly or implicitly expressed contractual rights of different members of the organization, which determine how costs and rewards will be shared between them, and the behavioral implications of possessing these rights. Another somewhat related approach to this problem is to consider the agency relationships within the firm, their costs, and behavioral consequences. These agency relationships commonly involve choice under uncertainty, and, contrary to the position once held by economists, the entrepreneur or owners of the business do not safeguard agents who provide productive services against all uninsurable risks. Employees' contracts can be terminated, and in some cases their rates of remuneration can be reduced. So the question arises as to how risk is to be shared between the owners and their agents in the firm, and how risk congruence as well as goal congruence is to be achieved. Hence it turns out that the question of motivating people to work toward organizational goals, of internalizing the organizational goals, is a prime and formidable example of a system of problems.

The problem of motivation is outside the ambit of this book but the evolution of thought on the question of motivation and incentives is briefly sketched in the appendix to this chapter.

CORRECTING PAST MISTAKES

Another reason for the desirability, if not necessity, of planning not mentioned in the foregoing is faulty decision making and ineffective control in the past. Since planning is here regarded as a dynamic process, the opportunity presents itself at each stage of the process to correct for shortcomings in planning or implementation of plans at previous stages. "We never can solve our problems; rather, we navigate through sets of interdependent problems, guided by the vision of a more desirable future" (Susman 1981: 150). Therefore, says Ackoff (1970: 16), one objective of planning should be to design an organization, management system, and information system that will minimize the need for "retrospective planning" aimed at correcting past deficiencies, while continuing to engage in prospective planning directed toward creating a desired future.

ACCEPTANCE OF PLANNING

It would be premature at this point to present a detailed account of current corporate planning practice. We still have a number of other aspects of planning to discuss: strategic and tactical planning, short-, medium-, and long-term planning, and different approaches to planning. For accounts of current planning practice readers are referred to Steiner's encyclopedic work (1969) and to Ansoff (1976–77). Rather, the intention here is to give preliminary notice that, in the business community, the utility of engaging in planning is by no means taken for granted everywhere.

First, however, we may note that the whole attitude to planning has been changing. It is no longer held in disrepute at the national level in the Western world and associated only with communism. Nor, as Ackoff notes (1974: 22) is it any longer assumed that planning has strong central government or central management as a concomitant. A sufficient reason for planning at the national government or top management level makes no appeal to a particular political or economic philosophy, but is based on the systems rationale stated earlier. The system is too complex, its interdependencies too numerous, and the rate of change of system and environment too great, *not* to do so. Some stages in the recent evolution of planning point toward a systems view. For example, there has been some evidence of a greater attachment to the idea of long-term planning, and program budgeting (PPBS) takes a systems approach. PPBS is described and modeled in Chapter 5 and the Appendix. Strategic planning has been given more emphasis than has tactical planning.

Among empirical studies, Modigliani and Cohen (1961) found that most U.S. firms surveyed engaged in a considerable amount of planning with respect to various parts of their operations, but principally production, sales, and capital investment. Plans were found to extend over varying periods of time, and seldom covered every aspect of operations, even for the very near future. It was frequently stated by the sample firms that plans were not binding on future decisions.

Cyert and March (1963) had some interesting observations to make about planning, although from a systems point of view they tended to be negative. Thus, while plans are described as "one of the major outputs of high levels in the organization as well as a significant output at other levels" (p. 104), they suggest that plans are used to bring about stability of decisions: a plan establishes a *prima facie* case for continuing existing decisions, unless there are quite exceptional reasons for not doing so. They also describe how firms try to minimize the need for predicting uncertain future events by taking decisions ("simulation in the raw") and using short-term feedback to make adjustments later.

Ackoff (1970) gained the impression from talking to many managers that most of them did not have a clear idea of what planning was or, more important, what it should be. He also found confusion over what a plan should contain, how planning should be conducted and organized, and what values could be derived from it.

There is evidence that many managers are not really "sold" on the importance of planning, or do not hold it to be important with any strength of conviction (Ackoff 1974: 33). In these circumstances they can hardly expect anyone else in their organizations to take it seriously.

In view of the widespread lack of acceptance of planning both in practice and in academic circles, Chapter 8 will be devoted to answering the arguments most commonly heard against it. The intervening chapters are needed to complete the description of the systems conceptualization of planning.

THE STATE OF THE ART

What is chiefly missing from the current practice of planning, already being referred to by some as "the old planning," can be traced to a failure to recognize the full implications of the firm as an open, purposeful system. The systems view asserts that the system of problems encountered in mapping out future operations must be treated together, and not isolated and treated independently. This applies to time periods as well as to segments of the business: Time periods are also interrelated. In short, there is still less than complete recognition of the system properties of the firm, and that the planning stage is the only opportunity the firm will get to take into account all the extensive interrelations that affect the system's behavior—to see the problem as a whole, complete with all these complications. We refer here to the interrelatedness of parts of the system (functions, decisions), and how well they fit together to form a functioning unitary entity, and to the relation of the firm to the larger whole of which it is a part. As Steiner notes

(1969: 725), no very acceptable rules are yet available to guide managers as to what elements of planning should be tightly related and what should be loosely related. Ackoff (1974: chs. 3 and 4) refers to the part–whole problem and the whole–larger whole problem as "humanization" and "environmentalization," respectively. By the first he means putting into the system's (i.e., planners') mind the system's relationship to its parts, and by the second the system's relationship to its suprasystem or systems. It can no longer be assumed that humans will always be prepared to adjust their objectives to those of the organizations that they serve. Rather, organizational objectives may have to be adjusted to those of their constituents. As we see in the Appendix, every system except the universe is part of one or more suprasystems. In current approaches to planning far less attention is given to the "environmentalization" problem than it deserves. The system's performance will be seen through the eyes of the people who carry out its functions and administer it, *and* through the eyes of the suprasystem or systems of which it forms a part. For example, a firm may be making handsome profits but its work force may be discontented and it may be inflicting quite intolerable levels of pollution on the local communities in the areas where it operates. If all expectations are to be reasonably satisfied, these relations must be incorporated into the firm's planning.

SUMMARY

Planning from a systems point of view—the "new planning"— emerges as *a major management function,* something that is absolutely essential if the firm is to adapt and learn effectively, not an option. As such it demands the utmost support of top and higher management. Strategic planning, defined in Chapter 4, is a particularly crucial element in this view. Uncertainty and dynamic change are important reasons why firms need to plan, but subordinate to the overriding system requirement. Planning should try to deal systemically with a large set of interrelated problems, and herein lies both its complexity and its necessity. This must thus be done at a point in time before actual decisions are taken. As one aspect of this systems rationale, planning is needed to integrate parts of the firm, coordinate related activities, and prevent the piecemeal taking of interrelated decisions. Plans are not the chief item of importance, since they rapidly become outdated. What is more important is the planning *process,* the bringing home to all involved, on an ongoing basis, of the firm's systemic properties, and how they affect its behavior. The more thoroughly these properties are instilled, the better chance the organization stands to adapt and learn. There must be a willingness and ability to abort plans continuously because the real objective of planning for an open system is selectively and continually to match the orientation of the system to the state of its changing environment. The firm must be continuously adapted. Hence in the case of an open system such as a firm *the need for planning is not just the need to solve a system of problems, but to do this in a way that constantly aligns the posture of the firm to the state of its environment in order to adapt for long-term survival.*

Other reasons for planning include the correction of past deficiencies, the measurement of performance, and possibly the provision of motivation. The last two are discussed further in Chapter 6. Above all, notice that most of the reasons given in support of planning—uncertainty, the need to integrate and coordinate interrelated parts of the firm, adaptation and learning, and correction of past mistakes—stem from the fact that the firm is a dynamic, open, purposeful system whose parts are also purposeful. Only two of the reasons—performance measurement and motivation—were not directly associated with the firm as a system.

The implicit or explicit systems logic underlying various budget models, types of plans, and approaches to planning will be further explored in the following four chapters.

APPENDIX: NOTE ON MOTIVATION AND INCENTIVE PROBLEMS

The evolution of thought on the question of the motivation of managers can be given some sort of perspective by tracing developments in the "theory of the firm." The main lines of development are discussed below.

In the *classical theory* the firm was run by an entrepreneur, or manager–risk bearer, whose objective was profit maximization in perfectly competitive markets. The entrepreneur provided or borrowed money capital and his functions were managing and risk bearing: He was supposed to safeguard employees who provided productive services against all uninsurable risks. He bore the residual risks. The sanctions of competitive markets ensured that employees had an automatic incentive to work with maximum effort. That is, strong motivation was provided by fear of dismissal for poor performance. Any conflict of goals between entrepreneur and employees was resolved in favor of the entrepreneur. There was no need for incentives.

A number of factors led to rejection of the classical model, among them the fact that the typical modern corporation is characterized by the divorce of ownership and control (Berle and Means 1932), the prevalence of imperfectly competitive markets and the development of theories of imperfect or monopolistic competition in the 1930s, and widespread dissent from the view that the economic behavior of firms is guided by a profit maximization objective.

The result was the development of *behavioral* or *managerial theories* of the firm (Penrose 1958; Simon 1959; Baumol 1959; Cyert and March 1963; Marris, 1964; Williamson, 1964); these theories are reviewed in Alchian (1965). The new theories had in common that they replaced or supplemented the traditional theory of the firm (which was really a theory of markets) by an inward-looking theory of the behavior of decision makers within the firm, acting in conditions of uncertainty. The notions of the entrepreneur, profit maximization, and sometimes even optimizing behavior of any kind, were rejected. Once decision making in the firm is seen as being undertaken by managers who are not security holders of the firm, and the assumption that all markets are perfectly competitive is removed, problems of control, motivation, and incentives arise. In these behavioral or managerial theories of the firm, more attention is given to managers acting in their own interests. But while the theories speculate about what the motives of managers might then be, many pay little attention to the problem of motivating managers to act in the interests of the firm. In Cyert and March (1963) the conflicting interests of members of the organizational coalition are brought into rough agreement on organizational objectives by offering pecuniary and/or nonpecuniary side payments to the active members of the coalition, generally leaving some unresolved conflict (see Chapter 3, "Conflicting Objectives and Goals" and "Conflict Resolution"). But the analysis does not extend to inquiring into the circumstances in which particular incentive schemes are likely to succeed in bringing about goal-congruent performance; and incentives are discussed without their concomitant, risk sharing.

The next two lines of development are sometimes not distinguished. They will be identified as the property rights approach and the theory of agency relationships approach. Although they have much in common (they are complementary to the point of overlapping), they developed independently, and so will be discussed separately. At the same time any division of contributions between the two is somewhat arbitrary. At any rate, we shall classify Coase (1937, 1960), and Alchian and Demsetz (1972), as important references in the property rights literature, which is reviewed in

Furubotn and Pejovich (1972); while notable contributions to the agency relationships literature (hereafter *agency theory*) include Wilson (1968), Ross (1973), Jensen and Meckling (1976), Mirrlees (1976), Holmström (1979), Demski and Feltham (1978), Baiman and Demski (1980a, 1980b), and Fama (1980). Useful reviews of agency theory will be found in Demski (1980: chapter 6), Baiman (1982), and in Kaplan (1982: chapters 16 and 17).

The *property rights* approach views the firm as a set of implicit or explicit contracts among factors of production. "Property rights" here refer to the relations, not between people and things as the term might suggest, but to the permissible behavioral relations between people arising from the existence of things, and relating to their use (Furubotn and Pejovich 1972). Specification of these rights determines how costs and rewards are allocated among members of the organization. In other words, the property rights approach purports to show that the content of contracts between members of the organization affects the allocation and utilization of resources *in specific and predictable ways* (Furubotn and Pejovich 1972). It assumes that systematic relations exist between property rights and the economic choices of members of the organization.

It is important to note that the unit of analysis is no longer the firm; nor are the interests of those holding ownership rights given exclusive attention. Rather, the focus is on individual participants, including the owners, each of whom is assumed to seek his own self-interests and to maximize his utility, subject to the existing organizational structure and to ensuring survival of the firm. Individual participants adjust to the economic environment, and the behavior of the firm is explained by observing the actions of individuals within the organization. This approach, then, is characterized by emphasis on the interconnectedness of ownership rights, incentives, and economic behavior. The presumption is that "property rights" influence incentives and behavior, and that once human motivations are known, the allocation and utilization of resources by the firm can be better understood. The implications for human motivation and resource allocation decisions of a number of alternative property rights assignments, and of changes in the content of property rights, have been worked out, and in some cases the formal equilibrium conditions of the firm have been established. In the perfect competition model of the classical firm one set of property rights governs the use of all resources, the entrepreneur possessing the ownership rights and arrogating for himself the entire direction of the firm. The cost of exchange, policing, and enforcing of cooperating (contractual) activities is zero: there are no transaction costs, and no control problem exists. The property rights approach departs from this view in recognizing non-zero transaction costs in most cases of interest, the possibility of discretionary behavior and shirking by managers, hence the need for control. Like the behavioral theory of Cyert and March, however, the property rights analysis builds on the traditional theory of the firm rather than replacing it completely.

As in the property rights literature, *agency theory* is concerned with contracts—agency relationships—under which one party (the principal) engages another party (the agent) to perform certain services on his behalf. The relationship may be between the owners and top management, or between top management and divisional or departmental managers. Performance of the service requires the principal to delegate some decision-making authority to the agent. Certain assumptions are made about the objectives of principals and agents (e.g., that they are both utility maximizers) and about the arguments of their utility functions (e.g., their relative preferences for pecuniary and nonpecuniary benefits, including leisure in the case of the agent). It is not usually possible for the principal—or indeed the agent—to ensure that the latter always acts in the best interests of the principal, without incurring some costs. By introducing appropriate incentives and by incurring monitoring costs the principal attempts to limit dysfunctional behavior on the part of the agent. The agent, for his part, may in some circumstances incur "bonding costs" to ensure that he does not act contrary to the principal's wishes, or to compensate the principal if he does. Together with any residual loss the principal experiences through the failure of the agent to fulfill his part of the bargain, these costs are collectively referred to as agency costs. They include all costs except that of the incentive.

The firm is seen in agency theory as a set of employment contracts between principals and agents (so far only as contracts between a single principal and a single agent), where each is assumed to be self-interest seeking (interpreted as seeking to maximize their own expected utility over a single period). The principal's utility function is defined over wealth alone (the monetary payoff from the agent's action less the agent's compensation), while the agent's utility function is defined over wealth and action (or "effort"), the latter term being intended to subsume all the agent's nonpecuniary benefits. It is further assumed that the agent's utility function is separable into his utility for wealth and disutility for effort (i.e., it is assumed that the agent's utility for nonpecuniary benefits is always on balance negative). Assumptions are made about attitudes to risk bearing (usually that the principal is risk neutral and the agent risk averse) and the respective beliefs of the two parties about the state of the world (they may have homogeneous beliefs or there may be an information asymmetry between them).

A relationship of this form has the nature of a noncooperative game: Both parties seek only to serve their self-interest, but their utility functions differ in their arguments. The principal's problem is to choose an incentive scheme such that his own expected utility is as large as possible when the agent maximizes his own expected utility by choosing a particular act (or effort level). The incentive must also ensure the agent at least as much expected utility as he could derive from employment outside the firm. Only things that are observable by both parties to the contract can be included as arguments in the compensation function; these jointly observable variables define the principal's monitoring capacity. The principal is assumed always to be able to observe the monetary payoff. He or she may or may not be able to observe the realized state of the world or the agent's act (effort level).

The self-serving action of the agent may not be in the best interests of the principal in several ways, due to uncertainty after actions have been taken and results realized. That is, there may be disagreement as to what constitutes a proper level of effort if the two parties have different risk attitudes, or different beliefs, or if the principal cannot directly observe the agent's effort. If the principal can observe only the payoff the agent could supply a less-than-optimal effort level from the principal's point of view and blame the poor result on an unfavorable state of the world (the "moral hazard" problem). This can be avoided if the agent is risk neutral. Again, even when the principal can observe the agent's effort level directly, the agent may have private information that she or he does not reveal, or misrepresents, to the principal, so that the latter is unable to determine whether the observed effort level was appropriate (the "adverse selection" problem). These problems can only be avoided by the principal installing an information system that removes all such ex post uncertainty.

A solution to the agency problem is called "first-best" if the sharing of both payoff and risk between principal and agent is such that neither can be made better off without making the other worse off (Pareto optimality). If there is information asymmetry between principal and agent, leading to moral hazard, and the agent is risk averse, only a "second-best" solution is usually possible. There must be a trade-off between incentive and risk sharing to induce the agent to provide the desired effort (the agent is offered a larger share of the payoff than in the first-best solution but must bear more of the risk of the uncertain payoff than he would wish).

According to the agency theory view the evaluation of an agent's performance may involve risk sharing as well as motivational (incentive) considerations, the two being interrelated. While agency theory offers important new insights, some of its prescriptions are controversial, for example the suggestion that (in "second-best" situations) managers should be required to share risk with their principals, the assumption that all managers have a disutility for effort (i.e., that they are "work shy"), and that they are motivated primarily by pecuniary benefits.

NOTES

1. This sentence, and the following one, require some explanation. Does "will," as it applies to decision making by individuals, also apply to decision making by groups and higher-order social systems, that is, to collective choices? Arrow (1963) investigated the formulation of group decisions or social preferences when there are three or more alternatives. The problem is how "best" to aggregate individual choices (preferences) into group or social choices (preferences). In his five famous axioms he stated the conditions he believed group/social choices/preference structures must satisfy to be "fair," or minimally acceptable. Individual and collective choices were described in terms of preference orderings of alternatives formed by the relation "is at least as well liked as" (i.e., preference included indifference).

Value judgments are involved in constructing the five axioms: Even if utility is measurable for an individual, there remains the problem of aggregating utilities. At best, individual utility functions are uniquely determined up to a linear transformation. This leaves us with an infinite number of possible indicators of individual utility; and aggregate utility depends on how these individual utility indicators are chosen. A value judgment is needed to render the individual utilities dimensionally compatible, a further value judgment to aggregate them according to any particular way.

Arrow's central result is negative. His Impossibility Theorem states that it is not, in general, possible to construct social preferences/collective choices that satisfy all five axioms; the conditions are inconsistent (see also Luce and Raiffa 1957: ch. 14; Henderson and Quandt 1980: 308–14). Consequently we have Arrow's "paradox of voting," in which the aggregate preference or collective decision is that of no single individual, or may be that of a minority (Arrow 1963: 2–3).

Yet social choice problems must somehow be resolved. How? In theory they can be resolved either by discarding one of the axioms as being too restrictive, or by formulating the problem in a different way. In practice, a business enterprise system seems to resolve the problem, and display corporate will, essentially by a combination of three devices:

(i) By one member of the organizational coalition emerging as dominant (in normal circumstances this is management), and acting as a (reasonably) resolute bloc. The will of the system reflects not merely rankings of preferences (an ordinal measure), as in Arrow's formulation of the problem, but also individual strengths of preferences (a cardinal measure). By "resolute bloc" is meant that differences in individual preference orderings within the management group are minimal, or at any rate are less dissimilar than those in other coalition groups. Added to this is the fact that some members of the coalition (e.g., stockholders) tend to be apathetic, and on important issues proxies are often solicited by management, thus leading to a self-perpetuating group. Of course this device partially violates one, and possibly two, of Arrow's axioms of "fairness" or rationality (the latter being identified with maximization of something), viz. nondictatorship and nonimposition.

(ii) By the capacity of a complex system to survive with a good deal of actual or latent internal conflict (i.e., very dissimilar preference orderings). As will be seen in Chapter 3 ("Conflicting Objectives and Goals" and "Conflict Resolution") it is not usually possible to define a joint preference ordering for the organizational coalition in a business enterprise. Indeed, opinion differs as to whether conflicts *need* to be resolved. For the conflicts normally appear to be, not about basic purposes or missions (ends), but about means of achieving them.

(iii) By the fact that, except in certain circumstances (e.g., a very high level of employment), business enterprises are able to exercise greater powers of persuasion over their constituents than society can. Except in very full-developed welfare states (e.g., Sweden), a worker's dependence on his employer is usually stronger than his dependence on the state to provide his basic needs.

2. Throughout the book "open system" will mean a system that is "open" in the Bertalanffy sense described in the Appendix, that is, a system that is open to entropy transfer and is able to become *negentropic*.

3. In view of this last statement it might be argued that the previously claimed advantage of organizing production by setting up a firm rather than by the price mechanism in external markets is not decisive after all. For once a firm is established, and particularly when it reaches a certain size, the centralization–decentralization problem arises; and one of the methods of coordinating a decentralized firm is by using an internal price system, that is, by transfer pricing. The degree of uncertainty existing between parts of a firm is, however, less than that between the firm and the external environment, for in the last resort operation of the transfer pricing system can be taken over by central management (e.g., by the use of decomposition techniques), which is in a position to know what all parts of the system are doing, and their interactions. In this way *apparent* independence of the parts can be maintained, and the advantages of decentralization can be secured (such as more intimate knowledge of local problems, higher morale and motivation) without its disadvantages (malcoordination, the parts acting in ignorance of what other parts are doing simultaneously, and dysfunctionally seeking their own goals rather than those of the system). But decentralization does not necessarily in-

volve use of a price system in all cases; coordination may be achieved by other means (see Mesarovic et al. 1970: 24–29, 197–99, where the conditions in which use of an internal pricing system as the appropriate means of coordination are shown to be a special case).

4. The difference between relations and functions can be stated as follows: in the (physical) relation $R(x,y)$, x and y are things; in the function $f(u,v)$, u and v are properties.

5. See D.H. Bogart (1980) for a description of feed processes.

6. We can, in fact, distinguish two notions of planning regarded as anticipatory decision making. The first concerns the anticipation of decisions to be taken in the future, and laying the administrative groundwork for these decisions in advance. Such decisions are more properly described as anticipated, and this aspect of planning as scenario-and-agenda setting. In addition there are the decisions taken now to profit from expected future opportunities, or to prevent or minimize the losses from expected future threats. These are anticipatory decisions in the literal sense. They differ from the former class in that they involve immediate commitment of resources, and hence greater risk. The systems rationale for planning covers both of these classes of decisions.

REFERENCES

Ackoff, R.L. 1969. "Institutional Functions and Societal Needs." In *Perspectives of Planning*, pp. 495–500. *See* Jantsch 1969.

_____. 1970. *A Concept of Corporate Planning.* New York: Wiley-Interscience.

_____. 1971. "Towards a System of Systems Concepts." *Management Science* 17: 661–71.

_____. 1974. *Redesigning the Future.* New York: Wiley-Interscience.

Alchian, A. 1965. "The Basis of Some Recent Advances in the Theory of Management of the Firm." *Journal of Industrial Economics* 14 (November): 30–41.

Alchian, A., and H. Demsetz. 1972. "Production, Information Costs, and Economic Organization." *American Economic Review* 62 (December): 777–95.

Ansoff, H.I. 1976–77. "The State of Practice in Planning Systems." *Sloan Management Review* 18: 1–24.

Arrow, K.J. 1963. *Social Choice and Individual Values,* 2d ed. New Haven, CT and London: Yale University Press.

Baiman, S. 1982. "Agency Research in Managerial Accounting: A Survey." *Journal of Accounting Literature* 1 (Spring): 154–213.

Baiman, S., and J.S. Demski. 1980a. "Variance Analysis Procedures as Motivation Devices." *Management Science* 26 (July): 840–48.

_____. 1980b. "Economically Optimal Performance Evaluation and Control Systems." *Journal of Accounting Research* 18 (supplement): 184–220.

Baumol, W.J. 1959. *Business Behavior, Value and Growth.* New York: Macmillan.

Beer, S. 1969. "The Aborting Corporate Plan." In *Perspectives of Planning*, pp. 395–422. *See* Jantsch 1969.

Berle, A.A., Jr. and G.C. Means. 1932. *The Modern Corporation and Private Property.* New York: Macmillan.

Bogart, D.H. 1980. "Feedback, Feedforward, and Feedwithin: Strategic Information in Systems." *Behavioral Science* 25: 237–49.

Bunge, M. and M. Garcia-Sucre. 1976. "Differentiation, Participation and Cohesion." *Quality and Quantity* 10: 171–78.

Coase, R.H. 1937. "The Nature of the Firm." *Economica* n.s. 4 (November): 386–405.

_____. 1960. "The Problem of Social Cost." *Journal of Law and Economics* 3 (October): 1–44.

Cyert, R.M. and J.G. March. 1963. *A Behavioral Theory of the Firm.* Englewood Cliffs, NJ: Prentice-Hall.

Demski, J.S. 1980. *Information Analysis,* 2d ed. Reading, MA: Addison-Wesley.

Demski, J.S., and G.A. Feltham. 1978. "Economic Incentives in Budgetary Control Systems." *Accounting Review* 53 (April): 336–59.

Fama, E.F. 1980. "Agency Problems and the Theory of the Firm." *Journal of Political Economy* 88 (March): 288–307.

Furubotn, E.G. and S. Pejovich. 1972. "Property Rights and Economic Theory: A Survey of Recent Literature." *Journal of Economic Literature* 10 (December): 1137–62.

Henderson, J.M. and R.E. Quandt. 1980. *Micro-Economic Theory, A Mathematical Approach,* 3d ed. New York: McGraw-Hill.

Holmström, B. 1979. "Moral Hazard and Observability." *The Bell Journal of Economics* 10 (Spring): 74–91.

Jantsch, E., ed. 1969. *Perspectives of Planning.* Paris: Organization for Economic Cooperation and Development.

Jensen, M.C. and W.H. Meckling. 1976. "Theory of the Firm: Managerial Behavior, Agency Costs and Ownership Structure." *Journal of Financial Economics* 3: 305–60.

Kaplan, R.S. 1982. *Advanced Management Accounting.* Englewood Cliffs, NJ: Prentice-Hall.

Luce, R.D. and H. Raiffa. 1957. *Games and Decisions.* New York: Wiley.

Marris, R. 1964. *The Economic Theory of Managerial Capitalism.* Glencoe, IL: Free Press.

Mesarovic, M.D., D. Macko, and Y. Takahara. 1970. *Theory of Hierarchical, Multilevel Systems.* New York: Academic Press.

Mirrlees, J.A. 1976. "The Optimal Structure of Incentives and Authority within an Organization." *Bell Journal of Economics* 7 (Spring): 105–31.

Modigliani, F. and K.J. Cohen. 1961. "The Role of Anticipations and Plans in Economic Behavior and Their Use in Economic Analysis and Forecasting." *Studies in Business Expectations and Planning,* no. 4. University of Illinois Bureau of Economic and Business Research.

Penrose, E.T. 1958. *The Theory of the Growth of the Firm.* Oxford: Blackwell.

Rosen, R. 1975. "Biological Systems as Paradigms for Adaptation." In *Adaptive Economic Models,* edited by R.H. Day and T. Groves, pp. 39–72. New York: Academic Press.

Ross, S.A. 1973. "The Economic Theory of Agency: The Principal's Problem." *American Economic Review* 62 (May): 134–39.

Simon, H.A. 1959. "Theories of Decision Making in Economics and Behavioral Science." *American Economic Review* 49 (June): 253–83.

Steiner, G.A. 1969. *Top Management Planning,* chapters 1, 3, 24. New York: Macmillan.

Susman, G.I. 1981. "Planned Change: Prospects for the 1980's." *Management Science* 27 (February): 139–54.

Williamson, O.E. 1964. *The Economics of Discretionary Behavior: Managerial Objectives in a Theory of the Firm.* Englewood Cliffs, NJ: Prentice-Hall.

Wilson, R. 1968. "On the Theory of Syndicates." *Econometrica* 36 (January): 119–32.

2
The Nature and Content of Planning

The nature and content of the activity known as planning can be viewed in two ways. We could, first, say that from a systems point of view planning is a process that begins with objectives. Several different types of planning objective can be identified, each with an underlying philosophy of what planning is intended to achieve, and each resulting in a different notion of what planning should include. Another approach would be to focus, not on objective and philosophy, but on the nature of the activity that generates the plans. These two approaches are overlapping, in that a particular objective and philosophy implies that planning is conducted in a certain way. Consequently there is a logistics problem in deciding which should be discussed first, or whether the two should be combined. We have decided that the second approach, concerned with the nature and content of the plan-generating activity, is more conveniently treated first. Planning objectives and philosophies are examined in the next chapter, where the reader will detect the correspondences.

Recognizing, then, that what constitutes planning is open to many different interpretations, we take as our starting point only the fact that this activity is concerned with the future, that plans are anticipatory decisions. The rest of this chapter identifies five different ways of regarding the future. These are arrayed in increasing order of acceptability from a systems point of view. It is assumed in the case of all five that at each new planning stage there is a review of past performance and feedback to see what can be learned from this.

INTUITION, JUDGMENT

To begin with, we could think of planning as being based on intuition and judgment acquired as a result of past experience. The reason for taking this as the least satisfactory method of planning for, and regarding, the future is that it makes no reference to the future at all and is, furthermore, entirely implicit. It is all in the minds of the planners, and hence not open to scrutiny. While one can be impressed by the way an experienced businessperson reaches a decision intuitively in a novel situation, and while decisions taken in this way are sometimes spectacularly successful, it is too much to expect that a large *system* of decisions with numerous interdependencies could be satisfactorily dealt with intuitively, or by informal judgment. The complexities are just too great. The literature of psychology is full of warnings about the possible biases inherent in human intuition and judgmental processes: Memory is limited and sometimes faulty, information search by humans is often superficial, human information processing often biased, while human judgment may also be biased, especially when dealing with information that is conceptual (Slovic 1972) or probabilistic (Cohen 1972; Hogarth 1975; Kahneman and Tversky 1972; Tversky and Kahneman 1974; Lichtenstein et al. 1977), and when the environment is unstable. Other surveys of this literature will be found in Slovic et al. (1977) and, in an accounting context, in Libby and Lewis (1977) and in the *Report of the Committee on Human Information Processing* (American Accounting Association 1977). No explicit forecasting is involved in this approach to planning. At the same time, we cannot categorically dismiss intuition and judgment as totally unacceptable in any part of the planning process, because this informal mode may have within it elements of imagination, experimentation, and creativity that other modes lack.

EXTRAPOLATION

Another way of planning for and interpreting the future is to assume that it will be like the past. That is, the firm either projects a recent trend or bases its plans on the immediately previous plan, with minor adjustments for foreseeable changes. The amount of foresight and forming of expectations involved is minimal. According to Cyert and March (1963: 111–12) and common experience, this approach to planning is widespread:

> A plan is a precedent. It defines the decisions of one year and thereby establishes a *prima facie* case for continuing existing decisions. Only in quite exceptional cases do firms re-examine the rationale of existing functions. . . . Because of these characteristics of plans and planning, the decisions within the firms have both temporal periodicity and consistency over time that they would not necessarily have otherwise.

A similar view is expressed by Hedberg and Jönsson (1978). They see firms' information and accounting systems as more stabilizing than destabilizing when the environment is relatively static, making the organization more insensitive to change, by filtering away conflicts, ambiguities, overlaps, and uncertainty, suppressing many relevant change signals, and killing initiatives to act on early warnings. In a changing environment the influence of the information and accounting systems tends, by the same token, to be destabilizing and dysfunctional. A firm's behavior is, in effect, seen as essentially state determined (this year's results depend on last year's results), with little acknowledgment of the fact that the firm is operating in a constantly changing environment, and that it is a purposeful system. It was to combat this view of planning that Arthur Burns, former chairman of the Federal Reserve Board, coined the term "zero-base budgeting" in 1969. If planning were conceived of as in Chapter 1 (i.e., as production of a continuously adapted set of anticipatory decisions), there would be no need for zero-base budgeting. Planning based largely on extrapolation must be given low marks on the grounds that, while we are aware that forecasting of uncertain future events is fraught with difficulties, one can usually make a better estimate of the future than that it will be very much the same as the past. In an unstable environment, history becomes a particularly unreliable predictor of the future.

PREDICTION

The next interpretation of planning involves anticipatory behavior: forecasting and estimating, and the forming of expectations. The future is taken to be given by the firm's predictions; it is regarded as largely uncontrollable. Goals are environment determined, and hence the system is not regarded as purposeful: The future according to the prediction is accepted, and the firm plans *for* that future. It does not plan a future partly of its own making. By forecasting the future, the firm hopes to reveal and clarify potential opportunities and threats, so that it can prepare for them in advance. This view of planning may also include contingency planning. The plan that is adopted reflects the firm's idea of the expected course of events, but other events are seen as possible, and so alternative plans are prepared for each of these other eventualities. That is, the firm's predictions include one to the effect that forecasts cannot be relied on. The appropriate plan can then be put into operation when "the future makes up its mind" (Ackoff 1970: 17).

The process by which the firm makes its predictions may be more or less sophisticated: There are more and less reliable forecasting techniques. But the validity of expectations depends on more than the particular forecasting method used. Faulty expectations may come about in a number of other ways: because too little information is collected, too little of the available information is used (insufficient communication), or because expectations are based on irrelevant data (weaknesses in search, collection, or initial screening activities, or incorrect conceptualization of the problem), or because the data collected, while relevant, have been seriously biased in the process, or because unpredictable events (natural disasters, major technological breakthroughs) have supervened. Cyert and March (1963: 111) remark as follows on this approach to planning:

> A plan is a goal. In classical economics the importance of planning predictions is obscured by the assumption that the predictions are always correct (and correct without benefit of interactions between the prediction itself and firm behavior). Outside of such a utopia . . . a planning prediction functions both as a prediction . . . and also as a goal. . . . Under some circumstances (and within limits) an organization can induce behavior designed to confirm its prediction (goal).

In the present discussion, however, our intention is to distinguish certain "pure" cases. We therefore see this approach to planning, when used alone, as essentially passive, accepting the environment as given. We distinguish this from planning without foresight (extrapolation) and, at the next level, from planning that recognizes the system properties of the firm.

SOLVING SYSTEMS OF PROBLEMS

The feature of this approach to planning is that it is the first point at which real notice is taken of the fact that the firm is a system, and that planning is a system of problems. Forecasting and contingent planning will be part of this approach. But, while emphasizing the systems approach, the firm is not yet recognized as a purposeful system, that is, goals are still to be environment determined.

This view coincides with the systems rationale for planning described in Chapter 1. That is, planning is regarded as an opportunity, the *only* opportunity, of solving a large set of interrelated problems, what Ackoff calls a "mess" (1974: 21). Many of the firm's functions or activities are interrelated. Planning from a systems point of view means taking these interdependencies into account. This can be done in two ways. We could, first, try to do it simultaneously, by including the significant effects of the interdependencies—the externalities—in the formulation of each of the related subplanning problems (see Collard 1973 for a discussion of externalities [or external effects] and how to deal with them). Alternatively, we could do it sequentially, by taking into account decisions made early in the planning process when making related decisions later in the process, and modifying the earlier decisions in light of the decisions made subsequently.

Strictly, we should deal not only with interdependencies between functions or activities in a single period but also with interperiod (intertemporal, dynamic) interdependencies as well, because one period's decisions cannot be regarded as a closed system, isolated from other periods' decisions. This would mean making planning dynamic; but there are difficult problems in attempting to do this formally for a complex organization (Chapter 4, "Frequency of Planning").

Regarding planning as the solution of a large set of interrelated decisions implies that planning is a process, rather than a single act, that must be carried on more or less continuously (recall the quotation in Chapter 1, under "Frequency of Plans").

Our characterization in the Appendix of a social organization as an open system leads us to believe that the inner and outer couplings of system components to each other and to the environment are never constant. The strength, and even the existence, of these relations is changing all the time (Weick 1974). It is highly unlikely that all the complex and changing interrelations between subplanning problems are effectively taken into account in practice. Existing planning practice is therefore, at best, seen as involving prediction, not as solving a system of problems.

Some examples will support this argument. First, there is the possibility that external variables connected to the system by two-way outer couplings will be regarded as part of the environment instead of part of the system, as they should be. Such a case is mentioned by Roberts (1964), and is unlikely to be unique. In this case it was shown that what were thought to be externally induced (hence uncontrollable) disturbances in fact originated within the firm, but were controllable only by extending the boundaries of the system beyond the organizational boundaries of the firm.

The case cited by Roberts was of a company manufacturing electrical components. Competition depended heavily on product reliability and *delivery time* rather than on price. The firm's customers were other firms who used the components in the manufacture of their products, a fact that was not considered in the firm's budgetary control system. What happened was that when customers received orders for their products they dispatched orders for components, the time at which these orders were placed depending partly on the lead time of the component manufacturer. Changes in lead time thus affected the rate at which customers released new orders, which in turn affected the company's lead time, forming a feedback loop that was not considered in the company's control system (Fig. 2.1).

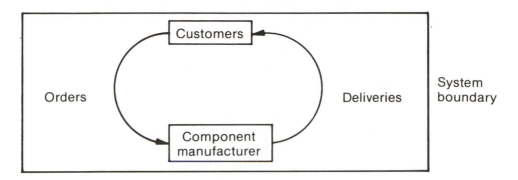

Fig. 2.1. Firm–customer feedback loop.

What was needed to eliminate these unnecessary fluctuations in the sales order rate was stabilization of lead time, and to do this customers' ordering decisions had to be treated as endogenous, inside the system (see Fig. A.1 in the Appendix). While this case refers to the control system rather than the planning system, precisely the same considerations apply in dealing with *two-way* outer couplings between planning system components and environment. Is this "interactive environment," which is part of the system, fully and accurately represented in the firm's planning deliberations?

The first reason for thinking that current planning practice is unlikely to consider all elements of the systems approach, then, is system misspecification. A second reason is that planning is unlikely to embrace all three levels in the hierarchy of system relations. Organizations, including firms, are purposeful systems: they choose both means and ends. Their parts (e.g., departments, functions) are also purposeful systems; and they are themselves part of a larger purposeful system or systems (an industry, economy, society). Three key problems in the management of organizations, says Ackoff, are how more effectively to achieve their own purposes, the purposes (or demands) of their parts, and the purposes of their suprasystem(s). He refers to these problems as the self-control problem, the humanization problem, and the environmentalization problem, respectively (Ackoff 1974: 18). Planning should encompass all three relations but probably seldom does in practice. For example, do budgets contribute to the solution of the humanization problem: are they set at a level designed to bring about an optimal balancing of the level of satisfaction of members' needs and the level of tension in the organization? Has allowance been made for members' personal goals that are incompatible with organizational goals? Are the organization structure, decision-making procedures and other operating rules, and role assignments conducive to achievement of the firm's goals? Recognizing that the firm and its parts are not completely programmable, is attention given to the question of motivation as an important element in management? What is the locus of motivation in the organization, and is it such as to encourage goal achievement or real progress toward goals? Does extrinsic motivation take the right form (monetary incentives are not always the most appropriate)? Is top management sure that the performance measures that are applied to parts of the organization are not inherently dysfunctional, serving to worsen performance rather than improve it? Is participation of people at all levels in the organization extended to the planning function, so that as many as possible may be convinced of the need to plan, and of the utility of the systems approach? Are managers given proper guidance as to what elements of the planning problem are tightly coupled and what elements loosely coupled (see the reference to Steiner in Chapter 1, "Behavioral Aspects: Motivation")? Some of these questions are further discussed in later chapters.

There are also the system–environment relations to consider. How much attention is given to these? In seeking constantly and selectively to match the orientation of the firm to its environment, is the firm's picture of this environment and of environment–system relations sufficiently detailed, accurate, and current? Does the firm have a sense of corporate responsibility? Does it consider how its activities and its products contribute to the problems of the suprasystem (e.g., waste and litter problems, creation of health hazards)? Is it contributing to social problems as well as to ecological and health problems? Does it have effective safety standards for its workers and its products?

These are some of the things that suggest that even in the case of firms that consider they are taking a systems approach to planning, some elements of this approach may be missing, or be given insufficient attention.

Regarding this "problem-solving" approach as a "pure" strategy, we note that the firm is still seen as taking an essentially passive view: It is planning *for* the future; it is not seeking to redesign the future, nor is it setting its own goals, but merely solving the system of problems that its environment, as seen through its forecasts, serves up to it.

PLANNING THE FUTURE

The final approach involves planning the future rather than planning *for* the future as in the previous categories. It includes forecasting, anticipatory planning, and problem solving as in the previous case, but instead of seeing the future as the firm's predictions suggest it is likely to be, the firm consciously designs its own desired future and prepares to bring it about. This calls for the ability to *explain* the system's behavior, not just predict it (Ackoff 1970: 44).

This view of planning gives full play to the potential of the open and purposeful system. In addition to passively (i.e., reactively) and actively adapting to a changing environment the firm now consciously seeks to redesign significant parts of its future environment as well. That is, as well as predicting potential opportunities and threats as in the previous two cases, it now creates opportunities and tries to prevent threats from developing. This kind of planning involves looking at the future with all constraints except the absolutely inescapable ones (and certainly all the self-imposed ones) relaxed. It is an idealistic view: The desired future state of the system may never be reached, but it can be continuously approached. The goals are proposed by the system itself, not set by the environment.

Heavier emphasis on everything that will lead to more effective adaptation and learning and to making the firm a more adaptive organization is the distinguishing feature of this kind of planning.

Information System

One requirement of this approach is that the information system must be designed to increase the firm's ability to learn and adapt rapidly: Information consists of differences that make a difference. We saw in Chapter 1 that this would mean more or less continuous planning. In the same way, the information system and decision modes should leave some discretion to decision makers. More generally, the information system must enable management quickly and efficiently to identify problems and their interrelationships, plan and make decisions, implement and control the decisions and plans once made, if the system is to adapt and learn effectively (Ackoff 1974: 32), and must not be mechanical and inflexible. It should enable the firm to learn from its own mistakes, be self-correcting, and become better at doing this over time. It should also increase the firm's ability to cope with variety in its environment—in short, to learn more about its changing environment, and to stimulate curiosity, experimentation, innovation, and creativity.

Probably most existing management information systems do not come close to meeting these needs by encouraging organizational flexibility rather than rigidity, ensuring that relevant information is communicated where it should be (between interdependent functions or activities), and not communicated where it should not be (unrelated functions). They should also provide sufficient information on the environment so that the system can seek selectively to match its orientation to the environment, if that is its objective, or at least keep it fully informed about its relevant environment if its objective is to change parts of that environment to its own design. In a rapidly changing environment, rigidly prescribed information search and collection routines and screening rules, and standard operating procedures, can exert strong inertial or even destabilizing effects, inhibiting adaptation and learning.

Hedberg and Jönsson (1978) have done some interesting research in this area on Swedish firms. They make the point that all information systems imply a "world view" as to what information, including characteristics of the environment, is relevant. These world views are not revised as the world changes; they resist change. There are also indications, say these researchers, that information systems hinder organizational search and filter out significant amounts of uncertainty, incompatible information, and change signals. They "make sense of environments which do not make sense," rendering them more homogeneous and explained than they really are. Systems designers are thus in a position to affect the quantity and quality of information received by organizational decision makers, and the organizational environment within which learning can take place (through the structures that are supported, and the modes of behavior that are encouraged). If, as suggested, they act dysfunctionally, the fit between "the complexity of cognitive structures" within the organization (the mapping of the environment into the organization) and the real world outside the organization is distorted. Changes in the environment may require organizations to restructure their models of the world, and change their internal structure, decision processes, and information systems. "Traditional accounting systems are small wonders of logic and consistency, much due to the fact that environments are perceived as rather simple, described by two essential variables: price and quantity . . ." (Hedberg and Jönsson, 1978).

This much seems beyond doubt, that firms need to devote considerable efforts to scanning their environments. Hedberg and Jönsson also make the point that more is not necessarily better: Access to more information and more advanced decision aids in no way ensures that decision makers will be better informed and make better decisions. This is particularly true of computerized systems, which tend to increase programmed behaviors and freeze defined organization structures (Mowshowitz 1976). Similar views concerning the frequently dysfunctional effects of information systems appear in Hedberg et al. (1976).

Other researchers also have noted that a desirable property of information systems for complex adaptive or learning systems is that they should provide for flexibility. Grinyer and Norburn (1975), in a study of 21 English firms, found their results suggested that a certain amount of ambiguity with respect to organizational roles and objectives could lead to better financial performance in many situations. In particular, the use of many informal information channels appeared to do this. The information system, it appears, is also likely to be more conducive to improved performance and adaptation if it provides for different cognitive types. That is, different individuals, and particularly persons with different educational backgrounds and representing different functions in the organization, have different learning styles, and these should be catered to (Kolb 1974; Wolfe 1976; Mason and Mitroff 1973). Consequently "pluralism, diversity of perspectives and measuring dimensions, and modest amounts of ambiguity and uncertainty appear to be desirable properties of trigger-rich information systems for organizations in changing environments" (Hedberg and Jönsson 1978).

The need to ensure flexibility extends to information filters (i.e., to decisions as to what information should be sought, what collected, what communicated, and the conscious or unconscious manipulation or biasing of information as it passes through the organization). In changing environments firms need to be able to change these filters as their strategies and action plans change.

Organization Structure

A second requirement for effective adaptation and learning concerns organization structure, a highly important variable. This refers to the inner couplings of system components, or, in Ackoff's words (1970: 13), "The way that the work done by an organization is divided into parts . . ., and how work is assigned to parts." Organizational structure must have the utmost flexibility, and be otherwise designed to facilitate adaptation and learning. Ackoff reiterates the point made by Beer (Chapter 1, "Frequency of Plans") that the organizational structure must be capable of carrying out the plan, and of adapting. On occasion the plan may require restructuring of the organization. If organization structure is not regarded as a variable it "may deprive the planner of his most powerful means of improving [the organization's] performance" (1970: 87). Adaptation, as Buckley (1968) pointed out, implies a willingness to maintain, destroy, or restructure internal structure as required by external events if the environment cannot be changed to the system's advantage.

Similar views are expressed by Hedberg et al. (1976). Continued viability requires that an organization remain cohesive without becoming rigid, and that its speed and direction of change approximate those of its environment. Long-term survival is maximized by what they call a "self-designing" organization, one that retains a fluid internal structure except when its inertia is deficient (the latter would cause it to respond too quickly to disturbances, or to respond to signals not warranting a response, or to overreact by taking stronger corrective measures than are necessary).

Their view of the organization is a process view: Processes play the key role. Behavior is generated by processes, and the latter may be broadly categorized as accelerator, decelerator, and stabilizer processes. Accelerator processes either speed up change in present directions or divert it into new directions. Decelerator processes reduce the speed of change in present directions, while stabilizer processes stabilize speed and direction of change. The best way to change organizational behavior, they suggest, is to focus on the change processes, and to modify these.

In their ideal self-designing organization (so-called because it constantly diagnoses its important problems, explores future options, and invents new solutions), long-term survival and adaptation can be achieved and serious future problems avoided by keeping processes dynamically balanced. What this means, specifically, is that processes should be balanced on six fulcra, which are overlapping to some extent. The self-designing organization should simultaneously seek *minimal* amounts of these six desirable characteristics:

(i) *minimal consensus*: "The usual organization seeks more consensus than is useful"; what is required is a balance between consensus and dissent.

(ii) *minimal contentment or satisfaction*: Too much attention to members' welfare leads to complacency and insensitivity to change signals, while discontent, when it becomes vocal, is a kind of crisis insurance, and a certain amount of tension aids adaptation (see Appendix).

(iii) *minimal affluence*: While a small amount of organizational slack[1] can be an asset, it must be kept in mind that most of the world's great civilizations arose in barren places, not in lush river valleys.

(iv) *minimal faith*: The organization should rely on its plans only minimally; "a realistic organization keeps itself ready to replace plans and goals in order to match and to exploit environmental unpredictability."

(v) *minimal consistency*: "The usual organization systematically avoids changes through inflexible policies, strict conformity to standard procedures . . ., clear and rationalized goals, reward structures that discourage risk taking, sharply delineated responsibilities . . ., punishment of dissent . . ., centralized control," whereas what is needed is utmost flexibility of organizational structure and a range of discretion in decision making.

(vi) *minimum rationality*: Excessive rationality may conflict with the need for flexibility in order to adapt. The models used to obtain rational solutions inevitably abstract from reality, may incorporate false assumptions, and they of course suppress alternative formulations; they also emphasize means to the exclusion of ends. An organization is too changeable a thing to be bound by such theoretical rigidities. And, as Ackoff says (1974: 21), decision problems do not come ready made, they have to be abstracted from real-life situations, and the key elements in the problem (obtained by asking the right questions) may not even have been identified.

This is a provocative view, and some may feel that the last argument is somewhat overstated. But otherwise it is generally consistent with what we should expect for an open, purposeful system. The orientation toward flexibility implies, the same authors add, that the organization should be induced "to act as if optimal is an impossible state," and its members should be thoroughly committed to impermanence. Among the key properties possessed by the self-designing organization, experimentation, arousal of curiosity, and disruption of complacency would be prominent.

SUMMARY

In this chapter we have distinguished five different approaches to planning in terms of what the planning task actually involves. They ranged from planning based on intuition and judgment to planning in the sense of actively seeking to shape the future, or significant elements of it, in an attempt to bring about some desired state. This latter approach was recognized as an idealistic one, unending but capable of successive approximation of the objective. It is unlikely that any firms yet practice this form of planning. Between these two extremes came the systems rationale for planning, which is that it is the only opportunity the firm has of "solving" its system of problems, of taking all the interrelatedness into account.

The five approaches distinguished were put forward as "pure" cases. In a given firm planning might contain elements of all five, or at least of the first four. The classification is not of course unique, but merely a convenient way of bringing out the features that planning for a complex, open, adaptive, and purposeful system should or should not desirably include. Thus Ackoff (1970: 56) distinguishes three attitudes toward the future which, ordered from the most to the least prevalent, are: (a) wait and see; (b) predict and prepare; and (c) make it happen.

Of the requirements for effective adaptation and learning other than ongoing, comprehensive planning, two were singled out as being of special importance. They concerned the necessary characteristics of the information system, and organizational structure.

In the next chapter we will look at planning in another way, by identifying several different types of planning objectives and their associated planning philosophies.

NOTES

1. According to Cyert and March (1963) organizations build up slack to absorb environmental change. An example of this is the top-heaviness of a firm. Thus, when demand drops sharply the staff of a production planning department could in one particular instance be reduced overnight from 3,000 to 150 with no adverse effects. Another example of slack is granting discretion to staff in investing company funds, resulting in some investment in pet schemes that is not economically viable. Firms in perfectly competitive equilibrium have zero organizational slack.

REFERENCES

Ackoff, R.L. 1970. *A Concept of Corporate Planning*. New York: Wiley-Interscience.

_____. 1974. *Redesigning the Future*. New York: Wiley-Interscience.

American Accounting Association. 1977. *Report of the Committee on Human Information Processing*. Sarasota, FL.

Buckley, W. 1968. "Society as a Complex Adaptive System." In *Modern Systems Research for the Behavioral Scientist,* edited by W. Buckley, pp. 490–513. Chicago: Aldine.

Cohen, J. 1972. *Psychological Probability: Or the Art of Doubt.* London: Allen & Unwin.

Collard, D.A. 1973. "External Effects." In *Readings in Management Decision,* edited by L.R. Amey, pp. 23–44. London: Longman.

Cyert, R.M. and J.G. March. 1963. *A Behavioral Theory of the Firm,* chs. 4–5. Englewood Cliffs, NJ: Prentice-Hall.

Grinyer, P.H. and D. Norburn. 1975. "Planning for Existing Markets: Perceptions of Executives and Financial Performance." *Journal of the Royal Statistical Society* series A138: 70–97.

Hedberg, B. and S. Jönsson. 1978. "Designing Semi-Confusing Information Systems for Organizations in Changing Environments." *Accounting, Organizations and Society* 3: 47–64.

Hedberg, B., P.C. Nystrom, and W.H. Starbuck. 1976. "Camping on Seesaws: Prescriptions for a Self-Designing Organization." *Administrative Science Quarterly* (March): 41–65.

Hogarth, R.M. 1975. "Cognitive Processes and the Assessment of Subjective Probability Distributions." *Journal of the American Statistical Association* 70: 271–89.

Kahneman, D. and A. Tversky. 1972. "Subjective Probability: A Judgment of Representativeness." *Cognitive Psychology* 3: 430–54.

Kolb, D.A. 1974. "On Management and the Learning Process." In *Organizational Psychology: A Book of Readings,* edited by D.A. Kolb, I.M. Rubin, and J.M. McIntyre. Englewood Cliffs, NJ: Prentice-Hall: 27–42.

Libby, R. and B.L. Lewis. 1977. "Human Information Processing Reseach in Accounting: The State of the Art." *Accounting, Organizations and Society* 2: 245–68.

Lichtenstein, S., B. Fischhoff, and L.D. Phillips. 1977. "Calibration of Probabilities: The State of the Art." In *Decision Making and Change in Human Affairs,* edited by H. Jungermann and G. de Zeew. Dordrecht, Holland: Reidel.

Mason, R.O. and I.I. Mitroff. 1973. "A Program for Research on Management Information Systems." *Management Science* 19: 475–87.

Mowshowitz, A. 1976. *The Conquest of Will: Information Processing in Human Affairs.* Reading, MA: Addison-Wesley.

Roberts, E.B. 1964. "Industrial Dynamics and the Design of Management Control Systems. In *Management Controls: New Directions in Basic Research,* edited by C.P. Bonini, R.K. Jaedicke, and H.M. Wagner, ch. 6. New York: McGraw-Hill.

Slovic, P. 1972. "Psychological Study of Human Judgment: Implications for Investment Decision Making." *Journal of Finance* 27: 779–99.

Slovic, P., B. Fischhoff, and S. Lichtenstein. 1977. "Behavioral Decision Theory." *Annual Review of Psychology* 28: 1–39.

Tversky, A. and D. Kahneman. 1974. "Judgment under Uncertainty: Heuristics and Biases." *Science* 185: 1124–31.

Weick, K.E. 1974. "Middle Range Theories of Social Systems." *Behavioral Science* 19: 357–67.

Wolfe, J. 1976. "Learning Styles Rewarded in a Complex Simulation with Implications for Business Policy and Organization Behavior Research." *Proceedings of the 36th Annual National Meeting of the Academy of Management.* August 11–14, Kansas City, Missouri.

3
The Aims of Planning

Having argued that planning is an essential part of system management, and examined a number of views as to what the planning task involves, we now go on to consider what *type* of planning objective business enterprises might adopt. The present discussion will be confined to types of objectives suggested in the literature. Each type of objective is associated with a particular planning philosophy or view of the purpose of the enterprise. No attempt is made to cover the literature exhaustively, only to present a number of different views emanating from influential writers on the subject. Our own views on the kind of objectives that would be most appropriate for business enterprises regarded as open, adaptive, and purposeful systems are the subject of Chapter 6. This chapter ends with some discussion of the resolution of conflicts over planning objectives within the firm.

THE NETWORK OF AIMS: SELECTED VIEWS

The contributions considered are those of Ackoff (1970, 1974), Steiner (1969), Ozbekhan (1969), Beer (1969), and Emery (1969). All these writers, in varying degrees, approach planning from a systems point of view.

Ackoff (1974) provides a structured view of general attitudes toward planning and a characterization of the type of objective associated with each. This framework gives us a useful starting point. Ackoff's categories are:

Planning philosophy	Type of planning objective
Inactivism	"Satisficing"
Reactivism	"Muddling through"
Preactivism	Optimizing
Interactivism	Idealizing

Each of the general attitudes appearing on the left is found in varying proportions in each individual and organization, according to Ackoff, and the mixture may change over time and from one situation to another. At any given time, however, one of the four is likely to be dominant in both individuals and organizations, and in different situations each one may be best.

As described by Ackoff, the inactivist or "do nothing" philosophy is to "ride with the tide," to seek stability—and survive. Inactivists are "satisfied with the way things are and the way they are going," believing intervention in the course of events is as likely to make things worse as to improve them. Ends are more likely to be fitted to means than conversely, and in selecting means the inactivist's principal criterion is feasibility rather than any notion of efficiency. ". . . ends are chosen that are appropriate to nearly available means" (Hirschman and Lindblom, 1969). This is "crisis management." In systems terms, this attitude amounts to a complete denial of the firm's open (hence adaptive if it is to survive) and purposeful properties. Ackoff associates this attitude to planning with an objective of "satisficing" on the basis that inactivists "are willing to let well enough alone." This is not quite the usual interpretation of "satisficing" as referring to a two-valued utility function (good enough, not good enough).

The second, or reactivist, attitude to planning represents a preference for a previous state over the one the firm is in, resistance to change, and attempts to unmake previous changes in order to regain some state best described as "the good old days." Continuing the metaphor used in the previous case, reactivists try to swim against the tide. In a rapidly changing environment, any organization that refuses to adapt cannot long survive. Once successful organizations, now in decline, are particularly susceptible to this point of view, says Ackoff. He characterizes their planning objective as "muddling through": "They prefer art to science: the art of muddling through to the science of management . . . they rely on common sense, intuition, and judgment based on long experience . . . [which] they believe . . . is the best teacher . . . ." Readers may recall the quotation from the sociologist Buckley (1968) in the Appendix (under the section "Complexity as degrees of freedom"), to the effect that a policy of "muddling through" is less likely to be disastrous, or immediately disastrous, in the case of social organizations than for systems of lesser complexity and consequently fewer degrees of freedom, always provided that environmental disturbances are not too great.

Preactivists, Ackoff's third category, have a more optimistic view of the future and less resistance to change. They are willing to believe the future will be better than the present or the past. They try to capitalize on this by predicting the future and preparing for it, exploiting future opportunities and avoiding potential threats. They seek to "ride in front of [the tide] and get to where it is going before it does." In systems terms there is at least implicit recognition here that the firm is an open system that must adapt to survive. But adaptation is directed toward a future or an environment that is regarded as essentially uncontrollable. In terms of the previous chapter's categories, the preactivist view of planning relates to prediction, and possibly to solving a system of problems also, but not to designing a desired future. Approached in this way, planning is based more on "logic, science, and experimentation than on common sense, intuition and judgment." The preactivist planner's objective is to optimize his position, taking the environment as largely uncontrollable.

Interactivism, the final philosophy, is concerned with designing a desired future and inventing ways of bringing it about. The firm is at last seen as a purposeful system. The corresponding planning objective is no longer to optimize in a largely uncontrollable environment, but to design and seek to bring about an idealized future that can never be attained, but can be continuously approached. As described by Ackoff, the interactivist sees this not as an exercise in utopianism but as a necessary step in setting long-range directions for continuous development, an attempt to redirect the tide. Planning here includes strong emphasis on restructuring the system—on trying to find the ideal form for the particular organization, a form that will increase its capacity to adapt and learn rapidly, on a continuing basis—as well as on inducing cooperative changes in the organization's environment. Four principles of planning recognized by the interactivist are that it should be ongoing, participative, integrated, and coordinated.

Ackoff gives a graphic example of interactivism by reference to the urban traffic problem. A preactivist planner would tend to assume a continued growth in demand for automotive transportation and no significant change in the automobile, and would suggest as remedies increasing the number and size of roads and expansion of other modes of transport. The interactivist would consider more radical remedies, such as changing the automobile and the city so that demand for transportation and roadways is modified. He seeks out root causes rather than symptoms.

Ackoff describes the circumstances in which each of these stylized views would be the most appropriate: inactivism if the course of events (the tide) is taking the system where it wants to go, as quickly as it wants to go; reactivism if it is taking the system where it does not want to go and it prefers to stay where it is or was; preactivism if events are taking the system in the right direction, but too slowly; interactivism if the system is not impressed by the past, present, or expected future *and* believes that that future can be made more attractive if it takes a hand in shaping it.

To Ackoff, planning *objectives* are desired future systems states (1970: 40–41). He distinguishes between "stylistic" objectives, which are valued for their own sake, and which he believes receive less attention in corporate planning than they deserve, and performance objectives, which are valued instrumentally. An example of the first would be the rejection by a company of a diversification plan that involved going into certain products because dealing with these products was not the company's "style," whereas a performance objective is some outcome that can be given operational meaning and measured, and is valued instrumentally in that it contributes to some other valued outcome.

Goals are dated objectives, that is, objectives whose attainment is desired by a specified time *within* the planning period. Objectives may be unattainable, but must be approachable, within the planning period; goals must be attainable within the planning period, but need not necessarily be attained. The phase of planning concerned with setting objectives and goals should specify explicitly what the objectives are, how they are to be translated into goals, and provide a schedule for the attainment of goals. In addition, goals need to be defined operationally (e.g., it is useless to tell the manager of a service department that the objective is to maximize profits), and measures need to be selected for evaluating progress toward goals.

Figure 3.1 displays another writer's idea of the network of aims of a business, arrayed in descending order of generality from the top of the pyramid.

Steiner (1969) provides a wealth of empirical material in the most comprehensive and authoritative work available on planning. He draws attention to a bewildering array of terms (*mission, direction, ultimate end, aims, purposes, objectives, goals*) which, moreover, are not defined consistently in the literature. His own interpretation is shown in Fig. 3.1.

The top three levels express the company's creed or philosophy. Preparation of a written statement of the ethical and operational philosophy of a company is something to which staff may contribute, but which must ultimately be determined by the senior executives, Steiner notes, adding:

> Once these statements are prepared they are not often changed. Perhaps
> they ought to be reviewed and changed more frequently . . . for they may

include company biases, dogmas, blind spots and obsolete standards, which should be eliminated.

Fig. 3.1. Network of business aims.

In order to survive the company must fulfill its basic socioeconomic purpose of satisfying consumer demands (i.e., support its suprasystem). It must do this, not philanthropically, but by using economic resources effectively and efficiently to pursue a mission, or line of business, and earn profits for its owners—indeed satisfy all its stakeholders. The statement of basic purposes is operationalized by selecting a mission or missions. For many large companies it would include some broad reference to the company's line of business (e.g., General Motors' "People building transportation to serve people"), its sense of social responsibility to the communities in which it does business and to society as a whole, and its responsibilities to its employees, in addition to its intention to achieve a continuous growth of profits. Firms are thinking more and more seriously about basic mission statements, says Steiner, because the alternatives included in corporate charters are usually too broad to serve as a basis for planning, and because specifying the basic mission(s) does, in fact, direct a company's efforts. He cites the case of the Cunard Line, which radically changed its line of business in 1966 by declaring that the passenger ship was no longer to be regarded "simply as a means of transport, but more as a floating resort in which people take a holiday and enjoy themselves," with transportation thrown in incidentally; "we find ourselves in a growth industry, the leisure industry." Deciding whether or not to change the basic mission or line(s) of business of a company is one of the most important tasks the chief executive has to perform, says Steiner. If a change is not made when needed, stagnation and bankruptcy may ensue; if a wise change is made, it can open up an entirely new horizon of profitable opportunities.

The value system or set of beliefs of top management considerably influences the direction in which a firm moves and the way it operates. They may also be partly responsible for the existence of multiple objectives. Value systems, says Steiner, are comparatively permanent bases for influencing behavior. They influence the way a manager perceives situations, solves problems and makes decisions, regards other individuals and groups, looks at his business, and decides on the direction in which it should go. As such, value systems have obvious relevance to the basic purposes top managers establish for their enterprises.

In Steiner's usage, as in Ackoff's, "objective" means a desired long-range state; "goals" or "targets" are desired short-range states. Objectives are usually established and revised annually as part of the planning process, short-range goals in the course of the budgeting process. Objectives may be set for every part of a business considered important enough to be the subject of plans (e.g, profitability, sales and markets, products, finance, manpower and personnel, stability, organization, research and development, public responsibility, management development, balance between goals and objectives—that is, short-range goals should make long-range objectives meaningful). This conspectus, it may be noted, covers system objectives, relations between system and suprasystem, the objectives of system components, and the needs of the business as a dynamic system. Both objectives and goals are expressed in specific, usually quantitative terms, and both are to be achieved by a specified time. Goals may exist for the business as a whole, for divisions or departments, and for individual performance. They are needed to guide and coordinate activity (in fact the whole pyramid of aims is designed to do this) and to set standards for performance.

The announcement of goals, objectives, and missions may also have motivating power, although influencing people's motivation is a complex matter that involves more than the setting of ends: Participation in planning, committed leadership, and the offer of suitable rewards for achievement are also helpful. Most, but not all, of the short-range goals are set forth in the annual budgets, and some goals may be nonquantifiable (e.g., developing better relations with suppliers, customers, or union leaders).

As stated above, there is an obvious need to give balanced attention to the different time horizons in planning. "Managements that become preoccupied with either end of the spectrum run grave dangers," warns Steiner. Too much attention to the distant future without considering the near-term leads to utopian (or "blue sky") planning; the reverse leads to *ad hoc* planning which may lose sight of its purpose. The time horizon is also relevant to the revision of aims: The shorter-range the aim, the greater the frequency with which it must be changed, although the need to maintain flexibility should apply to all of them. The whole network of aims changes over time; the only question is how frequently, and whether frequently enough. The network should also be integrated: goals should be related to objectives, objectives to missions, and missions to managerial values and basic purposes.

Ozbekhan (1969) defines things differently: In considering the purpose of planning only two systems are of interest, the plan, and the system in which the plan is embedded, which he calls the "environment." In Figure 3.2 these are represented by Ss and E-Ss respectively.

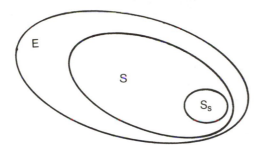

Fig. 3.2. Planning system and environment. Ss, planning system; S, human/social-centered aspects of environment; E, life/nature-centered and thing/technology-centered environments.

Hence "environment" includes not only the external environment (more precisely the true exogenous variables) but also the system being planned (e.g., the firm). Given this unusual definition, ". . . planning is a process whose function is to reduce entropy and increase organization within the environment" (Ozbekhan 1969: 111). Planning should change the "environment" in such a way that tendencies toward coherence in the "environment" are enhanced and those toward disintegration kept in check.

Note first that "coherence" (or integration) is here being used in a sense different from that defined in the Appendix and Chapter 1. As it was there described, integration involved relations between a system and its environment. In Ozbekhan's scheme of things there is nothing external to the system being planned, since "environment" means the firm plus its external environment. More to the point, a planning objective of seeking to decrease entropy within the "environment," of making the environment as well as the firm more organized, is surely utopian. For while the firm is always interested in changing itself only if it cannot change the external environment in its favor, the extent to which it can do this will be severely limited by what Beer (1969) terms "the cussedness of events." As he observes, the firm "has control over a mere fraction of the situation in which it inheres." It is very short on information—about itself, its external environment, what is going to happen, and when it will happen. What is sought is adaptation and survival of the *firm,* whatever the condition of its external environment, and the bringing of the two into a harmonious orientation is achieved mainly by changes within the firm. Even if the external environment were continuously stable, corporate planning would still be required because the firm's internal relations are never at rest, because the firm would still be faced with a system of problems to solve, and because even if the future were known with certainty it may not coincide with where the firm wants to go.

Beer is one of the leading proponents of the "new planning," that is planning whose aim is the continuous adaptation of the enterprise. This kind of planning, says Beer, is founded in organizational structure, because structure (inner couplings) is that which adapts. Plans will be changed, but it is the organization that adapts. And if the structure of an organization is not adaptive, the organization cannot effectively change its plans.

Few existing organization structures are likely to meet these demands, he considers. They were devised for an era in which the rate of technological change was slow and the environment relatively static. The metabolism of management needs to be speeded up to meet the increased rate of change in technology and society. A new form of organization structure is needed, one that is quicker and more effective in adapting.

Beer's answer is in terms of *controls* (a proposed five-tier hierarchy of controls) and is considered in detail in Chapter 5. The top three control levels correspond, in a planning context, to a planning for policies, strategies, and tactical operational objectives.

Beer makes extensive use of analogies between organizations and human beings, and seeks to describe and explain organizational behavior in physiological and neurophysiological terms, which he explains to the general reader in Beer (1972). As remarked elsewhere (Amey 1979: 100), it is valid to reason by analogy from human systems to organizations if we are dealing with motivated behavior: The problems are here essentially the same problems on a more complex scale. Analogies with nonmotivated or motivationally neutral human behavior, however, are unjustified, because there is no reason to believe that the two cases have enough in common for the explanation of one to provide at least a partial explanation of the other. It is also the case that certain important kinds of behavior in both humans and organizations (e.g., creativity) go beyond the feedback principle that Beer wishes to make the main determinant; they are autonomous.

Although Emery (1969) does not refer to planning per se, he makes two important points relevant to planning. One is the notion, shared by Ackoff and Steiner, that any attempt constantly to match the orientation of the firm to the state of its environment renders short-range goals and even long-range objectives expendable. There is, however, need for some focal condition, some organizing idea that will give everyone in the organization a sense of direction. The enterprise, being a purposeful system, must set itself a mission or missions "in terms of outcomes that are capable of achievement and yet are sufficiently beyond present performance to allow for some measurable degree of progress" (p. 10). The firm's purpose is not merely to adapt to its environment passively, or even by partly changing the environment. Rather it is to do these things while keeping some long-range general ideal constantly in view, an ideal that takes concrete shape through a succession of specific missions. This view seems to be close to Ackoff's idealizing objective, although Ackoff does not specify that this objective should take the form of a steady state as Emery does.

The second point made by Emery (Emery and Trist, 1969: chapter 12) is that, in addition to taking account of interrelatedness within the firm and relations between the firm and the environment, there are also interdependencies between parts of the environment, described as the "causal texture" of the environment. These processes which begin and end in the environment are among the determining conditions of the exchanges across the system-environment interface. A full understanding of organizational behavior, and effective planning, requires some knowledge of this area of external causal relationships as well as of the system and system-environment relations.

Emery's work ranks at the forefront of applications of systems thinking to organizations, and he was one of the pioneers in this area. He also describes an organization quite unambiguously as an open, purposeful system (others who view organizations in this way are Katz and Kahn [1966: chapter 2] and von Bertalanffy [1968]).

CONFLICTING OBJECTIVES AND GOALS

Following Steiner, it seems reasonable to envisage a network of corporate aims proceeding from high-level, very general basic purposes through a succession of lower-level aims that are narrower in their focus and increasingly precise. Conflicts among the basic socioeconomic purposes of a business are unlikely to arise, because of the very broad terms in which they are expressed, although a major environmental disturbance or a change in top management personnel could induce a change. The same goes for the missions by which these purposes are to be fulfilled. It is only when basic purposes and missions are elaborated into long-range objectives and short-term goals that conflicts usually arise.

Recalling that a firm is a system, with much interrelatedness between its parts, and that both the system and its parts are purposeful, we should not be surprised to find areas of conflict within it. In the Appendix it is stated that a certain amount of internal conflict and tension is normal in an open system, and is in fact one of the mechanisms that help it to adapt. In the present context, conflicts may arise in the process of *setting* objectives or goals, or in the course of their *implementation*; and the probability of conflict is increased by the fact that both human beings and organizations characteristically have multiple objectives.

More specifically, we can identify nine possible areas of conflict. The first arises from setting incompatible objectives or goals for a single planning period. The simultaneous optimization of two or more objectives that are functionally interrelated will usually be logically inconsistent. Thus short-range goals of maximizing profits and obtaining the largest market share may be incompatible. The remaining cases of conflict all arise from failure to formulate plans consistently for different levels, functions, or time periods, or because insufficient thought has been given to measurement problems.

If different planning periods, or planning stages in a single plan, are regarded as closed systems (not affected by or affecting other time periods), conflicts between short-range and long-range objectives are likely to result. A long-range objective of achieving some desired state in, say, 10 years' time is unlikely to be reached if annual goals are formulated without taking into account dynamic interdependencies between past, present, and future. Business operations are dynamic and sequential, the outcomes of decisions in one period becoming initial conditions that influence planning in the next period. Thus assets of various kinds, including inventories, are inherited from earlier periods. Second, actions planned for the current period may limit opportunities in future periods. If a firm deliberately cuts its programmed budget for maintenance expenditure this year it may reduce production in subsequent periods by causing excessive plant breakdowns. Third, actions planned for the current period may depend on action alternatives that the firm expects to have in subsequent periods. While future events cannot limit what is currently achievable, they may nevertheless limit what it is *desirable to achieve* if short-range plans are viewed as stepping stones toward the achievement of a long-range objective. Hence if the objective is to maximize profits over a 10-year period, it may be desirable to hold down sales and profits in the current period and build inventories if prices are confidently expected to rise in later years, in order to reap larger profits in those years. Unless all of these dynamic interdependencies are taken into account in formulating short-range goals, conflicts will be set up between goals and objectives.

A third source of conflicting objectives or goals arises when inappropriate performance measures induce dysfunctional behavior by parts of the firm, and incongruence of subgoals with goals. A frequently cited example of this occurs where a divisionalized firm has an ROI (return on investment) objective. The manager of a particular division with a stable ROI of 20 percent can improve his performance either by accepting only incremental projects that promise an ROI in excess of 20 percent or by disinvesting from projects that are currently yielding less than 20 percent. If the firm's cost of capital is 14 percent, the divisional manager is failing to support projects that would be acceptable to the firm, subject to risk considerations. Dysfunctional performance measures for parts of a business are very common in practice (Amey and Egginton 1973: chapter 17).

Another case is where objectives or goals have been specified in such a way as to make the measurement of performance in relation to them impossible. For example, it would be impossible to measure performance against an objective of maximizing the firm's long-term survival prospects · if the horizon had not been specified or "survival prospects" sufficiently defined.

Conflicts between the objectives or goals of different parts of a firm, or between subgoals and the firm's goals, are also introduced if plans are not functionally unified. By this we mean that plans may be consistent with each other in financial terms and, if they relate to different levels, their associated performance measures may not be dysfunctional, yet they may make it impossible for different functions to work together harmoniously. This may happen, for example, because inadequate or inconsistent administrative procedures cannot coordinate the functions and make the plans effective. We saw in Chapter 1 that one planning imperative was to bring about structural and functional unity.

Goals that are not operationally well defined, or not carefully enough delineated, may lead to further conflicts. As a result, different sections of the business may be pursuing inconsistent goals.

A major source of conflict, according to Steiner (1969: 186), results from the degree of priority placed on one or more aims by a firm with multiple aims. While most conflicts over ordering of aims may not be serious, some result in damage to the enterprise. For example, a key factor leading to the bankruptcy of many small firms has been the failure to balance growth, short-term working capital needs, and production costs. Incompatible priorities may also arise during the implementation of a plan. In translating objectives into goals a schedule is set up for the attainment of goals, and the annual budgets are likewise broken down into periods. In both cases unexpected lags (due, for example, to a shift in the seasonal pattern of sales, delays in deliveries of materials, or a strike by labor) may occasion conflicts between parts of the plan until such time as a revised plan can be drawn up.

A further source of potential conflict lies in the fact that most existing institutions "are not devised to undergo [change] gracefully" (Ozbekhan 1969: 137). Indicated adaptive responses to environmental disturbances or to new goals may be subverted if managers attempt to protect their own administrative positions by interpreting these events in terms of the organization's original charter or an infrequently updated aim. Such action may result, for example, if the adaptive solution is perceived as lying beyond the competence of existing personnel. If such action is allowed to go unchallenged, it will lead to neglect or distortion of the new goals, or to reactive or passive responses to environmental disturbances. If the firm's policy makers know or suspect this to be the case, they may develop built-in constraints to prevent it from happening: Every time new goals are set or a major environmental disturbance occurs, new planning entities may be set up to deal with them. This results in proliferating bureaucracy and conflict with entrenched interest groups.

The final source of conflict between goals to be mentioned here has received the lion's share of attention in the literature. This is the case of conflicts between personal and enterprise goals. A tremendous change has taken place in the way this type of conflict is viewed, both in economics and in organization theory (Cyert and March 1963: chapter 3; Steiner 1969: 186–95). Here we will merely summarize the stages in this process.

In economics, the neoclassical theory of the firm defined the organization as controlled by an entrepreneur assisted by a staff. The goals of the organization were the goals of the entrepreneur, and compliance with these goals was enforced by instructions from entrepreneur to staff through an internal control system, and by payments (wages, interest, etc.). Until comparatively recently the same view was held in management practice and in organization theory. Conflicts between personal and organizational objectives were regarded as inevitable. When they surfaced they were to be resolved in favor of the organization. A number of events have conspired to change these attitudes. We will consider the changes in organization theory first.

The early "scientific management" work in the 1930s by Mayo (1945, 1960), Roethlisberger and Dickson (1939), and others laid the groundwork for the new discipline of behavioral science, concerned with the individual in the organization, and his needs, objectives, and values compared with those of the organization. Most subsequent work has been sharply critical of the older view that individual objectives were to be considered as secondary to organizational objectives when the two were in conflict.

Among those who have taken issue with the classical view, some have argued that the needs of the individual and the formal organization are basically incompatible (Argyris 1957a, 1957b), others that they can be made congruent (McGregor 1960; Bennis 1966), while others have pointed out that the degree of conflict between individuals and organizations depends on the importance people attach to working for organizations (Dubin [1961: 78–81] points out that for many people a career in an organization is expected to fill only a minimal need, while for others it is their central life interest), or the level the individual occupies in the organizational hierarchy (Porter [1964] found from a study of 2,000 U.S. managers that, unsurprisingly, higher-level managers fulfilled their needs for recognition, autonomy, and self-realization more than managers at lower levels). In his well-known work on "organizational man," Whyte's (1957) central thesis was that modern business, especially larger corporations, forces individuals to behave as group standards dictate, at the expense of their individuality, creativity, and originality. Leavitt (1958: chapter 20) concluded that classical organization theory glossed over many complexities of human behavior, and many of its assumptions had been shown to be wrong (Cyert and March [1963: 16–18] summarize the three branches—sociological, social psychological, and administrative—of classical organization theory relevant to a revised theory of the firm).

It is apparent from this discussion that there has been a trend toward more democratic management, and a realization that people in organizations must be given a sense of belonging, a recognition of their personal worth and importance (see, e.g., Likert 1961). Steiner believes the pendulum has already swung too far in this respect, and elevates the man over the organization, pointing out that there are limits to the extent to which an organization can satisfy all the wants of individuals in it and still accomplish

> the basic aims society expects it to achieve. . . . [these] are predominantly economic and not social. . . . To expect business organizations to

satisfy all [the felt social and self-fulfillment needs of the people in them] is neither possible nor desirable. . . .

A similar view is expressed by Kast (1961: 59).

Two other studies have theorized about human motives and needs. McGregor (1960: chapter 3) characterized the classical view as Theory X, in which the individual was seen as disliking work and as having to be coerced with the threat of punishment to achieve organizational objectives. In place of this he proposed Theory Y, which assumes that work is as natural as play or rest, that individuals will serve objectives to which they are committed, and that commitment is a function of rewards related to achievement. A Theory Z, based on the Japanese, has recently been proposed in a book with that title.

According to Maslow (1943), this problem of enlisting human potential more fully in solving organizational problems is complicated by the fact that different individuals have different needs, and a single individual's needs may change or vary in intensity over time. As the individual progresses in the organization and becomes more affluent, and the lower needs (physiological, safety, affiliation) are met, the highest needs (esteem of others, self-fulfillment) assume greater importance, and they cannot be satisfied by offering higher pay or fringe benefits. Steiner believes a better reconciliation of individual and organizational objectives would result if greater emphasis were put on linking organizational objectives with the higher of Maslow's needs.

CONFLICT RESOLUTION

The description of the objective and goal formulation phase of planning in the first section of this chapter was deliberately left incomplete. The third part of this process concerns the elimination, or provision of means for resolving, conflicts between goals. Whether or not conflicting aims need to be resolved partly depends of course on how serious they are perceived to be. Steiner cites a 1959 study of over 600 U.S. scientists and engineers which found that 49 percent of the sample felt conflicts between their individual goals and enterprise goals were not serious, while 26 percent felt they were.

Ackoff (1970: 31) says firms frequently formulate objectives that, *at least under some circumstances,* are not compatible. If the conflicting pressures that result when managers attempt to cope with incompatible objectives become serious, intervention is required. This, he says, may take three forms. First, measures applied to different performance objectives and made on different scales can be transformed to a common scale, usually monetary. An example is given of a mail-order firm that wished simultaneously to minimize order-filling costs and delays in deliveries. The conflict was resolved by transforming the negative value of a delivery delay into a cost. Second, if the measures applied to different objectives are on a common scale, conflicts can often be resolved by formulating a higher-level objective expressed on that scale, and the contributions of each lower-level objective to this higher-level objective can be included in the formulation of the latter problem. Third, if neither of these methods succeeds, judgment is required to choose among the possible combinations of attainment levels of the non–jointly realizable objectives. One could also add that participation in planning, including goal setting, might reduce potential conflicts.

Thus far we have been implicitly assuming that conflicts among aims should be resolved if they are "serious." Deciding what is "serious" leads to some contrary views, two of which will be referred to. The first is that of Cyert and March (1963: chapter 3), and in order to present it we must first outline their view of the business organization. In their attempt to develop a theory that predicts and explains business decision-making behavior, the authors view the organization as a coalition of stakeholders—managers, workers, stockholders, suppliers, customers, government agencies. Over a relatively brief period of time, and for a particular decision, the major coalition members can be identified; over time the coalition may change (this is tantamount to saying that an open system cannot be defined once and for all). People have goals; collectivities of people do not. To suppose that a common or consensual goal will emerge from the coalition and be adopted as the organizational goal is, they claim, contrary to the empirical evidence. Different members of the coalition may have substantially different preference orderings (individual goals), and it will not usually be possible to define a joint preference ordering for the coalition. To the extent that coalition members do agree on organizational objectives, the objectives are likely to be vague, and behind this agreement there is likely to be considerable disagreement and uncertainty about subgoals. "*The existence of unresolved conflict is a conspicuous feature of organizations*" (p. 28). Different goals appear to be pursued at the same time, and most of these are of a "satisficing" nature. In a department store, for example, decisions that ought to be made simultaneously by a profit-maximizing firm were made sequentially and for different goals. The pricing objective differed from the output objective, and they were set at different times. Five different sets of decisions were tied to different objectives rather than to a single objective.

In Cyert and March's view, organizational coalitions and objectives
result from a more or less continuous process of bargaining. Some members of the coalition are active, some passive most of the time, and members also differ in the demands they make on the organization. Side payments to coalition members may take many different forms: money in the
form of stock options or year-end bonuses, privileged treatment, greater
authority, or favored policy commitments. The total value of side payments is a function of the composition of the coalition at any time. Cyert
and March believe a significant number of these side payments require the
organization to make policy commitments to active members of the coalition, and it is these that lead to the formation of organizational objectives.
They cite the entrance of labor unions in the United States into what were
traditionally viewed as management policy-making prerogatives (e.g., re-
quiring a firm to be investigated by independent management consultants),
and their demand for "payments" in the policy discretion area in addition to
the usual demands concerning wages and conditions of work. The objectives of a business emerge as a series of more or less independent constraints imposed on the organization through the process of bargaining
among coalition members, and elaborated over time in response to short-
run pressures (p. 43). It is of course implied that the coalition that emerges
at any time belongs to the subset of viable coalitions, those that meet the
minimal demands imposed on the system by its environment.

Over time organizational objectives so formed may change because of
changes in the composition of the ruling coalition, or because members' as-
piration levels change with experience. Cyert and March also believe organizational objectives are stabilized in various ways. One way is through
the internal control system (e.g., the budget), which performs the function
of enforcing the bargaining agreements, and which, in their view, operates
as a *mutual* control on superiors as well as subordinates: There are costs to
the department that exceed its budget, but there are also "severe costs to
other members of the coalition if the budget is not paid in full." Hence
budgets tend to be self-fulfilling. A second stabilizer is found in the allocation of functions. Role assignments define areas of jurisdiction and at the
same time constrain other members of the coalition from prohibiting action
within those limits. The allocation of discretion accordingly becomes
largely self-maintaining. Finally, because of frictions in the mutual adjustment of side payments and demands, and imperfections in factor markets,
the firm accumulates "organizational slack" (payments to members of the
coalition in excess of what is required to maintain the organization). Organizational slack "absorbs a substantial share of the potential variability in
the firm's establishment" (p. 38); and since the subset of viable coalitions is

a function of the environment, slack helps to perpetuate the existing coalition.

The conclusion to be drawn from Cyert and March's study is that most organizations, most of the time, exist and thrive with considerable latent conflict of goals: "Except at the level of nonoperational objectives, there is no internal consensus. The procedures for 'resolving' such conflict do not reduce all goals to a common dimension or even make them obviously internally consistent" (p. 117).

In Cyert and March's theory, consistency is facilitated by two characteristics of the organizational decision process: "satisficing" decision rules (i.e., choosing the first satisfactory alternative that comes along), and sequential (versus simultaneous) attention to goals: "The decentralization of decision-making (and goal attention), the sequential attention to goals, and the adjustment in organizational slack permit the business firm to make decisions without consistent goals under many (and perhaps most) conditions" (p. 43).

Thus Cyert and March agree with Ackoff that conflicts over goals are not always resolved, but differ by arguing that they *need not* be resolved. It is therefore of no use to take decisions simultaneously with respect to them. Also, based as it is on empirical observations, Cyert and March's theory puts less emphasis on planning than a systems approach would suggest it deserves: Management is characterized as "crisis management" (Ackoff's inactivist category). Planning is not seen to involve solving a set of interrelated problems; with different goals receiving attention sequentially there is no mechanism for revising decisions taken earlier in the planning process in the light of decisions taken later. In the short-run the firm uses a learned set of behavior rules, called standard operating procedures, to take "essentially contingent [i.e., ad hoc] decisions [i.e., of the "what gives?" kind, answered by rapid feedback]. Decisions are used as devices for learning about their hidden consequences (through outcries or other quick feedback—simulation in the raw)" (p. 110). These standard operating rules are changed in response to longer-run feedback, according to some more general rules. This constitutes the "long-run adaptive process by which the firm learns" (p. 113); and planning is viewed similarly:

> . . . plans, like other standard operating procedures, reduce a complex world to a somewhat simpler one. Within rather large limits, the organization substitutes the plan for the world—partly by making the world conform to the plan, partly by pretending that it does (p. 112).

It is possible to rationalize unresolved conflict of objectives between members of an organization without seeing it as the inevitable result of a bargaining process that leaves the organization weighed down with policy commitments. An alternative, more explicit, view that ignores bargaining over policy issues is that put forward by Hedberg et al. (referred to in Chapter 2, "Organization Structure"). Their "self-designing" organization maximizes its long-term viability by keeping a number of processes dynamically balanced. The organization actually seeks *minimal* consensus, contentment of its members, affluence, and consistency in the assignment of discretion, recognizing the value of a certain amount of dissent, discontent, flexibility in policies, and a range of discretion in decision making.

What emerges from the last view as important from a systems perspective is not the total harmonization of short-range goals or even long-range objectives, but that conditions are created in which individual objectives and goals are at least minimally met when enterprise objectives and goals are met, and that in pursuing its own objectives the firm also meets the demands of the environment. Insofar as complete harmonization of aims is called for, it should be sought, rather, in a strong all-around commitment to the *general* aims of the enterprise, its basic socioeconomic purposes and missions.

SUMMARY

In this chapter we have seen how a business may typically have a network of aims, ranging from the very broad and general to the very narrow and precise. The kinds of aims a business sets itself are influenced by the past, present, and potential future course of events, by the philosophy held by the planners, and their value systems. Four different philosophies were noted, roughly paralleling the ways the planning task was characterized in Chapter 2.

The operationalizing of a company's basic purposes in a mission or missions was seen as one of the most important tasks the chief executive has to perform. The mission is a long-range focal condition which, if carefully chosen and constantly kept in view, serves to give a sense of direction amid dynamic change, and may powerfully influence the firm's profitability. Because of their generality, basic purposes and missions are changed only infrequently, but if the firm is to be continuously adapted they may on occasion need to be changed dramatically (e.g., the Cunard Line).

The phase of planning concerned with setting the long-range objectives and short-range goals by which the mission is to be accomplished should specify what the objectives are, how they are to be translated into goals, and provide a schedule for the attainment of each. Goals need to be stated in an operationally meaningful form, and provision made for eliminating or resolving conflicts between objectives and goals. In setting objectives and goals, attention should be paid not only to the aims of the firm, but also to the needs of its members and of the environment. The causal texture of the environment should also be considered if planning is to be fully effective, and balanced attention should be given to the different time horizons of plans.

Conflicting objectives and goals may arise in the planning or in the implementation stage. Conflicts can arise because objectives are patently incompatible; those for one planning stage or period are inconsistent with those of a longer period; inappropriate performance measures make subgoals incongruent with goals; goals as specified make performance measurement impossible; plans are not functionally unified; goals are not operationally well defined; the priorities attached to different aims are not compatible; because high-level attempts to prevent reactivist responses at lower levels may lead to conflict; or because personal goals conflict with organizational goals. Opinions vary as to the degree to which such conflicts need to be resolved. That a good deal of unresolved conflict exists in most organizations seems not to be disputed. Cyert and March believe that organizational objectives are *formed* as a result of the bargaining that goes on over conflicting objectives, that active members of the organizational coalition are able to impose policy commitments on the organization to a significant extent. Organizations muddle along with internally inconsistent goals and much latent conflict of goals by having "satisficing" decision rules and treating goals sequentially.

A systems view of the problem would recognize that a certain amount of dissension, discontent, discretion, and flexibility within an organization has positive value, and would seek to create within the organization only conditions in which individual objectives are at least minimally met when enterprise objectives are met, and that in pursuing its own objectives the firm should also further the objectives of its suprasystem.

To the extent that they need to be resolved, objectives measured on a common scale may be harmonized by formulating a higher-level objective on that scale and including their contributions to this higher-level objective; and objectives measured on different scales can sometimes be transformed to a common monetary scale. If the measures are noncombinable, resolution of the conflict can only be a matter of judgment.

REFERENCES

Ackoff, R.L. 1970. *A Concept of Corporate Planning,* chapter 2. New York: Wiley-Interscience.

_____. 1974. *Redesigning the Future,* chapter 2. New York: Wiley-Interscience.

Amey, L.R. 1979. *Budget Planning and Control Systems.* London: Pitman.

Amey, L.R. and D.A. Egginton. 1973. *Management Accounting: A Conceptual Approach.* London: Longman.

Argyris, C. 1957a. "The Individual and Organization: Some Problems of Mutual Adjustment." *Administrative Science Quarterly* 2 (June): 1–24.

_____. 1957b. *Personality and Organization.* New York: Harper.

Beer, S. 1972. *Brain of the Firm.* London: Allen Lane (Penguin Press).

_____. 1969. "The Aborting Corporate Plan." In *Perspectives of Planning,* edited by E. Jantsch, pp. 395–422. Paris: OECD.

Bennis, W.G. 1966. *Changing Organizations.* New York: McGraw-Hill.

Bertalanffy, L. von. 1968. *General System Theory.* New York: Braziller.

Buckley, W. 1968. "Society as a Complex Adaptive System." In *Modern Systems Research for the Behavioral Scientist,* edited by W. Buckley, pp. 490–513. Chicago, IL: Aldine.

Cyert, R.M. and J.G. March. 1963. *A Behavioral Theory of the Firm,* chapters 3 and 6. Englewood Cliffs, NJ: Prentice-Hall.

Dubin, R. 1961. *Human Relations in Administration,* 2d ed. Englewood Cliffs, NJ: Prentice-Hall.

Emery, F.E., ed. 1969. *Systems Thinking,* Introduction. Harmondsworth, Middlesex: Penguin.

Emery, F.E. and E.L. Trist. 1969. "The Causal Texture of Organizational Environments." In *Systems Thinking. See* Emery 1969.

Hirschman, A.O. and E.C. Lindblom. 1969. "Economic Development, Research and Development, Policy Making: Some Converging Views." In *Systems Thinking. See* Emery 1969.

Kast, F.E. 1961. "Motivating the Organization Man." *Business Horizons* 4 (Spring).

Katz, D. and R.L. Kahn. 1966. *The Social Psychology of Organizations.* New York: Wiley.

Leavitt, H.J. 1958. *Managerial Psychology*. Chicago: University of Chicago Press.

Likert, R. 1961. *New Patterns of Management*. New York: McGraw-Hill.

Maslow, A.H. 1943. "The Theory of Human Motivation." *The Psychological Review* 50 (July): 370–96.

Mayo, E. 1945. *The Social Problems of an Industrial Civilization*. Boston, MA: Harvard University Graduate School of Business Administration.

_____. 1960. *The Human Problems of an Industrial Civilization*. New York: Viking Press.

McGregor, D. 1960. *The Human Side of Enterprise*. New York: McGraw-Hill.

Ozbekhan, H. 1969. "Toward a General Theory of Planning." In *Perspectives of Planning,* edited by E. Jantsch, pp. 45–155. Paris: OECD.

Porter, L.W. 1964. *Organizational Patterns of Managerial Job Attitudes*. New York: American Foundation for Management Research.

Roethlisberger, F.J. and W.J. Dickson. 1939. *Management and the Worker*. Cambridge, MA: Harvard University Press.

Steiner, G.A. 1969. *Top Management Planning,* chapters 6 and 7. New York: Macmillan.

Whyte, W.H. 1957. *The Organization Man*. New York: Doubleday Anchor.

4
Types of Planning and Plans

Planning, as we noted earlier, has many dimensions. Steiner (1969: 12) identifies five key dimensions as:

1. The subject of the plan (e.g., production, marketing)
2. The elements of the plan (charter, purpose, objective, strategy, policy, program, budget, procedure, rule)
3. The time range of the plan (short, medium, long)
4. The characteristics of the plan (ease of implementation, comprehensiveness, quantitative/qualitative, strategic/tactical, written/unwritten, flexible/inflexible, economical/excessively costly, etc.)
5. The organization to which the plan is applied (corporate, subsidiaries, functional groups, divisions, departments, product/project)

In this chapter we have selected certain types and characteristics of planning and plans as meriting further attention. The list does not coincide with Steiner's although some of his items will be found in it. More particularly, most of (2) above has already been discussed in Chapter 3; policy making and programming are considered in the second and third sections of this chapter, respectively, and (3) is the subject of the third section. The distinction between strategic and tactical planning is discussed as part of a broader classification in the second section, and flexibility of plans is considered in the fourth section.

Before embarking, three items that have been omitted from Steiner's list will be commented on briefly. First, Steiner notes that very few business plans are wholly quantitative, and that the higher the level in the firm at which plans are prepared the greater tends to be the significance of qual-

itative considerations. Second, apparently a large part of planning does not
result in written plans (Steiner 1969: 19; Barnard 1948: 166). A third important dimension is cost-benefit. This would need special attention in the
case of adaptive planning, which involves much forecasting, continuous
monitoring of the environment, and hence an enlarged information system,
experimentation (including simulations of combinations of possible future
events), as well as associated frequent changes in organization structure.
Any particular approach to planning is of course only justified if the costs of
planning are exceeded by its benefits.

THE "NEW" VERSUS THE "OLD" PLANNING

The first distinction we make is between the "new" planning and the
"old" planning. These are simply new labels for types of planning discussed in Chapter 2, that is, "where should we go" planning ("Planning the
Future") and "how to get there" planning ("Prediction"), respectively—in
other words designing of and preparation for the firm's own desired future,
and planning for a predicted future. The "new" planning thus involves "inventing" the future, that is, "acting in such a way as to make the future conform to some present vision of it" (Ozbekhan 1969: 129).

One of the reasons for the appearance of the "new" planning was recognition of the limitations of conventional planning, especially when
applied to complex social systems such as national economies and large
business enterprises. The "old" planning concentrated on changing variables within a given system, and was essentially short-term in scope. The
ends to which it was directed were forecasts, and the concern was for the
means of getting there, and the feasibility of action choices. At best, this
type of planning stops at prediction and problem solving, although in most
cases the full extent of problem interrelatedness escapes the orthodox planner. All too often "old" planning was the pursuit of expediency, in the form
of favorable short-term results, sometimes at the cost of unfavorable long-
term consequences. The simulated behavior of complex systems frequently
demonstrates the strength of long-range cause–effect relationships (Jantsch
1969: 21) so that an overemphasis on short-range goals will often be dysfunctional.

The second factor that led to the "new" planning was systems thinking: the recognition that organizations have systemic properties, and are
purposeful. The "new" planning seeks to change not only the variables
within a system (i.e., the system's global properties, or the system's con-

crete components), but also the system's internal structure (i.e., the material configuration, or interlinkage). It invents or creates its own ends, and hence contains a third hierarchical level of planning, called normative planning (see "Normative Planning," this chapter), not found in the "old" planning. In this respect there is no doubt that the computer, by offering the possibility of making conditional predictions of the behavior of a system under various artificially induced conditions, has made possible the testing of a variety of future scenarios that would previously have been infeasible or impossible. The "new" planning, as described in Chapter 2 (under "Planning the Future"), is more long-range and comprehensive than the old (i.e., it is three-level), and it is systemic (i.e., leads to integrated solutions), purposeful, ongoing, and is valued as an activity rather than for its product.

THE HIERARCHY OF PLANS

This section will discuss the hierarchical levels, or vertical integration, of the "new" planning. Here, as in the discussion of corporate aims, one encounters a number of different conceptions, and a use of common terms (like *strategy* and *policy*) to mean quite different things. The three-tier classification of plans presented here is somewhat eclectic: Only two of the writers to be referred to use all three of these terms. In the sequel we will describe what appears to be the emerging view, noting any significant divergences from it. What can be established at once without argument is that the sequence is to be understood as following a "top-down" order: Each level, starting with the normative level, provides the framework within which the next lower level takes place; it constrains the next lower level of planning. Since the ordering is hierarchical, strategic plans cannot be deduced from the lowest level or tactical plans, nor the normative or highest level from the strategic.

Normative Planning

"Normative planning" is mentioned explicitly by Ozbekhan and Jantsch (Jantsch 1969: 135–40 and 26, 30, 181, and 191, respectively). The common thread running through all descriptions of this highest-level planning is that it is *ends* planning, concerned with determining the ultimate ends or basic purposes of the firm—deciding what is wanted, or the design of a desired future. Beer (1969: 411–12) labels it simply "foresight." Steiner (1969: 32–33) does not give it a name, but refers to it as the premises or foundations of planning. To him it encompasses determination and review of the fundamental socioeconomic purpose of the enterprise, the value systems of top managers, and the evaluation of external and internal opportunities and problems, and of company strengths and weaknesses. Ozbekhan says the core of normative planning is norm seeking. It is primarily the exercise of value judgments to determine what *ought* to be done, or in other words what norms *ought* to be selected or invented. (Both Ozbekhan and Jantsch apply the term "policy making" to this activity; but, in deference to what we believe to be more common usage, we will confine the term "policy making" to means planning.)

The essential characteristics of normative planning are that it should be broad and imaginative. It must examine every feature of the firm in its environment that seems relevant to a consideration of its long-term future, and it must be capable of reflecting on totally new departures from the usual behavior of the firm (Beer 1969: 411). In short, normative planning is concerned with establishing the highest aims of the firm and, under the "new" planning, with inventing the desired future orientation of the firm to its environment. Ozbekhan (1969: 140) notes that most people who engage in this activity (normative planning) in a firm are ill-equipped to perform satisfactorily. Their training, mainly administrative and only rarely strategic, is not a good preparation for normative reasoning. Their experience is in reducing all issues to what they think *can* be done, not in instituting change inspired by what *ought* to be done (p. 139).

Strategic Planning

Strategic planning is described by Steiner (1969: 19) as relating to those plans having major importance in deploying resources. He adds (p. 34):

> Strategic planning is the process of determining the major objectives of an organization and the policies and strategies that will govern the acquisition, use, and disposition of resources to achieve those objectives. Objectives in the strategic planning process include missions . . . if they have not been determined previously [i.e., at the normative level], and the specific objectives that are sought. . . . Policies are broad guides to action, and strategies are the means to deploy resources.

Steiner prefers to include the determination of missions at the strategic stage. Thus strategic planning is *both means and ends oriented,* and covers matters of great importance in the pursuit of the company's basic purposes. The subject matter may be any aspect of the firm's activities, and of variable duration. Plans to acquire a major competitor within the next five years, or next month, are both strategic in nature.

Steiner lists some guidelines in developing strategies (pp. 260–61). A firm's strategies should be known and understood by all who need to know of them; they should be consistent with the firm's environment and with its internal strengths, objectives, policies, resources, and the personal values of its members. They should balance the acceptance of risk with profit potential, consistent with the firm's objectives and prospects, and should allow the maximum exercise of imagination and creativity by the planners. Finally, strategic plans should have timing attached to them, and not be open-ended.

Strategic Planning Versus Policy Making

We digress here to comment on the relationship between strategic planning and *policy making*. Ozbekhan (1969: 135, 138–39) is the exception in his interpretation of strategic planning. To him it means goal-setting functions, "part of what is usually called executive decision-making"; it involves the derivation of goals from objectives established at the normative stage. Thus Ozbekhan seems to be in a minority in classifying strategic planning as solely concerned with ends. To him, policy making belongs at the normative, not at the strategic, level.

Steiner defines business policies as guides to carrying out actions, while admitting that "policy" is a slippery concept, and that under certain circumstances policy and strategy may be synonymous (Steiner 1969: chapter 10). He does, however, insist on the distinction that "strategy" is principally reserved for deployment of resources of major importance to a company, while policies tend to be more diffuse. Procedures, standard operating plans, and rules differ from policies only in degree, Steiner says; all provide guidance as to how a particular problem should be dealt with. All are types of *standing plans*. In other words, there is a whole pyramid of business policies, ranging from major policy (lines of business), through functional policies (marketing, production, etc.), to procedures and standard operating plans (e.g., handling of incoming orders, servicing of customer complaints, use of company cars). In large companies there is usually a comprehensive, more or less integrated, structure of policies from the highest level of generality to the lowest level. At the very least, says Steiner, there should be some distinction drawn between basic (major) and routine policies.

Inquiry into the purposes and functions of policies and other standing plans reveals another important difference between policy and strategy (Steiner 1969: 270):

> Strategies select a major target and pinpoint a single approach to it. . . . On the other hand, a business of any size . . . must have literally thousands of "laws" to govern action. A web of up-to-date policies and procedures provides a framework within which managerial decisions . . . can be consistent with the basic purposes and objectives of the firm and the values of top managers.

As the firm grows, policies provide a means of countering the insularity that tends to develop among groups and organizational units, and of coordinating their efforts. Policies also reduce internal uncertainty by enabling one part of the organization to anticipate and predict actions in other parts with reasonable accuracy. Working within policy constraints, individual managers can take appropriate initiatives.

While policies may thus be seen as having positive value by aiding coordination and reducing internal uncertainties, a final judgment depends on what sort of policies they are, how "up-to-date" they are, and how flexible. The danger is that policies and indeed all "standing plans" will introduce inflexibility into the actions taken, will not allow sufficient discretion to those who must follow them, and will be changed only infrequently. If adaptation of the firm is the crux of planning, standing plans could very easily thwart this objective.

We conclude this digression by noting that policies may concern the environment of a firm as well as its internal organization (e.g., they may concern the public image of the business); in large firms they should guide the way planning takes place, how plans are revised and implemented; they should be continuously reviewed as part of the planning process; and they should accurately reflect the locus of authority in the organization.

Strategic Versus Tactical Planning

Another gray area is the distinction between *strategic* and *tactical planning*. The conceptual differences between the two are examined by Steiner (1969: 37–41) and Ackoff (1970: 4–5). Both agree that the distinction is blurred. To Steiner, strategic planning is conducted at the highest levels of management (at headquarters and in major divisions), and related exclusively to decisions taken at these levels, while tactical planning is done at, and relates to, lower management levels. Strategic planning is both ongoing and irregular, depending on the appearance of new ideas, management initiatives, or crises, whereas tactical planning occurs for the most part on a periodic cycle. Strategic planning gives greater rein to the subjective values of management and concerns a larger range of alternatives than tactical planning. Uncertainty is usually much greater and more difficult to minimize in strategic planning. Here the problems tend to be unstructured, one of a kind, whereas tactical planning deals with structured, often repetitive, problems. Strategic planning requires more information from outside the firm on relating to the environment; tactical planning relies more heavily on internally generated and historical data, particularly from the accounting system. It is carried out within the framework of strategic plans in the pursuit of objectives formulated therein, and mainly from a partial, functional unit point of view (e.g., the point of view of production or of marketing), whereas strategic planning is approached from a corporate point of view.

Ackoff makes the point that ultimately the distinction between *strategic* and *tactical* is relative. Thus the longer the effect of a plan and the more difficult it is to reverse, the more strategic it is; but *long* and *short* are themselves relative terms. Again, the greater the number of activities affected by a plan, the more strategic the plan is: Strategic planning is thus broad in scope, and tactical planning narrower. But *broad* and *narrow* are in turn also relative. Finally, tactical planning is concerned with selecting the means to pursue specified goals, while strategic planning involves both the setting of goals and the means of attaining them. But *means* and *ends* are again relative concepts. The example given by Ackoff is that advertising a product is a means to the end of selling it. But selling it is, in turn, a means to the end of earning profit; and profit may be a means to yet other ends.

Tactical Planning

Enough has already been said to convey the main features of tactical planning. The latter is exemplified in the preparation of annual operating and financial budgets, and in any "standing plans" and administrative procedures instituted during the annual budgeting process to ensure coordination at the operating level, and the implementation of decisions taken at all three levels (the normative, the strategic, and the tactical). In short, tactical planning is solely *means* planning, concerned with technical and administrative matters. *Means*, according to Ackoff (1970: 6), comprise the selection of "policies, procedures, and practices by which objectives and goals are to be pursued," this definition being understood as applying to both strategic and tactical planning.

Steiner (1969: 35–36) subdivides tactical planning into medium-range programming and short-term budgets and detailed functional plans. Medium-range programming is the process in which "detailed, coordinated, and comprehensive plans are made for selected functions of a business (e.g., production, sales, profits, personnel, capital expenditure) to deploy resources to reach objectives by following policies and strategies laid down in the strategic planning process." Medium-range programs and plans usually span a period of five years, with detailed plans for each year. If the timing of the planning cycle coincides with that of the budgeting cycle, short-term budgets may be the same as the first year of the medium-range programs. Short-term budgets typically cover sales, production and/ or purchases, expenses, cash, as well as income statement and balance sheet. These in turn imply the scheduling of sales, production and purchases, determination of inventory policy, manpower requirements, credit terms given and received, minimum cash requirements, quality standards, and so on. In Steiner's view, medium-range programming is directed towards subobjectives and substrategies, whereas short-range planning is concerned with goals or targets and procedures.

The picture that emerges of the hierarchy of planning is somewhat confused; the experts do not agree among themselves as to precisely what the two higher categories comprise, and there are semantic problems over common terminology. Yet the outlines of what appears to be a logical division of labor and priorities comes through. At the highest level, planning should be concerned with designing a desired future and with establishing ultimate ends, but not with how to get there. The lower levels have the task of devising means of getting there, and of converting the ultimate aims into (long-range) objectives and (short-range) goals, also of deciding on administrative rules of various kinds, from major policies down to very detailed and narrow operating rules. If the purpose of planning is constantly to adapt the enterprise to its environment, it seems clear that the main burden of doing that falls on the normative and strategic planners.

PLANNING HORIZONS

We have already made a number of references to plans of different duration. Some of these statements were that long-run planning is desirable because all too frequently a short focus results in decisions that bring favorable short-run results but have unpleasant long-run effects; that it is useful to distinguish between long-range aims (objectives) and short-range aims (goals), and necessary to give balanced attention to the different time horizons in planning.

Short Versus Long

Forrester (1969a: 235–54; see also Jantsch 1969: 503–10) believes, on the basis of studies he has made, that complex systems such as social systems are "devious and diabolical" in their behavior.[1] They have behavior characteristics that appear to be the same as those of simple systems but are really quite different. "Complex systems are counterintuitive," being remarkably insensitive to many of the usual system parameters and resistant to policy changes, but highly sensitive to a few parameters and to some changes in structure. He provides evidence from his work on planning for a city that seems to support the hypothesis that short-term planning, resulting in policies that are intuitively appealing and politically attractive, freeze and choke the system so that it declines in the longer run. He concludes that "planning for the near future (for such systems) will often conflict with planning for the more distant future," and that planning has usually been effective only in the short run, if at all. This is because "most planning criteria are derived from intuitive judgment, which will often be wrong because of the counter-intuitive nature of complex systems." Effective planning requires a deeper understanding of the internal dynamics of the system and identification of the relatively few variables to which the system is highly sensitive. Other remedies for this "planning paradox," Forrester believes, are more attention to what Ackoff calls the "humanization problem" (see Chapter 2, "Solving Systems of Problems") to counteract the widespread resistance of individuals to planning; less emphasis on the correction of immediate difficulties and more on finding the causes and removing them:

> Removing causes may take quite different actions from those aimed at alleviating symptoms. The cost of removing causes is often far less. The influence is much deeper. The improvements last longer. Good planning . . . will attempt to release the internal power, initiative . . . and human potential of the people in the system . . . instead of heaping more work . . . discipline . . . repression and . . . coordination on them in an effort to push back a . . . system that is still trying to go in the wrong direction.

The appendix to this chapter lists some possible further explanations of the "Forrester paradox" and examines one in detail, namely that the odd behavior observed by Forrester might be due to the multiple-time-scale properties of such systems.

Planning Horizon Versus Forecasting Horizon

In discussing the duration of plans we need, to begin with, to be clear about the difference between the forecasting (or anticipations) horizon and the planning horizon. There are two separate points here. The first is that companies, depending on the nature of their activities, sometimes make long-range projections that become premises in the planning process. Thus Steiner (1969: 21) says it is not unusual to find long-range projections of the economic environment, demand for the firm's products, or new technology of interest to the firm, extending 10 to 20 or more years into the future. Hence we should not be surprised to discover forecasts covering periods longer than the firm's longest plans.

A second point is discussed in connection with production planning by Modigliani and Hohn (1955), and in general terms by Modigliani and Cohen (1961). It involves looking at planning dynamically. Put simply, it is that the forecasting horizon is of variable duration for different activities of the firm, and need not be as long as the planning horizon; indeed it may be zero for some activities. The reasoning here is as follows. In the dynamic approach to planning (discussed later in this chapter—"Static Versus Dynamic Planning"), it used to be assumed (Hicks 1946) that the firm would determine the best possible plan for the entire future, act only on the first stage of this plan, and replan each year. Such extensive planning is now seen as unrealistic: Information gathering, including forecasting, is not a costless activity; and uncertainty usually mounts the longer the period considered.

Suppose instead that we set a planning horizon of T years, and try to optimize over this period. Then we need to know at each planning stage only what is necessary to determine the best possible course of action for the first year, where by "best possible" we mean that course of action which, provided there are appropriate plans in later periods of the T-internal, optimizes over the T periods.

Approaching the problem in this way, it is frequently sufficient to *plan* for only a subinterval, possibly a small subinterval, of the firm's entire future. Second, we need to *forecast* only those events that are expected to have a bearing on the optimality, over the T-period horizon, of the plan during the first period at each planning stage. All we need to do is ensure that any events in the future beyond the first period (components of future plans, future constraints) that affect the optimality over the horizon of first-period plans are included in formulating the planning problem at each stage. In this way the amount of forecasting necessary can be considerably reduced with no ill effects. In fact forecasting can be further reduced by eliminating not only formally irrelevant aspects of the future but also those that are cost-benefit irrelevant (see Amey 1979: 34–38). What emerges from this way of viewing planning will be a series of forecasts varying in length from zero to T periods, a detailed plan for the first period, and fragments of plans for the remaining T - 1 periods.

Determining the Planning Horizon

A remaining question is "How is the planning horizon determined?" Can we determine the horizon optimally, that is, arrive at the length of planning period that will yield the best results in the long run? There is a theoretical solution and a practical solution. Simulation offers a theoretical or approximate answer to this question. We could simulate the system under different planning horizons (for n periods, $n + 1$ periods, etc., the degree of confidence felt in forecasts suggesting the value of n). If the plan for $n + 1$ periods shows significant improvement, in terms of the firm's objective function, over an n-period plan, the process would be continued by planning for $n + 2$ periods, and so on, until extending the horizon causes no further improvement (i.e., an equilibrium value is approached). The horizon determined by this trial-and-error approach should yield results that are approximately long-run optimal. The costs of forecasting and planning under the different horizons should, of course, be included in the objective function.

Another suggested "theoretical" answer as to what is the "right" planning period is that it depends on the "commitment principle," that is, that planning should cover the period necessary "to foresee (through a series of (actions) the fulfillment of commitments involved in a decision" (Koontz and O'Donnell 1959). But, as Chamberlain (1963: 10) points out, planners also need to watch out for the release of resources when previously planned activities terminate; decisions will then have to be made as to how these resources are to be deployed. Accordingly, he argues that the planning period should be slightly longer than the length of the commitments assumed in any plan.

In practice we find no conscious attempt to determine planning periods optimally. According to Steiner (1969: 21), long-range *projections* (forecasts or extrapolations) of the economic environment may extend 10 to 20 years or more into the future, as already stated. Nor is it unusual to find long-range *objectives* set for 10 years ahead. But "it is very unusual . . . to find detailed plans extending much beyond five years." According to a 1966 survey of 420 U.S. companies by the National Planning Commission, the distribution of planning periods was as follows (these to be understood as the longest period for which plans are drawn up):

	%
No corporate plan	16
Less than 5 years	6
5 years	53
10 years	11
5 and 10 years	8
More than 10 years	6
	100

Source: National Planning Commission Survey, 1966, p. 29.

The long-range planning period in most companies, according to this survey, is thus five years. Steiner quotes the planning director of IBM who, when asked "Why five years?" replied, "Because four years seems too short and six years seems too long." A number of businesspeople told Steiner that five years was just about as far as they could see clearly enough to get involved in any detailed planning.

Several comments may be offered on the above. First, the businessperson's seemingly arbitrary choice of five years may be the result of a complex weighting of alternatives that are never made explicit, although if this were the case we should not expect the same period to be appropriate for many dissimilar companies. Indeed, technology changes that are faster in some industries than in others induce degrees of uncertainty that vary between companies. Thus, while a bakery may be able to plan 10 years ahead, a high-technology electronics firm cannot see that far ahead because of a higher rate of technological change.

Second, it is well known that while comprehensive *operational* plans tend to be drawn up for a fixed number of years, in many companies there are other, partial plans covering different time spans, the period depending on the subject matter of the plan and the nature of the business. There are also long-range forecasts, especially by firms in the basic industries and those producing a product of very high unit value or using inputs of high value (e.g., aircraft manufacturers and airlines). It is also true that the length of the planning period has been tending to increase for all firms over the years with the increase in size and complexity of firms, the greater complexity of the economic and social environments, the increasing rate of technological change, the greater magnitude of capital investment, and, in the more progressive firms, the desire to anticipate and bring about change to some more desired state.

About all we can conclude is that planning periods may vary from one functional area to another, although most short-range operational plans are for one year (possibly longer in the case of firms with a long production cycle, such as shipbuilding), and that the modal period for the longest plans in a company appears to be five years. Medium-range programming provides a schedule for linking the two. Partial forecasts may stretch much farther ahead. But we should not be overly concerned with current practice, because planning is in the process of undergoing a significant change, as indicated by the term *new planning*. What is important from a systems point of view is that effective adaptation requires fairly long-range plans in order to foresee potential opportunities and threats and allow time to prepare for them (this may take years), or prepare a future of the firm's devising, and to incorporate important long-term cause–effect relationships. In the interests of adaptation the firm should use a moving planning horizon (Amey and Egginton 1973: 166–68) so that all plans become what the accountants call "rolling" or "progressive."

FLEXIBILITY OF PLANS

We have seen in earlier chapters that flexibility in planning, decision modes, and organization structure comes at the top of the list of requirements for effective adaptation. This requires that plans can and will be changed quickly with changes in the environment that cannot be controlled, and that plans will also be flexibly implemented. The argument is sometimes heard that, since plans can never be accurate in every detail, what we should aim for are plans that are robust, less sensitive to their own inaccuracy or failure, yielding tolerably good results even when underlying forecasts prove to be wrong or assumptions invalid. This argument focuses on plans rather than on planning, which we earlier maintained was wrong. The need to adapt demands more or less continuous planning, and this process has the necessary flexibility to correct its own errors as it goes along.

By contrast, we have seen that firms commonly have a hierarchy of "standing plans," ranging from major policies through minor policies to standard operating plans and rules of various kinds. These constitute a potential source of inflexibility unless some degree of discretion is built into them.

FREQUENCY OF PLANNING

In practice, planning is done at discrete intervals, typically yearly. We have argued that it should be an ongoing process. This is because the firm's environment is changing more or less continuously, the organization itself is also constantly changing even without external disturbances, and because the firm is a whole made up of interrelated parts. A change anywhere in the system or in its environment is therefore likely to set off a chain reaction of consequential changes that require more or less continual plan revision. As Ackoff observes, ". . . no plan is ever final . . . planning is . . . a process that has no natural conclusion or end point" (1970: 3, 5).

STATIC VERSUS DYNAMIC PLANNING

A static approach to planning means that the entire planning period is treated as a single period, and the temporal environment (of the plan) or of the organization planned for is assumed to be constant over this period. A dynamic approach regards planning as relating to periods or stages with the environment changing over time.

The argument in favor of taking a dynamic approach to planning is that a business is a dynamic process, a "going concern," and there are dynamic aspects of its operations that should be taken into account. These aspects relate to a further kind of interrelatedness, that is, dynamic or intertemporal interdependence. That is, in addition to the systemic properties of the firm in any given period being taken into account, if planning is viewed dynamically the plan for period t is interrelated with the realizations of plans for periods $t-1, t-2, \ldots$, and with the plans for periods $t+1, t+2,$ . . . A static approach ignores these latter interdependencies, treating each period as a closed temporal system (or set of events) which neither affects nor is affected by actual or potential events in other periods. If these dynamic interdependencies are not taken into account in formulating the planning problem at each planning stage, achievement of the plan in one period could turn out to be prejudicial to performance in future periods. In other words, what needs to be done in the short run to maintain continuous adaptation over the long run may be very different from what is suggested by paying attention to the short run alone. That is, what is required in the short run for long-run adaptation may be counterintuitive, as Forrester remarked (this chapter, "Planning Horizons").

The nature of these dynamic interdependencies may be described as follows. First, for an established firm, the plan for period t will be affected by events in periods $t-1$, $t-2$, . . . in such a way that, in a dynamic model, the consequences of those earlier plans become the initial conditions for plans in period t. Thus the firm begins a planning period with certain assets and commitments inherited from the past. Second, the future may affect the T-optimality of plans that will be drawn up for period t, because certain parts of the plan for period t may affect, directly or indirectly, some future constraints, and hence the firm's opportunities in later periods. For example, if the firm dismisses part of its work force in period t and these workers move away and cannot be replaced, production possibilities in later periods are constrained. A further way in which the future interacts with the present is that if the firm is planning dynamically over a number of periods, alternatives open to the firm in the first period may depend on expected alternatives in subsequent periods. While future events cannot limit what it is possible to achieve in the present, expected future events, considered in the present, may limit what it is desirable to achieve if the objective is to optimize or achieve some desired result over an horizon of T periods.

To a first approximation, current corporate planning practice would have to be described as taking a static approach. If we consider the annual budgets drawn up by a firm, it is clear that the first kind of dynamic interdependence, that between past and present, is taken into account. There are also signs that the interrelatedness of future and present sometimes figures in planners' decisions, namely when they determine the amounts of, or put bounds on, at least some closing account balances. For example, desired ending inventory levels might give recognition to expected sales or product prices in subsequent periods, and the closing cash balance might be determined by the same sort of considerations. This could be interpreted as a rough attempt by the planners at intuiting interdependencies between present and future. The same sort of thing could be said about medium-range programs that specify and schedule the steps on the way to long-range objectives. Because of the complexity of the two-way interrelationships between present and future, however, it is inconceivable that such intuitive attempts to account for dynamic interdependencies can ever be other than incomplete. They may also be highly inaccurate because of the counterintuitive nature of long-run effects in complex systems; they may require greater understanding of the system than conventional planners possess.

Planning dynamically for a business enterprise, while desirable, would be extremely difficult to do. For all except very small businesses it may not be computationally possible, even if it were manageable analytically. A preliminary examination of the nature of the difficulties involved will be found in Amey (1979: 38–53).

SHOULD PLANNING BUDGETS AND CONTROL BUDGETS BE FORMALLY DISTINCT?

In this section we focus on tactical, short-range plans, as exemplified in the annual budgets. It is in relation to these that feedback control is usually exercised. Annual business budgets serve a number of different purposes: as plans, controls, motivating devices, coordinating devices, as a means of affirming authority and responsibility, and, subject to "standing plans," of distributing uncertainty within the organization. They may also serve to maintain a given organizational structure. The question arises: Can a single instrument simultaneously serve all these purposes with equal effectiveness? There is a strong presumption that, in view of the very diversity of the purposes, it cannot (Amey and Egginton 1973: 559–60).

We are particularly interested in the relationship between budgets as plans, controls, and motivating devices. Hopwood (1976: 41–45, 63–65) comments as follows on the potential conflict of purposes:

> The listing of purposes [served by budgets leads one] to question whether the diverse purposes are necessarily congruous. . . . Can the need for realistic budgets for planning and coordination, and for meaningful feedback for comparison with actual accomplishments, conflict with budgets playing a significant role in motivating performance and as a means for ensuring an active organizational atmosphere. . . . [For example,] budgets are only one of the many ways of motivating performance, but as a future oriented decision tool they are unique. Should their unique role be endangered because of an emphasis on their motivational potential? Ideally there is a need for separate budgets for motivational and planning purposes.

The same suggestion was made by Stedry (1960). Stedry quotes Charnes and Cooper as saying that "A good plan . . . does not necessarily yield a good control," that "good planning data and good control data are not necessarily the same." The best target for control purposes coincides with the planning target if and only if each person has an automatic incentive to work to this target. If budgeted performance based on a planned amount that is effectively unattainable (as it would be if it were the result of an optimization), no matter how great the reward for achieving it, with penalties for nonattainment, the expected value of the reward is zero and the net expected value of rewards and penalties negative. Such a control system would cause discontent, and workers would not agree to it. It would not be very effective even in the absence of penalties for nonattainment of objectives, because employees would still regard the target as unreasonable. They would therefore feel themselves to be under no compulsion to try to attain it, and their performance would be likely to drift farther and farther away from it.

Similar ideas have been expressed by Morris (1968). He contends that the concept of budgetary control is no longer a viable proposition because the majority of budgetary control systems are attempting to perform two different functions simultaneously: the functions of planning and of control. He differs from Hopwood in the kind of control target proposed. The budget most appropriate for financial planning, says Morris, is a statement of the most likely outcome of events. Target setting for control, on the other hand, must be based on some theory of human motivation. He would set control targets that demanded the highest possible levels of achievement, that is, optimal control targets: "From this control budget a separate (planning) budget would be produced which was more conservative." One can accept Morris's argument for the necessity of separating planning and control budgets without agreeing on the nature of the control targets he proposes. In particular we would argue against optimal targets for control for the reason given earlier.

Steiner (1969: 42) also recognizes the problem:

> . . . there is no question . . . that planning and control, both conceptually and operationally, are inextricably interwoven . . . [but] . . . despite this intermingling, planning and control must be distinguished both *conceptually* and operationally. Conceptually, . . . development of plans without proper control . . . may not only lead to poor results but to developments completely contrary to plans. . . . Perhaps of more . . . consequence, managerial relationships with people are considerably different as between planning and controlling (McGregor 1967: chapter 8). Furthermore, the philosophy, attitude, and pursuit of planning and control will differ very much depending on the centre of attention. . . . To fail to distinguish between planning and control conceptually and operationally may lead to a misunderstanding not only of the processes themselves but of the ways in which they interrelate. [Italics added]

We have elsewhere proposed that there should not only be separate planning and control budgets, but that they should be *formally* distinct (Amey 1979: 4–5). In practice accountants sometimes use what they call separate *planning* and *control budgets* by means of the device of budgeted variances. The budget including budgeted variances is the *planning budget*, without them it is the *control budget.* In other words, they specify a point at which the budget ceases to represent a plan and becomes a control. Both budgets, however, are based on the *same* model. Such a model does not enable us to achieve the separation we require, as we shall see if we look at the problem from a systems point of view. Recalling (from the Appendix, "What a System Is") the minimal model of a system,

$$\sigma = < C, E, S > \, ,$$

we note first that planning and control are both systems in the abstract sense. They are made up of interrelated parts (the plans or controls for different segments or functions in the business), and there is a synergy effect, that is, an effect whereby the combination achieves more than the sum of the separate parts. Consider the components of the ordered triple above for the planning and control systems in turn. There is no reason to suppose that the composition of the two systems will be identical—the control system may contain many more feedbacks, for example. The environment needs to be considered in some detail for planning purposes (planning involves modeling the environment), while the characteristic property of feedback control systems such as budgetary control is that the environment can be completely ignored, with attention confined to the controlled system. Nor is it likely that the structures of the two systems (i.e., the relations of system components to each other and to the environment), will be identical, given that the systems are likely to have different compositions and environments. If the planning and control systems differ significantly, it is unlikely that they can both be satisfactorily represented by a single abstract-system model. In fact, as we have seen, the essential purpose of planning is the continuous adaptation of the firm in a changing environment, while the essential purpose of control is prevention or correction of departures from such a plan on a continuing basis—in other words stabilization or regulation. These are clearly very different functions. Also, of course, planning as conventionally understood is concerned with *ex ante* situations while control (and performance measurement) is concerned with *ex post* situations, although performance can be measured against plans drawn up with hindsight after all the events in the planning period have occurred, and such a performance measure undoubtedly encourages adaptation more than the conventional measure of performance (Demski 1967; Itami 1977).

Further differences appear when we examine the planning–control interface. Plans and controls meet in the annual all-purpose budgets. In many businesses, particularly small ones, the entire planning process begins, and coincides, with the annual budgeting process. The latter is typically carried out by a budget committee comprising the managers of the main functional areas and the senior executive. This is a singularly inappropriate time to engage in other than purely tactical planning (Baxter 1968: 24). Apart from the time constraint (the committee usually meets about a month or two before year's end), the managers attending these budgetary hearings are partisan, anxious to protect their own special interests, and knowing that they must commit themselves to a performance target once the hearings are concluded. In contrast to this annual budgeting, which in practice is dominated by control considerations, planning requires its participants to subordinate their sectional interests and think only of furthering corporate objectives, of solving sets of interrelated problems, and, above all, of appropriately orienting the firm to its environment and to its members. The higher levels of planning (normative, strategic) should precede the annual budgeting process, to which they are logically prior as we saw above (this chapter, "The Hierarchy of Plans").

SUMMARY

The point has been made in earlier chapters that, far from being an optional activity, planning is an absolute necessity if a firm is to adapt successfully. For over a decade now the literature has been referring to the "new" planning, to distinguish this conception of "where we should go," purposeful planning *of* the future from the conventional ("old") "how to get there" planning *for* a predicted future. The two principal reasons for the change in attitude toward planning have been recognition of the limitations of the conventional planning when applied to complex social systems (its concentration on adjusting variables within a given system but not changing the system's organizational structure, and its heavy emphasis on the short term) and that business organizations are purposeful systems. The highest level of the "new" planning is not found in the "old" planning.

The emergent view of planning for complex systems consists of three vertically arrayed levels, each subordinated to the next highest. They are, from high to low, normative, strategic, and tactical planning, performed in that order. Normative planning is solely concerned with ends—the basic purposes of the firm, deciding what ought to be done, designing a desired future. Strategic planning is both means and ends oriented and is planning of major importance involving the deployment of resources. A company's missions and long-range objectives are seen as determined at this stage. Strategic planning is not to be understood as synonymous with long-range planning, although it will often have long-range effects. The distinction between strategic and tactical planning is not clear-cut; but tactical planning is entirely concerned with means, periodic (usually annual), and undertaken at lower levels in the organization than the other two. The annual budgeting process forms a substantial part, although not the whole, of tactical planning, which in a broader sense also includes medium-range programming.

Perhaps the main point to come out of this part of the discussion is that the main burden of seeking continuously to adapt the enterprise to its environment falls at the normative and strategic planning stages, and hence these are the activities of crucial importance to the survival and continued well-being of the firm.

"Policies" were interpreted as "standing plans," and policy making as straddling the strategic and tactical planning processes. Policies comprise a wide array of standing plans, ranging all the way from major policies through minor and functional policies to standard operating plans and procedures. While these standing plans reduce internal uncertainty, there is a danger that they may also create rigidities, and thus hinder the process of adaptation.

Firms sometimes make long-range *forecasts* of various kinds (e.g., of general economic activity, or the demand for their products) 10 or even 20 years ahead. These become premises in the planning process. The forecasting (or anticipations) horizon should be distinguished from the planning horizon. The current practice in corporate planning is characterized as essentially a static approach, and there the two horizons coincide. If the firm were to plan dynamically over a horizon covering T periods, forecasting would need to cover only those elements of the future beyond the first period that will affect the optimality, over the horizon, of first-period plans. Hence forecasts would vary in length from zero to T periods. Dynamic planning would be desirable, because it takes into account interrelationships between periods which, if omitted, may be prejudicial to performance in future periods. However, dynamic planning would be extremely difficult to implement; and its comparative advantages are lessened if planning, while formally static, is done on an ongoing basis as suggested here. The need remains, of course, to make short-range plans, medium-range programs, and long-range plans mutually consistent.

There is no detectable attempt by firms to set their planning horizons optimally. Based on surveys, the modal period for the longest corporate plans appears to be five years, with considerable variability on either side of this number. We are referring to comprehensive detailed plans. Partial plans (e.g., for sales or capital expenditure) may be of longer duration. The great majority of short-range plans are for one year. What is important, of course, is the planning process rather than the content or duration of plans per se. The "new" planning, as stated earlier, tends to be more long-range than the "old." The reasons for this are that effective adaptation frequently requires a fairly long period in order to allow time to prepare for potential opportunities and threats, and because planning that is too short-term in focus often has adverse long-term effects—and long-range cause–effect relationships are thought to exert a powerful influence on the behavior of complex systems.

Flexibility, in the interest of adaptation, is an attribute that applies as much to planning as to all other aspects of the firm. It is more important that plans should be flexible than that they should be robust. Because both the organization and the environment are constantly changing, planning should be continual rather than at widely separated discrete intervals as in current practice.

It is at the tactical level that plans and controls interface: Tactical plans, in the form of short-term budgets, commonly serve as both plans and controls. Indeed, they may serve other purposes as well: as motivating devices, coordinating devices, and as stabilizers. Particularly if budgets are largely extrapolations, they serve to perpetuate existing activities and a given organizational structure. There is a strong presumption that, in view of the diversity of purposes budgets are required to serve, a single budget or set of budgets cannot simultaneously fulfill all of these purposes effectively. It was argued that the budgets that constitute the (tactical) plan should be made formally distinct from the budgets used for control, that is, they should be based on different models. Reasons were adduced for believing that the models used in the planning system and in the control system, while related, are usually not at all similar. The systems have very different functions. Planning is (or should be) concerned with the continuous adaptation of the firm—control with regulation: the prevention or correction of departures from a continuously updated plan.

APPENDIX: WHY DO SOCIAL SYSTEMS APPEAR TO BEHAVE COUNTERINTUITIVELY?

Forrester (1975) says that social systems behave counterintuitively. Actions taken to alleviate problems often make matters worse. This, at least, we have all observed! Forrester's own remedies include adopting a longer planning horizon (more than 10 years); gaining greater understanding of system dynamics and identifying the relatively few variables that influence the system's behavior dramatically; more attention to human relations; and greater attention to finding and removing causes of difficulties and less to alleviating symptoms.

A number of other possible explanations of the phenomenon come to mind. The plans made by social systems are not systemic, and not continually revised. Decisions are taken in isolation, not within a framework of (updated) plans. The structure of the system, and particularly the interdependencies between parts of the system and between system and environment, are not well understood. Or it may be that once decisions are taken, control is not effective. A combination of these reasons might go some way toward explaining the Forrester phenomenon.

Another possible explanation, which will be examined in more detail, is that social systems often have important multiple-time-scale properties. Over a relatively short period the system's behavior is dominated by a set of fast variables associated with the operating units of the organization, but in the longer run, behavior is dominated by a set of slow variables associated with the higher levels of the hierarchy (strategy and policy making). This could account for the appearance of a behavior that is quite different in the long run from that in the short run. It also has important implications for planning (contrary to Ackoff and the main discussion here, not all planning needs to be systemic) and for control (additional "strategic" controls are needed for the slow variables).

The motivation for the technical analysis of this view will now be presented, followed by some concluding remarks.

Simon and Ando (1961) present the first discussion of multiple-time-scale properties. Simon (1969) presents much evidence showing that complexity in physical, biological, and social systems frequently takes the form of hierarchy, the system being composed of interrelated subsystems, each of which in turn is hierarchical in structure until some lowest level of elementary subsystem is reached. Such systems are, moreover, weakly coupled: interactions within subsystems are (in the short run) much stronger than interactions between subsystems, a characteristic noted also by Ashby (1960: 192–96).

Simon and Ando describe such systems as nearly decomposable, and assert that "there is every reason to believe . . . that near decomposability is a very common characteristic of dynamic systems that exist in the real world. . . ." Nearly decomposable systems have the characteristic that interactions between subsystems are weak but not negligible and, as we shall see presently, they have important multiple-time-scale properties. The local (intra-subsystem) behavior of such systems is fast (high-frequency) compared with the systemwide low-frequency behavior caused by the weak coupling of the subsystems. The slow behavior is described by an aggregate model in which each subsystem is represented by a single variable ("index").

Nearly decomposable systems are then viewed as composite systems formed by the superposition of terms representing interactions between variables within each subsystem and terms representing interactions between subsystems. Simon and Ando conclude that, over a relatively short period, the first group of terms dominates the behavior of the system and as a result each subsystem can be regarded as approximately independent. Over a longer period the second group of terms dominates the system's behavior. Each subsystem converges to, or oscillates around, a state of equilibrium (the variables within each subsystem move roughly proportionately), enabling the variables within each subsystem to be aggregated into a single index representing the subsystem. The system as a whole slowly drifts under the influence of the subsystem couplings, which in the long run are not necessarily weak. This is what is meant by the system exhibiting multi-time-scale behavior. The superposition of the two models separates short-run dynamics from long-run dynamics. The ratio of the strength of interactions between subsystems to that of interactions within subsystems determines the ratio of the speeds of the slow to the fast phenomena (Peponides and Kokotovic 1983).

In order to describe this behavior more precisely, it is first necessary to give a formal description of "near decomposability." This is most simply done in terms of linear systems, to which Simon and Ando confined their attention. Then, in recognition of the fact that economic systems including business enterprises usually have significant nonlinearities, a point made by Forrester in reference to all social systems, Simon and Ando's analysis will be generalized to nonlinear systems. Peponides and Kokotovic have already performed this task very thoroughly, and accordingly their analysis will be followed here, with only the addition of some points to make it comprehensible to a wider audience.

Simon and Ando consider a linear system to be represented by an equation of the form $x(t + 1) = x(t)P$, where P is a matrix of constant coefficients. The dynamic characteristics of this system depend on the properties of the matrix P, particularly the patterns of zeros or near-zeros. They assume that the system represented by the above equation is a closed system and that P is a square matrix ($n \times n$).

The matrix $P*$ is said to be (completely) decomposable if after an appropriate permutation of rows and columns it can be written in the form

$$P* = \begin{bmatrix} P_1* & & & & & \\ & \cdot & & & & \\ & & P_2* & & & \\ & & & \cdot & & \\ & & & & \cdot & \\ & & & & & P_I* & \\ & & & & & & \cdot \\ & & & & & & & P_N* \end{bmatrix}$$

where the P_I*s are the square submatrices and the off-diagonal elements are all zeros. Consider now a slightly altered matrix, P:

$$P = P* + \epsilon C$$

where C is an arbitrary matrix of the same dimension as $P*$, ϵ is a very small positive number, and ϵC marks the upper bound of the off-diagonal elements. Matrix P is nearly decomposable. Simon and Ando then examine the dynamic behavior of closed linear systems described by the equation $x(t + 1) = x(t)P$, with P defined as above.

Analysis of Nonlinear Weakly Coupled Systems

A nonlinear (and continuous) generalization of this nearly decomposable system, following Peponides and Kokotovic, may be described by an equation of the general form

$$\frac{dx_i}{d\tau} = f_i(x_i, \epsilon) + \epsilon g_i(x, \epsilon), \qquad i = 1, \ldots, N \qquad 4.1$$

where $x = [x_1^T, \ldots, x_N^T]^T$, τ denotes time, ϵ is a small positive number as before, and $\epsilon g_i(x, \epsilon)$ are the weak couplings between subsystems. The functions f_i are defined in a domain $D_i \times [0, \epsilon_0] \subset R^{n_i} \times R$, functions g_i are defined on

$$D \times [0, \ \epsilon_0] \subset R^n \times R,$$

and

$$n = \sum_{i=1}^{N} n_i;$$

f_i and g_i are assumed to be appropriately differentiable (smooth).

Weakly coupled subsystems and diagonal dominance (as shown above in the matrix P^*) are related to time scales. The multi-time-scale behavior of systems like Equation 4.1 can be illustrated by considering a particular system represented by the equations

$$\frac{dx_i}{dt} = \hat{f}_i(x_i) + \hat{h}_i(x_i) + B_i u_i \qquad\qquad 4.2$$

$$y_i = C_i x_i, \qquad i = 1, \ldots, N$$

where x_i (state variables) are as defined earlier, the control variables denoted by u_i and the output variables by y_i. It will be assumed that u_i and y_i have the same dimensions (m_i) and that $C_i B_i$ are nonsingular for all i. We will suppose that this system has high gain (highly amplified) output feedback control, described by

$$u_i = \frac{1}{\epsilon} y_i \qquad i = 1, \ldots, N \qquad\qquad 4.3$$

By substituting 4.3 into 4.2 and rescaling time to $\tau = t / \epsilon$ one obtains

$$\frac{dx_i}{d\tau} = B_i C_i x_i + \epsilon \cdot [\hat{f}_i(x_i) + \hat{h}_i(x)]. \qquad\qquad 4.4$$

If the dimension of u_i and y_i is less than n_i, each isolated subsystem, represented by the first term on the right of 4.4,

$$\frac{dx_i}{d\tau} = B_i C_i x_i, \qquad\qquad 4.5$$

has a continuum of equilibrium points (rather than isolated equilibria), that is every point in the null space of C_i, denoted $\mathfrak{N}$ (C_i), is an equilibrium point of subsystem i. Peponides and Kokotovic show that this leads to the appearance of different time scale in the system's behavior. The slow motion of x_i will occur near $\mathfrak{N}$ (C_i). Equation 4.4 has the property that the time paths of Equation 4.5 satisfy:

$$V_i x_i (\tau) = V_i x_i (0), \qquad \tau \geq 0, \qquad\qquad 4.6$$

where V_i, the basis matrix of the null space of C_i, is defined by $V_i B_i = 0$. For each $x_i (0)$, Equation 4.6 defines an invariant manifold of Equation 4.5. (The term *manifold,* which occurs again in the later analysis, will be unfamiliar to many social scientists. Encountered mainly in topology, a manifold can for present purposes be intuitively thought of as a surface or set of objects.) These two properties (a continuum of equilibrium points and the relations of Equation 4.6) are common in dynamic economic models and in Markov chains (Peponides and Kokotovic 1983). This example provides the basis for the following crucial assumption. For every isolated subsystem of Equation 4.1,

$$\frac{dx_i}{d\tau} = f_i (x_i, 0), \qquad i = 1, \ldots, N \qquad\qquad 4.7$$

it is assumed that the following equilibrium and conservation relations apply:

1. The set of equilibrium points

$$S_i = \{ x_i | f_i (x_i, 0) = 0 \} \qquad\qquad 4.8$$

is a v_i-dimensional equilibrium manifold of Equation 4.7, $0 < v_i < n_i$, that is, there exists a smooth function $\phi_i: R_i^n \to R_i^n - {}_i^Y$ such that

$$\phi_i (x_i) = 0 \text{ if and only if } f_i(x_i, 0) = 0. \qquad\qquad 4.9$$

2. There exists a function $\sigma_i: R^n{}_i \to R^v{}_i$ such that

$$F_i = \{ x_i \mid \sigma_i(x_i = \sigma_i [x_i(0)] \} \qquad\qquad 4.10$$

is a family of invariant manifolds of Equation 4.7 parameterized on $\sigma_i [x_i(0)]$, where

$$\nu =_{/i+1}^{N} \sum \nu_i > 0.$$

Also S_i and F_i are nontangential, that is,

$$\text{rank} \begin{bmatrix} \phi_{ix} \\ \\ \sigma_{ix} \end{bmatrix} = n, \text{ all } x_i \epsilon D_i, \qquad\qquad 4.11$$

where ϕ_{ix} and σ_{ix} are the Jacobian matrices of ϕ_i and σ_i.

Singular perturbation techniques are used to show that when assumptions 1 and 2 are satisfied system 4.1 will exhibit multi-time-scale behavior. To put system 4.1 into standard singularly perturbed form, the following new coordinates are introduced:

$$y_i = \sigma_i(x_i)$$

$$z_i = \phi_i(x_i) \qquad i = 1, \ldots, N$$
4.12

In its singularly perturbed form the system has ν predominantly slow variables y, and

$$\rho = \sum_{i=1}^{\rho} \rho_i$$

predominantly fast variables z, as will be proved. Moreover, the quasi–steady-state $\bar{z}(t)$ of z is zero. (The qualifier "quasi" distinguishes the singularly perturbed system from the actual system, a bar indicating the quasi–steady-state value.) The proofs now follow.

It is first shown that y_i is a slow variable. Since the time paths of 4.7 satisfy the condition

$$\sigma_i[x_i(\tau)] = \sigma_i[x_i(0)], \text{ all } \tau \geq 0. \qquad\qquad 4.13$$

then

$$\frac{\partial \sigma_i}{\partial x_i} f_i(x_i, 0) = 0. \qquad\qquad 4.14$$

Taking the derivatives of y_i along the time paths of Equation 4.1, and making use of the mean value theorem in ϵ for each component of f_i gives

$$\frac{dy_i}{dt} = \frac{1}{\epsilon}\frac{dy_i}{d\tau} = \frac{1}{\epsilon}\frac{\partial \sigma_i}{\partial x_i} \quad [f_i(x_i, \epsilon) + \epsilon g_1(x, \epsilon)]$$

$$= \frac{\partial \sigma_i}{\partial x_i}\frac{[\partial f_i + g_i(x_i, \epsilon)]}{\partial \epsilon} \qquad 4.15$$

It can be seen from Equation 4.15, Peponides and Kokotovic assert, that in the slow time $t = \epsilon \tau$, dy_i/dt is o (1), and hence y_i is a slow variable. This needs further explanation. First, the notation o (1) means "of order of magnitude one," which in turn means "is a constant or zero"—in other words that dy_i/dt is bounded above and below. The reasoning is then that if dy_i/dt is o (1), $dy_i/\epsilon\, d\tau$ is o(1), and $dy_i/d\tau$ is o (ϵ). Since ϵ is, by definition, a small positive number, this establishes that y_i is a slow variable.

Denoting the inverse transformation of Equation 4.12, which exists because of Equation 4.11 by $x_i = \gamma_i (y_i, z_i)$, we obtain from Equation 4.12

$$\epsilon \frac{dz_i}{dt} = \frac{\partial \phi_i}{\partial x_i} [f_i(\gamma_i(y_i, z_i), \epsilon) + \epsilon g_i(\gamma(y, z), \epsilon)] \qquad 4.16$$

$$= G_i(y_i, z_i, \epsilon) + \epsilon H_i(y, z, \epsilon);$$

and since

$$\left.\frac{\partial G_i}{\partial z_i}\right|_{\epsilon = 0}$$

is nonsingular (otherwise the equilibrium manifold of Equation 4.15, Equation 4.16 would have dimension greater than ν_i, which would lead to a contradiction since Equation 4.12 is a nonsingular transformation), the z_i are fast variables. It also follows from the fact that $x_i \in S$ if and only if $x_i = \gamma_i(y_i, 0)$ that $f_i[\gamma_i(y_i, 0), 0] = 0$ and

$$G_i(y_i, 0, 0) = 0, \qquad 4.17$$

which implies that $\bar{z}_i(t) = 0$.

When the system has been put into the standard singularly perturbed form:

$$\frac{dy_i}{dt} = \frac{\partial \sigma_i}{\partial x_i} \frac{\{\partial f_i[\gamma_i(y_i, z_i), \epsilon] + g_i[\gamma(y, z), \epsilon]\}}{\partial \epsilon}$$

$$= J_i(y, z, \epsilon) \tag{4.18}$$

$$\epsilon \frac{dz_i}{dt} = \frac{\partial \phi_i}{\partial x_i} \quad \{f_i[\gamma_i(y_i, z_i), \epsilon] + \epsilon g_i[\gamma(y, z), \epsilon]\}$$

$$= G_i(y_i, z_i, \epsilon) + \epsilon H_i(y, z, \epsilon), \tag{4.19}$$

the reduced order fast and slow models describing the short-run and long-run behavior of the system, respectively, can be defined. The quasi–steady-state $\bar{z}$ of z, obtained by setting $\epsilon = 0$ in Equation 4.19, is zero, and the slow model is

$$\frac{d\bar{y}_i}{dt} = J_i(\bar{y}, 0, 0), \qquad i = 1, \ldots, N \tag{4.20}$$

Rescaling back to the "stretched time scale" τ and setting $\epsilon = 0$ again in 4.19 gives the fast model

$$\frac{d\bar{z}_i}{d\tau} = G_i(y_i, \bar{z}_i, 0), \qquad i = 1, \ldots, N \tag{4.21}$$

in which y_i appears as a parameter.

It will be noted that J_i is a function of the whole vector $\bar{y}$, whereas G_i is a function of the single variable $\bar{z}_i$ only. Thus the separation of time scales results in a decomposition in which parts (aggregate variables, "indexes") from every subsystem are combined to form a "slow core," the y variables, while the rest of each subsystem forms a "fast residue," the z_i variables, the slow motion having been removed from each subsystem. The slow core describes the slow behavior of the system as a whole due to the weak couplings between subsystems; the fast residues describe the local dynamics of subsystems that are strongly connected internally. In the short run the latter dominate the behavior of the system; in the long run the slow core is dominant.

Comments

While near decomposability is a rather restrictive condition to impose on a system, Simon (1969) nevertheless maintains that such systems are far from rare in the world of social and physical systems. Whether a particular social system such as a large business enterprise can be characterized in this way of course depends on how good an approximation one insists on (how small ϵ is required to be).

It would appear that separation of short-run from long-run dynamics is a potentially powerful tool for seeking effective adaptation and long-run survival of business enterprises and social organizations in general, meriting further study and empirical testing. One may at least speculate that Forrester's claim that social systems often behave counterintuitively over the long run may show he did not recognize that the characteristic weak couplings of these systems cause multi-time-scale behavior that might, before separation into its components, appear very confusing and even reverse itself over time. What *does* answer to the description "counterintuitive" is that a general property of nearly decomposable systems is that they may often be strongly coupled in the long-run scale while being weakly coupled in the short run.

For those who, like the author, are interested in the control of business enterprises, the foregoing analysis points up the need for an extension of the conventional control procedures. These procedures focus exclusively on the short run. There is no systematic monitoring of performance in the long run (beyond one year) except as a succession of these short-run reviews and, rather haphazardly, through annual and medium-term planning (budgeting). In practice medium-term budgeting (up to five years, say) is nonsystemic and not fully comprehensive. Certainly there is no awareness in accounting circles of the aggregation problems inherent in correctly identifying the "slow core," or a general recognition of the need to control against the slow drift of the system under the influence of weak couplings between subsystems if long-run adaptation is to be more than a chance event. Together with systemic planning, such long-run control should go a long way toward preventing the self-reversing phenomenon Forrester found to be so common.

What form this long-run control should take in a business enterprise, and what effect, if any, its implementation would have on the form of the conventional short-run controls, raises a number of interesting questions, the answers to which are not all obvious at this stage. The control variables u_i in Equation 4.3 would have to be divided into a slow part and a fast part. From an information-processing point of view, decisions should be factored in such a way that the higher-frequency ones (short-run dynamics) are associated with the operating parts of the organization (production and service departments), while the lower-frequency ones (long-run dynamics) are associated with the strategy- and policy-making parts, located higher up in the organizational hierarchy (Simon 1969: 477). If this analysis is correct, conventional short-run controls would remain essentially unchanged (which is not to say their form should not be changed at all), and long-run controls would be devised and superimposed to regulate the strategic and policy-making functions through aggregate variables.

It should also be noted that the analysis of Peponides and Kokotovic, like that of Simon and Ando, was confined to closed systems. As Simon (1969) observes, to the extent that an organization is effectively adaptive, its behavior will reflect characteristics largely of its environment, in light of its goals. In other words, for effective adaptation an organization must selectively (i.e., in light of its goals) map the environment into itself, as structure or as information, more or less continuously, comprehensively, and quickly. Once the model presented here is modified to take account of the open-system nature of organizations, and specifically of the couplings between the environment and the organization, one would have to see whether the system still qualified for the description of nearly decomposable, although the presumption is that it would. It is this characteristic on which the decomposition into fast and slow time scales depends.

One may conjecture that the model of hierarchical, nearly decomposable systems is likely to be more appropriate to a more homogeneous and stable (hence more predictable) environment than to diverse and rapidly changing environments. This is based on the proposition that there is no one best organizational design, but several, and that their suitability is determined by the extent of the match between organization form and the demands of the environment (Lawrence and Lorsch 1967). Nor would the "nearly decomposable" description fit organizations in which the work of different stages (subunits of the system) is highly interdependent, as is claimed to be the case in high-technology industries (Ouchi 1980).

The implications of this discussion for planning would seem to be twofold, assuming that the system to be planned is nearly decomposable.

First, planning does not need to have a horizon of more than 10 years, as Forrester suggests, but to be conceived differently, namely in terms of those (aggregate) variables that account for the slow drift of the system. In addition to the usual tactical planning, these variables should be monitored and planned annually. Second, the discussion tells us that the low-frequency dynamics of the system associated with strategy formation and more generally with all top-level management decisions are likely to dominate the firm's behavior in the long run. A firm would therefore be unwise to neglect these elements in its planning. Yet in practice we commonly find the reverse to be true: more attention given to tactical planning of the "fast residues," and very little planning directed at the "slow core." What may be broadly termed "strategic planning" therefore deserves much more attention.

NOTE

1. According to Forrester (1975), social systems belong to the class called multiple-loop nonlinear feedback systems, which are "far more complex and harder to understand than our technological systems." The history of human evolution has not prepared us to interpret the dynamic behavior of such systems but computer models can enable us to do so. ". . . we now do know enough to make useful models of social systems . . . and substantial supporting evidence is beginning to accumulate that the proper use of models of social systems can lead to far better systems. . . ." Forrester notes the following characteristics of social systems: (a) they are inherently insensitive to most policy changes that attempt to alter their behavior, tending to draw our attention to the very points at which intervention will fail. The system presents us with an apparently plausible cause of trouble that we often discover later is not an underlying cause but a symptom, being produced by the feedback-loop dynamics of a larger system; (b) social systems seem to have a few sensitive influence points through which the behavior of the system can be changed. But we often attempt to effect change in a system through points that have little leverage for change, and the real influence points are not in the locations where most people expect them to be; (c) even if we succeed in identifying a sensitive point where influence can be exerted, there is a high probability that a person guided by intuition and judgment will alter the system in the wrong direction (e.g., in an urban system housing is a sensitive control point. To revive the economy of a city it appears that the amount of low-income housing must be reduced rather than increased); (d) there is usually a fundamental conflict between the short-term and long-term consequences of a policy change: "A policy that produces improvement in the short-run, within five to ten years, is usually one that degrades the system in the long-run, beyond ten years. Likewise, policies . . . that produce long-run im-

provement may initially depress the behavior of the system." A change that has opposite effects in the short run and in the long run "can eventually cause deepening difficulties after a sequence of short-term actions."

REFERENCES

Ackoff, R.L. 1970. *A Concept of Corporate Planning.* New York: Wiley-Interscience.

Amey, L.R. 1979. *Budget Planning and Control Systems.* London: Pitman.

Amey, L.R. and D.A. Egginton. 1973. *Management Accounting: A Conceptual Approach.* London: Longman.

Ashby, W.R. 1960. *Design for a Brain,* pp. 192–96. London: Chapman & Hall.

Barnard, C.I. 1948. *Organization and Management.* Cambridge, MA: Harvard University Press.

Baxter, R.F. 1968. *Proceedings of the Third Annual Symposium on Planning.* Providence, RI: The Institute of Management Sciences.

Beer, S. 1969. "The Aborting Corporate Plan." In *Perspectives of Planning,* pp. 397–422. *See* Jantsch 1969.

Chamberlain, N. 1963. *Managerial Long-Range Planning,* edited by G.A. Steiner. New York: McGraw-Hill: 10.

Demski, J.S. 1967. "An Accounting System Structured on a Linear Programming Model." *Accounting Review* 42 (October): 701–12.

Forrester, J.W. 1969. "Planning Under the Dynamic Influences of Complex Social Systems." In *Perspectives of Planning,* pp. 235–54. *See* Jantsch 1969.

———. 1969b. "A New Corporate Design." In *Perspectives of Planning,* pp. 423–45. *See* Jantsch 1969.

———. 1975. "Counterintuitive Behavior of Social Systems." In *Collected Papers of J.W. Forrester.* Cambridge, MA: Wright-Allen Press.

Hicks, J.R. 1946. *Value and Capital,* 2d ed. London: Oxford University Press.

Hopwood, A.G. 1976. *Accounting and Human Behaviour.* Englewood Cliffs, NJ: Prentice-Hall.

Itami, H. 1977. *Adaptive Behavior: Management Control and Information Analysis.* Sarasota, FL: American Accounting Association, Studies in Accounting Research no. 15.

Jantsch, E. 1969. "Synopsis"; "Integrative Planning of Technology"; and "Adaptive Institutions for Shaping the Future." In *Perspectives of Planning*, edited by E. Jantsch, pp. 13–22, 177–200, 461–91. Paris: OECD.

Kokotovic, P.V. 1981. "Subsystems, Time Scales and Multimodelling." *Automatica* 17: 789–95.

Koontz, H. and C. O'Donnell. 1959. *Principles of Management*. New York: McGraw-Hill.

Lawrence, P.R. and J.W. Lorsch. 1967. *Organization and Environment: Managing Differentiation and Integration*. Boston, MA: Harvard Graduate School of Business Administration.

McGregor, D. 1967. *The Professional Manager*. New York: McGraw-Hill.

Modigliani, F. and K.J. Cohen. 1961. "The Role of Anticipations and Plans in Economic Behavior and Their Use in Economic Analysis and Forecasting." *Studies in Business Expectations and Planning*, no. 4. Bureau of Economic and Business Research, University of Illinois.

Modigliani, F. and F.E. Hohn. 1955. "Production Planning over Time and the Nature of the Expectation and Planning Horizon." *Econometrica* 23: 46–66.

Morris, R.D.F. 1968. "Budgetary Control is Obsolete." *The Accountant* (May 18): 654–56.

Ouchi, W.G. 1980. "Markets, Bureaucracies and Clans." *Administrative Science Quarterly* (March): 129–41.

Ozbekhan, H. 1969. "Toward a General Theory of Planning." In *Perspectives of Planning*, pp. 45–155. *See* Jantsch 1969.

Peponides, G.M. and P.V. Kokotovic. 1983. "Weak Connections, Time Scales, and Aggregation of Nonlinear Systems." *IEEE Transactions on Systems, Man, and Cybernetics* SMC-13 (July–August): 527–32.

Simon, H.A. and A. Ando. 1961. "Aggregation of Variables in Dynamic Systems." *Econometrica* 29 (April): 111–38.

Simon, H.A. 1969. "The Architecture of Complexity." In *The Sciences of the Artificial*, edited by H.A. Simon, pp. 84–118. Cambridge, MA: MIT Press.

Stedry, A.C. 1960. *Budget Control and Cost Behavior*. Englewood Cliffs, NJ: Prentice-Hall.

Steiner, G.A. 1969. *Top Management Planning*. New York: Macmillan.

Tilles, S. 1968. "The State of the Art." *Proceedings of the Tenth Annual Symposium on Planning*, New York, June 8–9, 1967) edited by R.F. Baxter, pp. 9–28. Providence, RI: The Institute of Management Sciences.

5
Some Planning Models

In previous chapters planning was described as an ongoing process for solving systems of problems and adapting the firm to its changing environment. This chapter is concerned with modeling the planning process. We use the term *model* in the broadest sense to mean any representation of reality other than reproducing it. "Models" of the planning process are abstractions of the process as it exists (operational, or descriptive, model) or as we feel it ought to be (conceptual, or normative, model). This broad definition will permit us to consider models represented mathematically, diagrammatically, or in words.

All of the models surveyed here are conceptual models, and most of them are decision models. Some, however, are predictive models which, on the basis of some assumed permanence in structural relationships, make projections of future behavior. Ultimately, predictive models are inappropriate for planning, since planning is anticipatory decision making, a series of adapted "dry runs."

In Chapter 1 ("The systems rationale for planning") we quoted Ackoff's (1970) characterization of this process. There the set of decisions was seen as very large, too large to be handled as a single problem. The planning process had therefore to be split up into stages to be performed sequentially by a single planning body, or simultaneously by a number of different planning bodies, or some combination of these approaches. Many of the decisions were also seen as interrelated. As a result, the whole planning problem could not be broken down into independent subproblems because the latter are not independent. Therefore the interdependencies had either to be taken into account in formulating the subproblems, if they were to be solved simultaneously, or else subplans drawn up at earlier stages of the process had to be reviewed and modified in light of subplans prepared at later stages.

The models discussed here differ in their scope, in the "decision space" to which they refer, and we have made this our main principle of classification. "Global" models span the whole space consisting of the normative, strategic, and tactical planning levels, or at least the last two. Partial models refer to the single tactical level, to the narrower decision space of production planning as it is represented in microeconomics or in accounting (the break-even model), or even to the narrower and more detailed budgeting models. This classification, based on a multilevel decision space, it will be noted, subsumes another relating to the duration of plans, that is, to segments of the production planning period. Our intention is to present a reasonably wide selection of different types of corporate planning models, while not seeking to be exhaustive.

Another way in which the models vary is that some are concerned solely with planning while others are integrated models of planning and control.

THE USEFULNESS OF MODELS IN PLANNING

The main justification for the use of models in planning is the same as that for modeling generally, namely that by abstracting from reality we may gain greater insights into the nature of that reality. This statement applies, in particular, to conceptual (i.e., normative) models. Implied in this proposition of course is the belief that a plan derived from the abstraction will translate into desired or satisfactory behavior in the real world. As Ackoff explains (1970: 10), experimentation is needed to gain insight and control over a large system. But the latter cannot be tested in a laboratory or, as a whole, in its natural environment. Experiments must therefore be conducted on a *model* of the system, a representation of what the system is like. An experiment conducted on a model of the system is called a *simulation*. Alternatively, it may be possible to solve the model by *mathematical analysis* without experimenting. Of course, whether the model can be solved analytically depends on the scope of the model and the analytical methods available for solving it. The models of large, complex systems will often make analytical solutions impossible. It is then necessary to resort to computer simulation on the model to determine the changing state of the system (Forrester 1969: 243). While Forrester is referring to the system as a whole, it seems likely that the computer may be of great assistance even in the partial planning problems at different levels (normative, strategic, tactical), given the immensity of the problem presented by the corporate planning process for a large corporation. J.C. Emery (1969: 151, 156–57), referring to the work of Morton (1967), comments as follows on these possibilities:

> The meagre evidence that we have suggests that a symbiosis between man and computer will prove especially powerful and fruitful in coping with the enormously complex problems encountered in higher-level organizational planning [and] the time now seems ripe for a major improvement in [the latter]. Information technology has advanced to a point that large man-machine planning systems are technically and economically feasible. Such a system could provide major improvements in the planning process. The effect on organizational behaviour could be profound. The planning process largely governs behaviour, and therefore fundamental improvements in performance must come principally through better planning [while] the generation of substantially better plans is so complex a task that only through an elaborate man-machine system can we hope to come to grips with it. Such a system will provide an efficient means of performing a sequential, iterative search through a hierarchical plan space of the organization.

Another reason for examining some models of planning is that it affords an opportunity of comparing different approaches, as exemplified, for example, in adaptive systems planning, program planning and budgeting systems (PPBS), production planning in microeconomics, and budgeting in accounting.

SPECIFYING COST IN PLANNING MODELS

Before commencing the survey we call attention to several points concerning the meaning of *cost* in different types of planning models. Since costs feature in all or most planning models it is important that we have a clear understanding of what this term includes so that we can properly interpret the models and the results (plans) that they yield. The specification of costs varies, depending on three different circumstances: on whether the planning model takes the form of a decision model, on whether a decision-type planning model lists all alternatives or focuses on a single alternative, and on whether uncertainty (specifically, the planners' attitude to risk taking) is built into the model explicitly. We will consider these in turn.

Listing Versus Imputing Alternatives in Decision Models: Explicit Versus Implicit Costs

Most planning models that have the form of decision models list all the planning alternatives under consideration, in terms of their costs and benefits. An example would be the linear programming budget models discussed later. The costs to be included in this kind of model differ from those in a decision model that focuses on a single alternative and compares it with the rest. Let us consider an example. Suppose a student is faced with the choice of whether or not to attend graduate school. Regarding this as a planning problem, what are his/her costs *ex ante* (i.e., the anticipated or expected, versus actual or incurred, costs)?

If the planning model takes the form of a decision model we require data on all the feasible alternatives. Assume that the alternative of remaining idle is lower-valued than those of getting employment now or attending graduate school, and that these are the only feasible alternatives. We could, first, set down in two columns the expected lifetime earnings, discounted to the present, of attending and not attending, subtracting from the former column the estimated costs of tuition, books, living expenses, travel, and so on, and from the latter any expenses to be incurred in earning employment income. Note that these costs are entirely objective, in the sense of estimates of payments that will eventually be incurred if the alternative in question is chosen. The student should choose the alternative offering the highest discounted net receipts.

Alternatively, the student could focus just on the alternative of attending, and compare it implicitly with not attending. Here we would set down the discounted lifetime earnings minus the costs to be expected by attending. Costs would include the items referred to above plus a subjective cost which we will call an implicit opportunity cost, that is, the present value of the income, net of expenses, foregone by remaining a student for two more years. The reason this is not included in the first (taxonomic or alternative-display) approach follows from the definition of "opportunity cost" as the highest net receipts foregone by choosing this particular alternative. But by arraying, in the first approach, all the alternatives in terms of their receipts and objective costs to determine the highest-valued, the student avoids this hurdle. Another reason is that income foregone is a subjective cost, that is, the decision maker's *own* estimate (not the market's) of the highest-valued alternative foregone, a valuation not observable by anyone else. For the student to choose to attend under this second approach the net receipts need only be positive (Table 5.1).

Table 5.1. Decision-relevant costs

First Approach: Comparing attending with not attending
(explicit, objective comparison)

	Attend	Don't Attend
Discounted lifetime earnings	E_1	E_2
less avoidable outlay costs	C_1	C_2
	$E_1 - C_1$	$E_2 - C_2$

Attend if $(E_1 - C_1) > (E_2 - C_2)$

Second Approach: Attending, compared with not attending
(implicit, subjective comparison)

Discounted lifetime earnings by attending	E_1
less avoidable outlay costs of attending	C_1
less implicit opportunity cost (net income foregone by attending)	$E_2 - C_2$
	$E_1 - E_2 + C_2 - C_1$

Attend if $(E_1 - E_2 + C_2 - C_1) > 0$

Source: Compiled by the author.

We can take this argument a step further by saying that in any problem of choice *all* the costs involved, the "relevant costs," are opportunity costs. They will comprise explicit opportunity costs (i.e., avoidable outlay costs), items like expected tuition fees, if we are listing all alternatives, or explicit *and implicit* opportunity costs if we are not. Explicit opportunity costs eventually become *ex post* (i.e. actual) costs; implicit opportunity costs do not. (In the literature the term *opportunity cost* is often reserved to describe what we have here called *implicit opportunity costs.*) The latter vanish at the moment of choice, because the alternative to which they refer is eliminated by the act of choice.

The same plan or decision will result from either of these approaches. The difference between the specification of costs in the two cases is worth remembering, however, for while most of the decision-type planning models discussed in the sequel are examples of the taxonomic approach that lists all alternatives, other planning models do require the inclusion of implicit opportunity costs. An example would be an inventory planning model using the optimal inventory formula, where costs would include the implicit opportunity cost of the capital to be tied up in inventories. This model *implicitly* compares various inventory levels with a single alternative of investing funds at the highest return obtainable.

PRE-DECISION COSTS IN DECISION MODELS AND POST-DECISION COSTS IN PREDICTIVE MODELS: BOTH EX ANTE

A second point is that the costs to be included will differ depending on whether the planning model takes the form of a decision model. There are in fact two different kinds of *ex ante* (or expected) costs, one pre-decision, the other post-decision. Let us consider some examples to illustrate the difference. We have, on the one hand, the neoclassical economic theory of the firm in the *short run* and accounting budgets, the results produced by the annual budgeting process. In each of these cases the costs represented are *post-decision* but still *ex ante*. That is, they represent the expected costs of certain courses of action *which have already been decided upon*. It follows that they do not include implicit opportunity costs; in other words all costs are objective. The short-run economic theory of the firm is not a theory of choice, because it neither assumes alternative courses of action nor allows alternative outcomes. Given the objective, and assuming economic rationality, its results (the decision rule for price-output determination) follow automatically. Given a profit maximization objective, they follow trivially. It is a *predictive* theory: Given objective data on prices and quantities and the firm's objective (profit maximization), it predicts the properties of the equilibrium relationships that tend to become established by market processes.

On the other hand we have, in the pre-decision, *ex ante* category, costs in the neoclassical theory of the firm in the *long run*, costs in planning models that take the form of decision models like the inventory planning model, and "relevant costs" for decision making that focus on a single alternative. Here "cost" includes both explicit and implicit opportunity costs. These costs are *ex ante* and *pre-decision*. The difference is illustrated in Figures

5.1a and 5.1b, showing the equilibrium of a profit-maximizing firm in the short and long run:

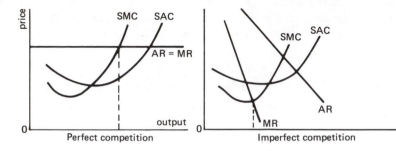

Fig. 5.1a. Short-run equilibrium of the firm.

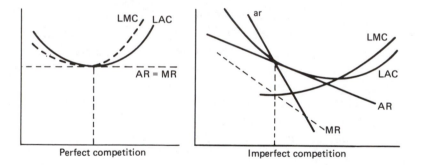

Fig. 5.1b. Long-run equilibrium of the firm. Key: AR, average revenue (= price), assuming competitors' prices remain fixed; ar, average revenue, competitors' prices same as this firm's; MR, marginal revenue; SAC, short-run average cost; SMC, short-run marginal cost; LAC, long-run average cost; LMC, long-run marginal cost.

In Fig. 5.1a costs include only explicit opportunity costs; in Fig. 5.1b they include both explicit and implicit opportunity costs. Implicit opportunity cost is represented by what is generally called "normal profit." Normal profit is the highest net receipts that could be earned by transferring the capital invested in the firm to the next-best use, net of the costs of transferring it. Unless revenues clear all costs including this normal profit, *on the average in the long run* the owners of the business would be better off transferring their investment elsewhere. In the short run this is not the case, because in the short run the firm cannot suddenly transfer capital to another use should income fall below this level. Eventually, however, as the period considered lengthens, a return on the capital invested at least equal to the highest rate that capital could earn outside the firm, allowing for any difference in risk, must be a condition for continued production in this firm, and therefore a cost.

These ideas are spelled out more fully in Amey (1980). Their significance to us here is that we should be careful in specifying and interpreting costs in different kinds of planning models. They will differ as between predictive and decision models.

Constant Costs and Revenues: The Circumstances in Which They Are Relevant

A third point about cost specification relates only to decision-type planning models. It concerns fixed costs, or more precisely costs (and revenues) that are constant over all the alternatives considered by the model. Should these costs be included in the model? The answer depends on whether the firm takes risk into account explicitly in a utility (or preference) function and, if it does, on whether that utility function is linear. We can characterize the two cases to be considered as planning where uncertainty is not allowed for explicitly and the objective function is a monetary one (such as profit or wealth maximization), and planning that allows for uncertainty explicitly and has a probabilistic objective, of say, expected utility maximization.

In the first, or deterministic, case we can follow an "incremental approach" and safely ignore costs and revenues that are constant over all alternative plans. We consider only the revenues and costs that change from one alternative to another. It might be dangerous to do this, however, if the firm takes uncertainty into account explicitly and has a nonlinear utility function (or more precisely if its utility function has certain nonlinear forms). If the dollar amounts of the constant items involved are substantial relative to the incremental amounts, failure to include them might lead to different, and suboptimal, plans. This is because omission of these constant costs or revenues from the data of the problem has the effect of making a different portion of the utility curve (representing nonconstant costs or revenues) correspond to given plans. The marginal utilities, represented by the slope of the curve, may be substantially different over this section of the curve from what they were when the items were included. Comparison of alternative plans may thereby be distorted so that the position that maximizes expected utility no longer represents the optimal plan. So in this case constant costs and revenues should be included in formulating the planning problem.[1]

In practice, firms seldom have models of the normative or strategic planning process; their models are only of tactical planning, which are usually deterministic. Since accounting budgets that represent this tactical planning rarely take uncertainty into account, if the firm seeks to optimize some objective expressed in monetary terms, it is a matter of indifference whether constant costs and revenues are included. Keep in mind, however, that most budgets in practice do not seek to optimize.

GLOBAL, OR MULTILEVEL, PLANNING MODELS

As previous stated, *global* is intended to mean a planning model that is not only comprehensive in the sense of being companywide, embracing all operating activities, but also spans the three hierarchical levels of planning already identified (normative, strategic, and tactical) or at least the last two (since the normative level is a relative newcomer to the list).

Beer's Cybernetic, Organismic Model: Planning by Controlling; Motivation Ignored

Beer has produced a generalized design of an adaptive organization that he calls the cybernetic firm. It is described in Beer 1969a: 397–422; 1969b: 31–54; 1972). This five-tiered integrated planning and control model was suggested to Beer by his studies of the physiology of the human brain and other related neurological systems; he traces isomorphisms between the human brain and the brain or command system of the firm. The model is displayed in Figure 5.2.

Given that planning should be described as an ongoing process whereby an enterprise adapts to a changing environment, and that the enterprise must be structurally capable of adaptation, Beer asks how the enterprise should be organized. His answer is that it should be organized cybernetically (i.e., in terms of feedback mechanisms) and as hierarchies of command that take the form of five interlocking control systems, each of which is assigned a particular role. This kind of organizational structure, Beer claims, is adaptive.

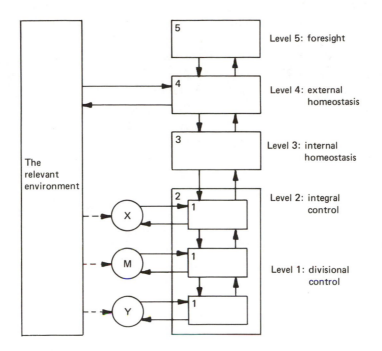

Level 5: foresight

Level 4: external
homeostasis

Level 3: internal
homeostasis

Level 2: integral
control

Level 1: divisional
control

The relevant environment

Fig. 5.2. Beer's integrated planning and control model.

In Figure 5.2, X, M, and Y denote divisions or subsystems of the firm, M representing a management unit and X and Y operating divisions. The column of boxes on the right represents the planning and control systems. System 1 controllers regulate resource allocation decisions and associated risk calculations in the divisions, after receiving instructions (a budget program) from higher management. This is seen as essentially a horizontal command axis. System 2, which performs integral control, operates on the interactions between divisions to harmonize their behavior. The control performed by System 3, called *internal homeostasis,* acts to modify the behavior of the divisions to align it with the firm's objective. *Homeostasis* means the ability to hold some critical variable within certain prescribed limits necessary for survival of the firm. Systems 1 and 2 act as filters to report upward only on what is exceptional. Armed with instructions from top management about particular goals, with a superior view of the environment, and with these exception reports, System 3 reoptimizes in light of the firm's overall objectives and transmits fresh instructions downward. Problems such as the allocation of resources between divisions and determination of transfer prices are solved at level 3. System 4 performs external homeostasis, which is a staff function taking into account the interactions between the environment and the firm *corporately,* as distinct from its operating divisions. It collects and analyzes information on the environment and decides on strategies. System 5, the final element, is concerned with "every feature of the *company in its environment* which seems relevant to a consideration of the firm's long-term future." Its task is to invent and test possible future scenarios, as described in earlier chapters.

Hence Beer's "cybernetic firm" has a control structure consisting of "machines controlling machines controlling machines controlling machines controlling machines having their own intrinsic control." Beer describes level 4 as corporate planning, which he sees as maintaining a minimum gap between now (level 3) and then (level 5). In terms of our earlier discussion, however, levels 5, 4, and 3 may each be seen as a type of corporate planning, approximating what we have called normative, strategic, and tactical planning, respectively.

The weakness of this otherwise interesting conceptual model lies in Beer's analogy with the human brain, implying that the system being planned for (the firm) is an organism (see, for example, Beer 1969a, xix: "This model of an organic adaptable system is argued to be isomorphic with any other such system—such as society itself. [In other words] the control problems of the body, the firm, and the government are cybernetically indistinguishable"). The analogy does not hold, however. The parts of an organization, unlike the parts of the human body, are purposeful. Hence, as Ackoff has pointed out (Lawrence 1969: 24–25), plans for an organization cannot be effectively implemented unless they have the support of its parts. Consequently in organizational planning "it is essential to consider the *incentives* that are built into the system." Control of an organization must be richer than control of an organism; the parts must be properly *motivated* if they are to perform in the desired way. If the organization structure does not conform to the particular capabilities of people the structure may have to be changed. It is only at a very high level of generality, as in Beer's model, that we can talk about one type of structure for all organizations, Ackoff argues. When we become more specific and look at a particular organization, the characteristics of the personnel may dominate the design of its structure.

Ackoff's Adaptive-Management, System Model: Planning as Coordination

Ackoff's own views have been quoted extensively in the foregoing and should by now be familiar. The nearest he appears to come to modeling his ideas is in a diagram, not of a planning system as such, but of what he calls an adaptive management system (Ackoff 1970: 120–21; Jantsch 1969: 27), or an adaptive-learning control system (Ackoff 1974: 230). The adaptive management system has three components: a decision subsystem, a management information subsystem, and a control subsystem. Elsewhere, Ackoff addresses the problem of coordinating planning at different levels in the organization (e.g., corporate level, division, department) by means of planning review boards (Ackoff 1970: 133–37).

Ruefli's Goal-Decomposition, PPBS Model: Planning (or Goal) Structure versus Control (or Organization) Structure

Ruefli (1971: 161–209) has developed the only formal model of a planning programming budgeting system (PPBS) of which we are aware, and this affords us an opportunity to comment on program budgeting and PPBS. Essentially, PPBS covers only the lower two levels of the hierarchy of planning (i.e., strategic and tactical planning). It includes the determination of missions, the setting of major objectives, and medium- and short-term goals, but not determination of the basic purposes of the firm nor the design of its desired future. The normative level is missing.

Program budgeting (PB), it may be recalled, was developed at the RAND Corporation in the United States as an attempt to control and rationalize defense spending, and reduce inefficiencies (Novick 1954, 1956; Hitch and McKean 1960). The suggestion was that this could be done by focusing on the outputs or mission of the organization rather than following the traditional input or "line of expenditure" approach—"top down" rather than "bottom up." PB was motivated by the assumption that, under existing budgeting processes, planning and control of resources by subdivisions of an organization would be effective only if we strongly separate the missions of organizational subdivisions by redefining these subdivisions. In other words, it recognized that an information system monitoring the performance of organizational subdivisions alone (i.e., of units determined only on the basis of existing organization structure) is useless for the planning and control of missions that involve more than one subdivision. An alternative, and the one adopted, was not to change the existing organizational structure (i.e., restructure the organization along mission lines) but rather to add mission-oriented budgeting to the budgeting process. Essentially this meant superimposing a mission-oriented information system on the existing one based on organizational subdivisions, rather than changing the organizational structure.

PPBS developed from PB by extending the planning period beyond the one-year budget period. Prior to the introduction of PPBS the scope of formal planning was confined to the next fiscal year. Under PPBS, budget estimates continue to be made for one year, but in light of planned activities and commitments over a number of years. This does not, however, affect the information system which, if based on organization structure, is not appropriate for planning and control. Moreover, although PPBS, by its title, proposes to combine planning and budgeting in a program (i.e., decision versus organizational structure) format, in practice they are *implemented* in the traditional budget (i.e., administrative-organization) format. Several questions arise here. One is whether the increased efficiency in resource allocation expected from the program format outweighs the increased information costs (of producing a separate set of plans and budgets on this basis and translating them to the traditional format incorporated in the existing budgeting process). Another is whether this latter step subverts the program format by giving the program categories too inaccurate a representation at the implementation stage, making it necessary to put the existing budgeting process on this basis also. These problems are likely to remain because the program format seems to have clear advantages for planning and programming, while budgets in the traditional form are considered by many to be necessary for detailed financial control.

Our main interest in Ruefli's model, reproduced in the appendix to this chapter, is that it reflects the basic assumptions of PPBS that the structure of the information system and its relation to the organizational structure is an important determinant of behavior. The organization modeled by Ruefli is hierarchical, consisting of a central unit (top management) and m divisional managements, each responsible for n operating units. The central unit sets initial goal levels for each of the divisional management units and allocates resources to them. They each solve a goal programming problem, which is to minimize the deviations from these goals. Solution of this problem yields shadow prices which are sent to the central unit and to the operating units under the division's command. The operating units solve a linear programming problem in which these shadow prices are used to select operating proposals. These are sent to the divisional management units for approval. At the same time the central unit uses the shadow prices in a linear programming problem to revise the goal levels set for the divisions. This process continues until deviations from the divisional management goals are at a minimum, and no actions by the operating units or the central unit will reduce deviations from goals of the organization as a whole.

Ruefli's goal decomposition model, consisting of these three separate models, recognizes that an organization is composed of a series of information systems, and that the information systems must be made interdependent when the tasks associated with them are interdependent. The model is an explicit representation of the relation between different information structures and the organization structure. Formally, Ruefli's model amounts to a combination of Dantzig and Wolfe's (1960) decomposition algorithm and goal programming.[2]

PPBS has been criticized for stating that the best organizational structure for planning is one designed around programs (means of fulfilling missions), without showing how to design the optimal program structure. Moreover, it does not show how the program structure, desirable for planning but less efficient for control than the traditional budget format, should relate to the latter. This problem is not likely to be solved the other way around for, considering how they arise (to serve an administrative role), there is little reason for thinking that traditional organizational structures will conform at all closely to mission-determined (i.e., objective- or decision-determined) structures.

We close by summarizing the argument of PPB: (1) program budgeting is necessary to improve decision making; traditional budget categories do not do this; (2) classification of budgetary items is a key to rational program budgeting; changes in classification can be made to produce desired changes in behavior; (3) program budgeting specifies one information structure (based on programs) as being superior for planning and programming purposes; (4) a particular information structure implies a particular organizational structure—the two are interrelated; (5) if an information structure based on programs does not match the existing organizational structure, there are two possibilities: (a) the organization can be restructured to match the information structure, or (b) the existing organizational structure can be retained, and some means established for translating information from the program budget to the traditional budget categories. As stated earlier, PPBS has in practice compromised by following possibility (b).

Anthony's Planning cum Control Model:
Are Planning and Control Inseparable?

Anthony's study (1965) arose out of a concern over the ambivalence in the way planning and control were related in the literature and in practice up to that time. On the one hand some writers claimed that planning and control were separate functions, although they were bound to admit that they were interrelated, since control is usually exercised in relation to a plan. On the other hand there were writers who, recognizing this interrelationship, went the other way and regarded planning and control as inseparable, a single function. Anthony observed (pp. 10–11):

> The trouble essentially is that, although planning and control are definable abstractions and are easily understood as calling for different types of *mental* activity, they do not relate to separate major categories of activities actually carried on in an organization, either at different times, or by different people, or for different situations.

This is a fair description of conventional practice. His suggested framework for studying planning and control was as shown in Fig. 5.3.

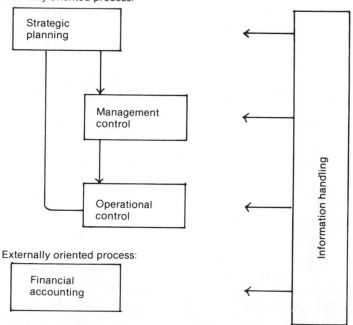

Fig. 5.3. Planning and control processes in organizations.

This model spans just the two lower levels of our hierarchy of planning, strategic and tactical. Strategic planning is defined by Anthony in the same way as by Steiner, as deciding on corporate objectives and on the resources needed to attain them. The categories of management control and operational control do not correspond to Steiner's medium- and short-range planning, however. Management control in Anthony's scheme means execution of policies formed at the strategic level. It is concerned with individuals (managers) and nonprogrammed decisions, taken by following set rules and procedures, that is, with ensuring that specific tasks such as production scheduling, order processing, and inventory control are carried out effectively and efficiently. (The terms *efficiency* and *effectiveness* are used by Anthony in the generally accepted sense to mean, respectively, optimal relationships between input and output, and the accomplishment of a specific end result.) Hence, in terms of Steiner's classification, *management control* covers medium-range programming and the non-automatic part of short-range budgeting, while *operational control* is the remainder of short-range budgeting (that part which is automatic).

All of Anthony's categories are functions whose inputs and outputs are both informational, but he prefers to treat "information handling" as a separate category because "some important generalizations can be made about handling data . . . that are independent of the intended use of the data."

At the time it was written this was a commendable attempt to bring some sort of definition to a gray area of management and accounting, namely by regarding budgets as both plans and controls and relating them to the normative. Beyond that observation we cannot say that Anthony's framework is presently very helpful. His management control, for example, includes budgeting, which is a planning activity, and the same is true of his operational control. While agreeing that planning and control may not be separable activities in practice, we do not agree with Anthony that this is as it should be. As already stated in Chapter 4 ("Should planning budgets and control budgets be formally distinct?"), we believe with Steiner that planning and control must be distinguished, both conceptually and operationally. Granted Anthony's claim (in the passage quoted) that they have certain things in common, we would argue that those things should occur at different times, that they have an entirely different nature, and may or may not be undertaken by different people.

Ther main criticism of the Anthony framework, however, is simply that it has been overtaken by subsequent events, notably by the considerable development in systems theory and systems thinking. Anthony refers to systems (p. 4), but gives a dictionary definition that misses the essential features. Likewise he mentions cybernetics (p. 8) and quotes J.D. Thompson et al. (1959) who refer to an organization's "system properties"; but the ideas are not developed. Organizational structure is treated as a given, not as an important variable to be manipulated. With the trend toward increasing specialization of knowledge and the explosion of publications, it is not surprising that important new ideas developed in disciplines remote from accounting or business administration tend to gain widespread attention only after a considerable lag.

With the recognition that firms are open systems, the role of planning is, as we have seen, greatly enhanced. Its task is to bear the brunt of adapting the firm to its environment, and this needs to be done on an ongoing basis. We then have two ongoing processes, planning and control, the first concerned with deciding what should be done now to make desired ends happen in an uncertain future (Steiner 1969: 18), the second with seeing that they are implemented as intended by the continually adapted plans. It would be pointless to suppose that these two processes could be conceptually and operationally rolled into one. The systems approach also forces to the forefront of our attention the importance of the interdependencies within the firm and the dangers in ignoring them, and that the overriding objective of the firm must be to adapt, an imperative of which Anthony (1965: 29) was clearly aware.

Other Global Planning Models

Steiner's conceptual model (1969: chapter 2) has been alluded to already, primarily in Chapters 3 and 4. The diagram with which he illustrates it is reproduced as Figure 5.4, and needs no explanation.

Other global planning models will be referred to only briefly. Gilmore and Brandenberg (1962) are believed to have made the first comprehensive conceptualization of corporate planning. Their model, which is extremely detailed, distinguishes four major phases of planning: formulating the economic mission and performance objectives; determining competitive strategy and deriving associated goals for the various functional areas; specification of a program of action (a search for efficient means of implementing the competitive strategy); and reappraisal (determining when and to what extent the plan should be modified). The model also requires specification of synergy points, namely points where performance of several programs is likely to exceed the sum of individual performances.

The Stanford Research Institute model (Stewart 1963) covers strategic, corporate development, and operational planning, but includes in strategic planning some of the elements of normative planning (notably determination of basic company purpose). The corporate development plan includes some, but not all of the elements normally included in strategic planning (e.g., diversification, divestment, and R & D).

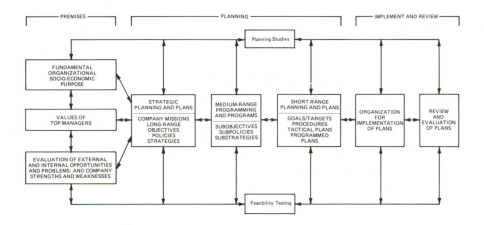

Fig. 5.4. Steiner's conceptual model for business planning.

Ozbekhan's attempt to construct a general theory of planning has already been described in Chapter 3 ("The Network of Aims: Selected Views") (Ozbekhan 1969). He is one of two writers who recognize a normative level of planning as well as strategic and tactical. His model differs from the descriptions we have presented of this three-level planning hierarchy chiefly in that to him the system under study and the environment are parts of a total system, which he calls the ecosystem. Ozbekhan believes that since normative planning can bring the system and its environment into harmony (make them more compatible), it should play an evolutionary role. In anticipating and preparing to meet future opportunities and threats the system must not restrict itself to economic and technological considerations but must be prepared to change its *value system* whenever its traditional values give indication of becoming irrelevant or of lagging behind emergent new norms in society.

Branch (1962, 1966, 1969) has written extensively on planning from a systems point of view. A weakness in his approach, as in Beer's, is that he treats an organization as a type of organism. As we show in the Appendix ("Degree of Complexity"), an organization is of greater complexity for, unlike an organism, its parts are also purposeful. If we followed the Beer and Branch approach we would be ignoring one of the most perplexing

problems presented by organizational planning, that a plan cannot be successfully implemented unless the parts of the organization are motivated,
that is unless the plan has their support and cooperation. Support and cooperation cannot, in our kind of society, be taken for granted; they must be induced by building motivation into the system somewhere, and providing
incentives to influence the behavior of managers and operatives in the desired way.

PARTIAL, OR SINGLE-LEVEL, PLANNING MODELS

The remaining group of models relates to only one level in the planning hierarchy, the lowest level, which we have called tactical planning.
Most of these models can be called budget models, for they have approximately the same coverage as the annual accounting budgets, and are constrained by the firm's strategic and normative plans.

Break-Even and the More General Goal Programming
Models: The First Kind of Linear Model

Most readers will be familiar with the basic break-even planning
model. This model, it will be recalled, assumes that cost and revenue functions are linear over some relevant range of activity, measured by sales, and
that all costs can ultimately be classified as either strictly fixed or strictly
variable. In the basic model it is possible to have semi-fixed (or step) costs,
but not semi-variable costs (represented by line segments of different
slopes). The analysis does not allow for the holding of inventories, or more
strictly for inventory change over the planning period, nor for the existence
of any constraints. But the analysis is very short-run, that is, valid only so
long as input and product prices and certain other things (e.g., productiv-
ity) remain constant. Thus the lack of constraints is a serious omission. The
model centers around the idea of the break-even (or zero profit) point, and
offers a "satisficing" solution to the firm's planning problem: Any solution
to the right of the break-even point is, in effect, good enough.

The analysis works best for a firm producing a single product. In the
case of a typical multiproduct firm, unless the contribution margin ratios
([price - unit variable cost]/price) are equal for all products, a new variable,
sales mix, must be introduced. The sales mix proportions are then used as
weights in calculating the weighted average contribution margin ratio over

all products. Use of any average, of course, results in some loss of information. A constant sales mix is assumed at all levels of operation. Formulas for the calculation of break-even sales for single- and multiproduct firms under certainty are presented in the appendix to this chapter.

Several extensions of the basic model may be mentioned. First, if the cost and/or revenue functions are not even approximately linear over the relevant range of sales, the curves may be linearized by converting them into a series of piecewise line segments. This enables semivariable as well as semi-fixed costs to be accommodated. The break-even point(s) are then determined by goal programming, as shown by Ijiri (1965: 15–28).

A second extension is to introduce uncertainty into the model. However, since the basic model is naive, the utility of doing this is questionable, and there is no empirical evidence of its use. The first attempts to introduce uncertainty into the break-even model were by Bierman (1963) and Jaedicke and Robichek (1964). In the appendix to this chapter there is an explanation of Jaedicke and Robichek's results for the case where all variables in the break-even model are random variables, and specifically their expression for the variance of net income. The appendix also draws attention to a weakness in the analysis and to subsequent developments.

A target level of profit may be substituted for zero profit in the model. If a single-product firm is planning for a target profit of X dollars before tax, the basic formula becomes $Q = (F + X)/(P - V)$, where Q is the number of units sold; F is the total fixed costs; P is the price per unit; and V is the variable cost per unit, $(P - V)$ is contribution margin per unit, and has its counterpart in the multiproduct and probabilistic versions of the analysis.

Ijiri (1965) shows how the case of a firm with a single goal and multiple subgoals may be handled by using goal programming (pp. 28–37) or generalized matrix inverses (pp. 54–62). Goal programming is a type of linear programming in which the roles of structural variables and slack variables are reversed. In goal programming the slack variables, representing deviations from goals, form the objective function, and it is the slack variables that drive the ordinary (structural) variables, not the other way around. Goal programming is an improvement over break-even analysis for it allows constraints to be introduced into the problem. It contains break-even analysis as a special case, since in goal programming the goal(s) and subgoal(s) are not necessarily of a break-even nature but, as in break-even analysis, the solution is essentially a "satisficing" rather than an optimizing one. One tries to make the deviations from goal(s) as small as possible, but not necessarily zero. It is thanks to this feature that the case of a firm whose multiple objectives are incompatible can be solved, once we order and weight the goals (Ijiri 1965: 44–50).

Input-Output Models: The First Kind of Linear, Dualistic Model. Macroeconomic, Mostly Static, Models Inappropriate for Forecasting Behavior of a Single Firm

This section and the next discuss two different types of models that both exploit the duality principle of double-entry bookkeeping by means of double subscripted variables, and both assume linear relationships. The one to be considered in this section employs *matrix methods* and is called inter-industry or input-output analysis. In order to assess its relevance to *corporate* planning it is desirable to look first at its origin.

The theory of input-output analysis was developed in the early 1950s by Leontief. The analysis relies on the availability of census data on inter-industry production transactions throughout the economy. The analysis is in fact applied almost exclusively to empirical data on production: Purchases and sales of financial assets and payments other than for value received are excluded. An input-output table is a kind of double-entry record, or matrix, of all the transactions in goods and services in an economy in a given year, with the industrial sector treated in some detail.

Table 5.2 gives a breakdown of sales and costs for an economy as a whole and for the *n* industries within it for a given year. Each industry is represented by a row and a column. Looking down a column reveals the inputs to, or cost structure of, the industry, that is, how much it bought from each of the other industries, and the amounts of imported goods used, wages paid, profits earned, and so on. Looking along a row gives the sales analysis for the industry (the proportions of its output sold to other industries, to domestic consumers and to the export market). Notice that the analysis differs from national income analysis, which excludes all intermediate transactions. Input-output analysis tries to show these intermediate transactions in as much detail as possible. The main theoretical basis of input-output analysis has a singularly systems ring, in that in the last resort all economic activity is interdependent. Because the number in a particular cell is at the same time both an input and an output, the sum of the rows and the sum of the columns must balance. Also the total sales (= outputs) of industry i, ($i = 1, 2, \ldots, n$) to all other industries and to final consumers must equal the total purchases (inputs) of industry i from all other industries and from outside the industrial sector (the latter category includes labor, in-

Table 5.2. Inter-industry relations of country Z in 198X, $ mill.

Purchases by (inputs) / Sales by (outputs)	Industries (intermediate buyers) 1 2 3 ... j ... n	Private consump-tion	Govt. consump-tion	Gross invest-ment	Exports	Total output
Industries			Final Demand			
1	0			b_1		x_1
2	0			b_2		x_2
3	0			b_3		x_3
.				.		.
.	y_{ij}			.		.
.				.		.
n	0			b_n		x_n
Imports, wages, salaries / Profits, rents / Indirect taxes less subsidies				0		b
Total input	x_1 x_2 x_3 ... . x_n			b		$\Sigma x + b$

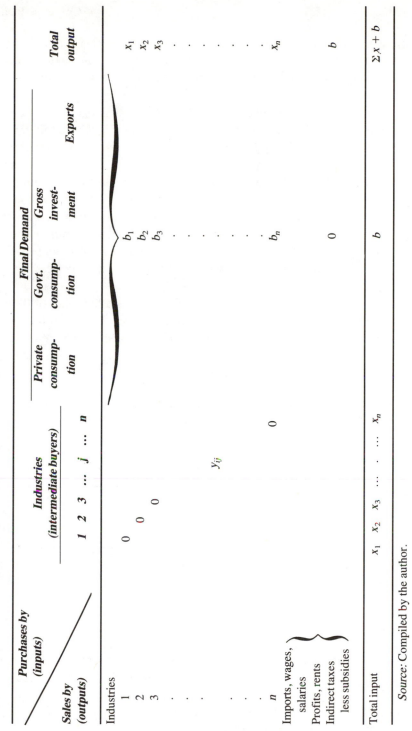

Source: Compiled by the author.

direct taxes, imported goods, and profits). Hence the totals of both row and column i are x_i, and the row and column totals for the nonindustrial sector are b. Transactions within an industry are excluded, hence the diagonal row of zeros.

Once the input-output table is constructed it is used in government economic planning. Input-output was first used in the United States to determine the effects throughout the economy of expanded rearmament, the extent to which other production would have to contract, and the bottlenecks that might arise. It also enabled governments committed to maintaining full employment to determine the detailed consequences throughout the economy of given changes in effective demand, and offered governments the prospect of controlling scarce materials more effectively in wartime. In short, input-output analysis enabled governments to define the technological constraints within which economic policies may be formed.

The input-output table presented above is a static model of the economy. It can be made dynamic by including inventories of capital goods.[3]

So much for the origins and general description of the model. To see how this model can be used for forecasting, consider a portion of an input-output table for a simple three-industry economy:

Sold by \ Purchased by	Industry			Final demand	Total output
	1	2	3		
Industry					
1	y_{11}	y_{12}	y_{13}	b_1	x_1
2	y_{21}	y_{22}	y_{23}	b_2	x_2
3	y_{31}	y_{32}	y_{33}	b_3	x_3

y_{ij} denotes the output of industry i purchased by industry j, and b_i denotes the external (exogenous) demand for the output of industry i. (As already stated, $y_{11} = y_{22} = y_{33} = 0$. If the y's stood for outputs of information rather than of goods and services, we would say this was a system without feedback.) Looking along row i we have the relation

$$x_i = \sum_j y_{ij} + b_i, \qquad i = 1, 2, 3; \qquad\qquad 5.1$$

which says that the total amount, x_i, which industry i must produce to meet final demand exactly is the sum of its sales to all other industries $\sum_j y_{ij}$, and to consumers at home and abroad, b_i.

The next step is to express each industry's inputs ($y_{ij}, i = 1, \ldots, n$) as a ratio of its output (x_j). Thus for industry 2 the ratios will be $y_{12}/x_2 = a_{12}$; $y_{22}/x_2 = a_{22} = 0$; and $y_{32}/x_2 = a_{32}$. Clearly $a_{12} + a_{22} + a_{32}$ must equal one. This gives us the relation

$$y_{ij} = a_{ij}x_j, \qquad \text{all } i \text{ and } j, \qquad\qquad 5.2$$

which says that the input from industry i to industry j is a constant fraction, a_{ij}, of industry j's output. That is, the type of production function used in input-output analysis assumes that all inputs are used in fixed proportions.[4] We will return to these a_{ij} technological coefficients later; they play a crucial role in the analysis.

Substituting Equation 5.2 into Equation 5.1 gives

$$x_i = \sum_j a_{ij}x_j + b_i, \qquad i = 1, 2, 3$$

or in matrix notation,

$$(I - A) x = b, \qquad\qquad 5.3$$

where A is the submatrix of technological coefficients:

$$A = \begin{bmatrix} a_{11} & a_{12} & a_{13} \\ a_{21} & a_{22} & a_{23} \\ a_{31} & a_{32} & a_{33} \end{bmatrix} = \begin{bmatrix} 0 & a_{12} & a_{13} \\ a_{21} & 0 & a_{23} \\ a_{31} & a_{32} & 0 \end{bmatrix},$$

x is the vector $[x_1, x_2, x_3]$, b the vector $[b_1, b_2, b_3]$, and I is the identity matrix.

The final step is to put numerical values on the final demands, b. Then, provided the inverse of $(I - A)$ exists, we may solve Equation 5.3 for x, the outputs of each industry required to meet these final demands. The solution is

$$x = (I - A)^{-1}b \qquad\qquad\qquad 5.4$$

where the superscript -1 denotes the matrix inverse. In ordinary notation Equation 5.4 can be written

$$x_i = \sum_j a_{ij}b_j \qquad i = 1, 2, 3 \qquad\qquad 5.5$$

where a_{ij} denotes the elements of $(I - A)^{-1}$. Equation 5.5 says that the gross output of industry i needed to meet final (or exogenous) demands depends linearly on these final demands. The coefficients a_{ij} are based on the input ratios, a_{ij}, of all industries.

Forecasting based on the input-output table rests on the fundamental assumption that the input ratios, a_{ij}, are technologically fixed, that is, that a given change in output of any one industry will call for proportionate changes in the input from each of the other industries, and that technological conditions will remain unchanged for the period of the forecast. The whole analysis depends on this assumption; without it the system is indeterminate. The input ratios are assumed to remain constant irrespective of changes in relative prices of inputs. More generally, changes in input prices or in the scale or composition of production will not lead to substitution of inputs within industries. Prices are regarded as neutral.

Input-output forecasting may take various forms: in terms of Table 5.2, forecasting the pattern of final demand given the outputs of all industries, or forecasting what the individual inputs/outputs (y_{ij}) will be for given levels of final demand;[5] showing what will be the effect on the total output of any industry of a change in the final demand for the output of one or more other industries; or, instead of treating prices as neutral, regarding quantities as neutral and studying the effects on prices of changes in costs.

Planning for the economy or for particular industries hinges on the assumption that the a_{ij}'s will remain constant over the forecasting period. Early input-output forecasting experience suggested that in most circumstances it is possible to assume the a_{ij}'s to be constant for three to five years. The reason is that, over the field of industry as a whole and for broad industry groups, technological change is usually slower than is commonly supposed. If anything does happen to change the input-output ratios significantly during the period of a forecast, the forecast's accuracy will diminish accordingly. Such a change raises a practical dilemma, namely that the input-output table for an economy is likely to be sufficiently detailed but quickly out of date, or up to date but insufficiently detailed to be of practical value.

A number of writers have suggested using the input-output model described above to draw up plans for a single firm (Shank 1972: chapter 5; Livingstone 1969; Farag 1968; Feltham 1970; Butterworth and Sigloch 1971). As the first of them notes (p. 96), "there is still much controversy as to whether the ideas [of input-output analysis] can really be transferred out of a macro context." Our own feeling is that it is very doubtful. The case for input-output analysis is generally put exclusively on its merits as a general equilibrium model describing interdependence *throughout the economy*. When we come down to the level of a single industry, the usefulness of this analysis is less apparent. The useful life of a specific model is short, with forecasting on the basis of relative constancy of the input ratios over a period of three to five years, avoiding serious error only for the least interdependent industries.

Finally, there is a systems rationale for rejecting uncritical use of the input-output model. By coming down to the level of a single firm, we would be ignoring not only interdependencies between the "industry" and other industries, but also between firms in the same industry. This is a serious drawback because constancies that *may* hold over large systems of interdependent parts are extremely unlikely to do so over a single part. Nevertheless projections of the behavior of the single part made just one year ahead, as in annual budgeting where they are based on fixed input ratios, may not go seriously astray. But bear in mind the external interdependencies overlooked even at the level of a single industry, for a fairly fine industry classification will still lump together a number of very dissimilar firms, as most firms operate in several industries. Our conclusion therefore is that while input-output analysis (or what boils down to just matrix methods) may have uses in the firm (e.g., in cost allocation between interacting departments, see Livingstone 1969), planning should not be one of them. It is also likely to be a poor vehicle for planning in the firm in light of our earlier remarks (Chapter 2) that planning is more than prediction. Indeed, for an adaptive, open, purposeful system planning should involve having a hand in designing the future, not regarding the environment as essentially uncontrollable.

Linear Programming Budget Models: The Second Type of Linear, Dualistic Model

Linear programming (LP) models are the second type of linear model that incorporate the duality principle of double-entry bookkeeping. They have been proposed by a number of writers in the accounting and management science literature, the earliest of whom appears to have been Stedry

(1960: chapter 5). Other models were developed by Charnes et al. (1963); Ijiri et al. (1963); Ijiri (1965); Amey (1969); and Colantoni et al. (1969). Two other LP models, those of Demski (1967) and Itami (1977), are presented in the context of performance evaluation and control. The appeal of the LP model form derives from the fact that it has a very efficient solution method.

Our intention here is not to comment on these models individually. Readers who wish to gain a reasonably complete view of the form these models may take are referred to Amey (1969), where LP models are presented for (1) a unitary firm and (2) a divisionalized firm and, in each case, in the form of (3) a single-period model and (4) a multiperiod model.

It seems more appropriate here to comment on some of the distinguishing features of LP planning models as applied to accounting systems. In the general form of the LP problem a firm is represented as engaged in a number of "activities" or "processes," an "activity" being a given method of production or the production of a given product. In the accounting-based models, by contrast, the firm is decomposed into sets of aggregated transactions (e.g., total sales of product A, total purchases of material B). The variables of the problem thus become transactions instead of activities. The entire transactions of the firm are represented by a set of transaction variables, x_{ij}, where the subscripts denote the accounts to be debited and credited. Different conventions are used as to which subscript denotes which side of the transaction. It would be consistent with the usage for input-output analysis presented earlier for the first subscript to represent the account to be credited. However, the order of subscripts does not matter as long as it is followed consistently.

When using an LP formulation of an accounting problem it is necessary to eliminate all transactions consisting of a debit and credit to the same account (contra entries), so that $x_{ii} = 0$, for all i. It is also necessary to represent all compound transactions, those consisting of m debits and n credits, where $m \neq n$, into simple entries involving a single debit and credit. Ijiri (1965: 84) has shown how this may be done. One further adjustment may be needed to deal with unrestricted variables. Recall that in LP all variables are constrained to be nonnegative. However, in the planning problem for a firm with a large number of transaction variables and constraints we may not know before solving the problem whether a particular transaction variable will be a debit or a credit in the solution. For example, since a bank balance may end up as a debit or credit, the transaction variable "bank interest" may also be a debit (interest paid) or credit (interest received). Therefore if we represented bank interest by a single variable we might violate the nonnegativity constraint. To overcome this difficulty we replace the variable for bank interest by two variables of opposite sign, each of which is required to be nonnegative. Thus if the firm's bank interest account is denoted by the subscript i and bank account by j, we replace the single variable for bank interest by $x_{ij} - x_{ji}$. Since by definition these variables are mutually exclusive, bank interest is thereby permitted to have any sign.

To complete the notational modifications we need only introduce a symbol for beginning account balances; these could be represented by B_s for account s.

In the LP formulation of the budget problem the constraints will include the usual resource, institutional, and market demand constraints and various accounting relationships and balance requirements (e.g., that sales cannot exceed beginning inventory plus production minus required ending inventory).

A final note of caution is in order. The LP formulation should not be used unless the linearity assumptions are met, at least approximately. This requirement is not as restrictive as it sounds, however, because substantial nonlinearities can be linearized, in the way stated in this chapter (Break-even and the More General Goal Programming Models: the First Kind of Linear Model"), although this complicates the problem. Linearity requires that (1) the objective function must be linear, which implies that the prices of inputs and outputs are constant over the range of operation and time period considered; (2) that all constraints are linear, implying that there are constant returns to scale in each transaction variable; and (3) the transactions are independent, meaning that the total resources used in the joint performance of several transactions equal the resources used when each transaction is undertaken separately.

Simulation Models for Complex Planning Problems

In the first section of this chapter we referred to Ackoff's description of simulation as experiments conducted on a model of a system. Such experiments are feasible when the firm's planning problem is so complex that it cannot be solved mathematically. The model on which the experiments are performed, the simulation model, is a representation of the structure, including the interrelationships between components, of the system. Alternative plans are tested by giving the model a series of dry runs on a computer. The simulation method thus has great versatility. But, needless to say, everything depends on whether the representation captures the essential features of the system's behavior.

The earliest budget simulation models were developed by Mattessich (1961, 1964). Further discussion or examples of the use of simulation models for corporate planning will be found in the work of Forrester (1961, 1969), Cyert and March (1963: 128–236), and J.C. Emery (1969: 145–57). More recent work includes Naylor (1976a, 1976b, 1976c), Naylor and Mansfield (1976), Naylor and Schauland (1976a, 1976b), and Naylor and Seaks (1979).

Microeconomic Models: Contrasted Among Themselves and With Accounting Models

We now turn to economic planning models, where we need to be aware of the different uses economists make of the term *plan*. Some economists (e.g., Schneider 1966: 123–24, 193) talk about the firm's short-run and long-run *production plans* that result from short-run and long-run equilibrium analysis of the (profit-maximizing) firm. The single-period LP models presented in Amey (1969: 160–73) yield such plans. Other economists (e.g., Modigliani and Cohen 1961; Cohen and Cyert 1965) understand "plans" to denote *decisions that are subject to revision*. This is a dynamic view of planning. Such planning is conducted periodically and consists in solving a multiperiod dynamic optimization problem. The solutions for the first period provide a set of decisions for the current period; those for periods 2 through the horizon period T constitute the firm's future plans. Data on periods 2 to T are included in formulating the planning problem at time $t = 0$ only in order to select the set of period 1 decisions that will be optimal over the horizon of T periods. But not all authors agree on which aspects of the future (beyond the end of the first period) should be included in formulating the problem at $t = 0$. Hicks (1946) includes all aspects, Modigliani and Cohen (1961) only "relevant" aspects (those that will affect the optimality over the horizon of period 1 decisions). Further discussion of these two alternatives is provided in Amey (1979: chapter 2).

Beyond this diversity in the meaning of *planning* as understood by economists we find a number of differences in approaches to planning as presupposed by the economic theories of the firm, on one hand, and by annual accounting budgets, on the other. Some of these differences are set out in Table 5.3. A fuller discussion appears in Amey and Egginton (1973: chapter 5).

Production Scheduling Models:
Planning the Plan's Implementation

It should be borne in mind that part of planning is the determination of a timetable or schedule as to when the different parts of the plan are to be carried out. In the case of production, this means determining not only the rate of production for the year, but how this total is to be allocated throughout the year. The latter is what is considered in the production scheduling (or production smoothing) problem. The problem is to determine how, when future sales orders are expected not to occur at a steady rate throughout the planning period, the firm should optimally absorb these fluctuations. (In the absence of such action, production rates would be subject to the full force of sales fluctuations, with adverse effects on unit costs.) If cost functions are approximately linear, this problem may be formulated as a transportation-type LP problem, where the object is to determine the production schedule that satisfies the technological constraints, meets the demand requirements, and minimizes the sum of production and storage costs (see, for example, Magee and Boodman 1967: Appendix C). Another well-known model, that of Holt et al. (1960), allows the various costs relevant to the problem to be either linear or quadratic and introduces uncertainty explicitly. This is a dynamic model.

Project Planning Models: Planning a Specific Part
of Production or the Production of a Specific Thing

At an even more micro level than the annual tactical plans for a business are plans for individual projects. These constitute project planning, which may be for parts of production, R & D, capital projects, and so on. The most interesting types of project planning model are those that take the form of networks. Charnes and Cooper (1967: 24–52) have applied such a model to an accounting system by showing how the latter can be fitted to a network. Moreover, they show how the problem of finding the critical path through a network may be formulated as an LP problem (see also Ijiri 1965: 92–94; Hadley 1962: chapter 10).

Network planning models are of particular interest because of the importance of controlling time at the planning and scheduling stages. A number of examples of this come to mind. In a very large and complex manufacturing operation such as building a supersonic aircraft, where there

Table 5.3. Economic and accounting approaches to planning: differences and similarities

Aspect of planning ＼ Approach to planning	Economics	Accounting
Planning objective	Explicit, usually optimizing	Implicit, "satisficing"
Type of model used	Normative (i.e., suggestive)	Descriptive (i.e., factual)
Coverage of model	Only flow (income statement) variables in static model; both stock (balance sheet) and flow variables in dynamic model; flow variables denote only goods flows	Stock and flow variables; flow variables denote cash flows as well as goods flows
Degree of aggregation	Plans not disaggregated for different parts of the firm or for different segments of the planning period	Both types of plans are disaggregated
Interdependencies between different activities	Always taken into account	Only sometimes taken into account
Set of alternatives considered	Complete	Incomplete
The role of prices	Prices represented as variables (except if the firm is a "price-taker")	Prices represented as constants
State of information (randomness of variables)	Models are for the most part deterministic	Models are crudely and and unsystematically stochastic

Table 5.3. (Cont.)

Aspect of planning / Approach to planning	Economics	Accounting
Type of data gathered	The two models may have different rules specifying the type of data (e.g., "cost" in economic plans may not be the same as "expense" in accounting budgets). Thus they may describe the same future events differently.	
Information-gathering and computation costs	Usually ignored	
Organizational structure	Not a variable	

Source: Compiled by the author.

might be a large number of subcontractors, close control of time is necessary to prevent the occurrence of bottlenecks and delays which would have a "snowball" effect. Another example would be construction work to fulfill a contract on which there is a fixed completion date and penalties for overrunning it. Research and development work is a further case where control of time is very important, for there is a tendency for delays to occur at the transition stages between R & D, and between development and commercial exploitation. Network planning need not, however, be confined to time (scheduling), but may cover additional dimensions, such as dollars and physical units.

Planning Models in Practice: Conventional Budgets' Lack of a Systems View

Having reviewed a number of conceptual planning models it is now appropriate to examine planning models in practice. These are restricted largely to budget models, for few models are found at the normative and strategic levels of planning, which are less susceptible to modeling because the problems faced there are less well structured. The budget models consist largely of the conventional annual accounting budgets of firms. Our objective in examining these (partial) planning models is to uncover the explicit or implicit systems logic underlying them.

We begin with the general observation that, to the extent that there is no *explicit* recognition in the budget model that in seeking to serve its own ends the firm should at least minimally serve the ends of its environment and of its parts, the model does not really represent the essential characteristics of a system at all. The whole–larger whole and part–whole relationships are not at all well articulated. Contrast typical accounting budgets, regarded as plans, with the minimal model of a system described in the first section of the Appendix at the end of the book ($\sigma = \langle C, E, S \rangle$), and ask how well the elements on the right are represented. It is at once evident that E, and the part of S consisting of the outer couplings, are very poorly represented.

But suppose, for a moment, that we could regard the budget model as a representation, albeit a poor one, of a system. What kind of system would it be? First of all it would be relatively closed, since few and infrequent exchanges with the environment are represented by the model (the environment is not richly represented, as we may recall from the reference to Hedberg and Jönsson in Chapter 2, "Information System").

Second, traditional budgets do not regard the firm as an adaptive system. Failure to so regard the firm results in the normative and, to a lesser extent, strategic levels of planning not being well developed in practice. It also results in tactical budgets themselves not being systematically adapted and often being mere extrapolations, in numerous standard rules being employed in implementing them, and in organizational structure not being regarded as a variable in planning. All this leads to inflexibility, the opposite of what is required for effective adaptation.

Third, we note that the conventional accounting budget model largely agrees with what we would expect as far as inner couplings are concerned. That is, the individual budgets, with the exception of the cash budget, are somewhat loosely coupled, affecting one another only weakly in most cases, while within any given budget the components are tightly coupled (see the discussion in section "Type of Behavior" in the Appendix at the end of the book). This is all to the good, as the time it takes the firm to adapt is thereby decreased.

Finally, it would appear that conventional budget models only *formally* treat the parts of the system (as well as the system as a whole) as purposeful, without articulating how goal-directed behavior is to be brought about, and by assuming a consistency between subobjectives (e.g., of divisions) and the overall system objective, which is more apparent than real.

The performance measures typically selected for evaluation of the subsystems are often dysfunctional, encouraging the latter to act in ways inconsistent with the achievement of organizational objectives.

In sum, conventional accounting budgets are generally weak in terms of systems logic, the weakness being all the more evident in light of the "new planning." Although the evidence is skimpy, one gains the impression that they are probably not drawn up within constraints imposed by well-conceived strategic and normative plans. It is these stages, rather than tactical budgeting, that, in the total planning process, most contribute to effective adaptation of the firm.

SUMMARY

In this chapter we have surveyed a number of models that can be used by firms for planning. They have, with the exception of the last, all been conceptual models, each suggesting a different way of planning. Our emphasis on conceptual matters seems justified since the whole conception of planning is undergoing an important change. Business enterprises are now recognized as systems of organized complexity, of which a number of models are required. By modeling the planning process of such systems we abstract from reality, and such abstraction is seen to be necessary in order to gain greater insights into the nature of the reality. Such insights are needed, of course, only to the extent that the plan yielded by a model translates into behavior of the kind desired in the real world.

Almost all planning models have a common element: costs. However, models will vary in what they show as costs, and a clear understanding is needed of what these costs are in order to properly interpret the models. As we have shown, what a planning model includes in costs will depend on whether or not the model is a decision model; if so, whether it lists all the planning alternatives or concentrates on one; and whether or not the model allows for risk preference explicitly. The options are conveniently summarized in Tables 5.4 and 5.5.

Our classification of planning models has been based on the hierarchical nature of planning (normative-strategic-tactical). We have classified models as "global" if they span all three levels of planning or at least the lower two, and partial if they relate only to tactical planning.

The more or less global planning models chosen for comment were those of Beer, Ackoff, Ruefli, Anthony, Steiner, Gilmore and Brandenberg, the Stanford Research Institute (see Stewart 1963), Ozbekhan, and Branch. Beer's otherwise interesting cybernetic model suffers from regard-

ing the firm as an organism. This analogy is faulty for, as we have seen
from the Appendix on systems, organizations differ from organisms in that
their parts are also purposeful. Thus Beer cannot address the important
problem of how to implement plans effectively which, in an organization,
involves questions of motivation and incentives. Branch's models are similarly flawed.

**Table 5.4. Type of cost included in different types of
planning models**

Type of planning model	Objective costs only	Objective costs plus implicit opportunity costs
(i) Decision model		
(a) Listing all alternatives	X	
(b) Focusing on single alternative		X
(ii) Nondecision model (e.g., a predictive planning model such as a conventional accounting budget)	X	

Source: Compiled by the author.

**Table 5.5. Role of constant costs (and revenues) in different
types of planning models**

Type of planning model	Need not be included	Should be included
(i) Deterministic model	X	
(ii) Stochastic model		X

Entry (ii) is an approximation, subject to the qualification in note 1.
Source: Compiled by the author.

Ruefli's model of a program planning and budgeting system (PPBS) is of interest because it focuses on the fundamental incompatibility, noted in formulating our systems model in the next chapter, between the structure of an output-, objective-, or decision-oriented information system and an existing organizational structure built along administrative, bureaucratic lines. The goal decomposition model provides a bridge between the two, a means of translating information from the program or "decision" structure to traditional budget categories that match organization structure.

Anthony's 1965 model is based on his observation that planning and control are often inseparable activities in practice but he does not challenge this state of affairs. Hence this model is limited to the strategic and tactical levels of the "old planning," and is passed over by the new systems insights. Under the systems view, as we have seen, planning comes into its own as a major function. Planning thus only *implies* control, which means that the two are related but not inseparable.

A number of partial, or single-level planning models were examined that suggest different approaches to tactical planning. Some (the linear programming models and the dynamic microeconomic models) have an optimizing objective, while others (the break-even, and the more general goal programming) have a "satisficing" objective. All but a few (e.g., the dynamic economic models) are similar, however, in that the planning horizon is typically one year or less, and thus shorter than in the case of normative and most strategic planning.

The goal programming model was shown to be more general than break-even analysis, for in it the goals are not necessarily of a break-even nature. This model is versatile, and can be used to represent a firm with a single goal and multiple subgoals, or a firm with a number of incompatible goals. (In the latter case the planning problem can be formulated so that the firm comes as close as possible to achieving all of its goals in some prescribed order). Goal programming is one kind of linear programming, and a reminder was given that, just as in LP, the linearity assumptions must be met at least approximately, or any nonlinearities must be linearizable.

The LP form, for its part, lends itself readily to the representation of accounting systems thanks to the device of substituting transactions for "activities." The model can be made multiperiod if desired and has a very efficient solution method. It is therefore frequently found in the literature and in practice.

Use of the input-output model generally rests exclusively on its merits as a general equilibrium model of the whole economy for purposes of economic forecasting. The model's appropriateness for corporate planning is doubtful, among other reasons because it overlooks interdependency with the environment, which is great in the case of the single firm. In addition, the "new planning" that we have been espousing asserts that planning should be more than prediction.

The other partial models surveyed included simulation models, microeconomic, mostly dynamic, models and, at an even more micro level, network planning models for projects. Production scheduling models were also briefly referred to, because planning includes deciding not only what shall be done but also when it shall be done.

After surveying all the *conceptual* or normative models, we slightly redressed the balance toward the practical, or descriptive, side by examining conventional accounting budget models and the implicit or explicit systems logic underlying them. It was concluded that, if they included planning at all, such planning was appropriate for a relatively closed, nonadaptive, loosely coupled system in which the purposefulness of the parts is more apparent than real. Conventional budget models were pronounced weak in terms of their systems logic, especially in light of the "new planning," where the future is partly made and not just reacted to.

APPENDIX: GOAL DECOMPOSITION MODEL; BREAK-EVEN MODELS

Goal Decomposition Model of a Planning Programming and Budgeting System (Ruefli)

The vector-matrix model comprises the submodels of equations 5.6, 5.7, and 5.8 below. There is one central unit and m management units, each responsible for n operating units (or projects). Thus management unit k has responsibility for n_k projects, each of which is measured on m_k attribute dimensions (Fig. 5.5).

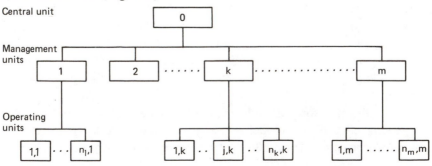

Fig. 5.5. The vector-matrix model.

Management unit k (k = 1, . . ., m)

$$\min w_k^+ y_k^+ + w_k^- y_k^-$$

subject to

$$\sum_{j=1}^{n_k} a_{jk} x_{jk} - I y_k^+ + I y_k^- = g_k$$

$$(k = 1, . . ., m) \qquad\qquad\qquad 5.6$$

$$0 \leq x_{jk} \leq 1, \qquad \text{for all } j \text{ and } k$$

$$y_k^+, y_k^- \geq 0$$

where y_k^+, y_k^- are (m_k x 1) vectors representing, respectively, positive and negative deviations by the kth management unit from its centrally determined goals; w_k^+, w_k^- are (1 x m_k) vectors representing weights assigned to the positive and negative deviations of the kth management unit from its goals; a_{jk} is an (m_k x 1) vector of the attribute levels (unit cost or contribution) of the jth project undertaken by the kth management unit; x_{jk} is the level at which project j is operated, expressed as a proportion of the maximal level; g_k is an (m_k x 1) vector of goal levels for the kth management unit; and I is the identity matrix. Solution of this goal programming problem at stage t yields an (m_k x 1) vector of shadow prices, $\pi_k^{(t)}$, associated with the first constraint.

Operating Unit j, k, (the unit responsible for carrying out the jth project of the kth management unit)

$$min \ \pi_k^{(t)} a_{jk}$$

subject to

$$D_{jk} a_{jk} \geq f_{jk}$$

$$\qquad\qquad\qquad 5.7$$

$$a_{jk} \geq 0$$

where D_{jk} is an (m_{jk} x m_k matrix of technological coefficients; f_{jk} is an (m_{jk} x 1) vector of restrictions; and $\pi_k^{(t)}$ is an (m_k x 1) vector of shadow prices yielded by Equation 5.6 at any stage t.

Central Unit

$$\max \sum_{k=1}^{m} \pi \, {}_{k}^{(t)} g_{k}$$

subject to

$$\sum_{k} P_{k} \, g_{k} \leq g_{0} \hspace{5cm} 5.8$$

$$g_{k} \geq 0, \qquad k = 1, \ldots, m$$

where P_{k} are (m_{0} x m_{k}) matrices of coefficients relating the goal levels of the management units to each other and to the corporate goals; g_{0} is an (m_{0} x 1) vector of corporate goals; and $\pi \, {}_{k}^{(t)}$ are the shadow prices derived from Equation 5.6 at stage t. That is, the central unit has to find the goal levels, $g_{k}, k = 1, \ldots, m$ of the management units such that, when each is given its proper weight (the P_{k}'s are transformation rates or weights), they will sum to the corporate goal.

In other words, coordination of activities is sought by goal setting on the part of the central unit and price setting on the part of the management units. Essentially what PPBS says is that an organization whose missions require the participation of multiple organization units needs some mechanism for achieving coordination. Such a mechanism is provided in the above model, although there are other ways of achieving coordination, and the above is not necessarily the best way.

Formulas for Break-Even Sales Under Certainty

Q is the number of units sold; P is the price per unit; V is the variable cost per unit; F is the total fixed costs; $P - V$ is the contribution margin per unit; and $(P - V)/P$ is the contribution margin ratio (CMR).

Break-Even Sales for a Single-Product Firm
Under Uncertainty

Q, P, V and F are now all random variables. If we write C for $P - V$, then net income $Z = QC - F$, and Z is also a random variable. There are two cases to consider:

(i) If Q and C are statistically independent,

$$E(Z) = E(Q) E(C) - E(F) \qquad 5.9$$

that is, if Q and C do not covary, the expected value of their product equals the product of their expectations. The variance of Z in this case (Q and C uncorrelated) is

$$\text{var}(Z) = \text{var}(Q)\text{var}(C) + E(Q)^2 \text{var}(C) + E(C)^2\text{var}(Q) \qquad 5.10$$

(ii) If Q and C are correlated,

$$E(Z) = E(Q) E(C) + \text{cov}(Q,C) - E(F) \qquad 5.11$$

where $\text{cov}(Q,C) = E(QC) - E(Q) E(C)$. Since the expression for var(Z) is much more complicated than in Equation 5.10 we do not show it.

We will henceforth concentrate on case (i) and explain how Equation 5.10 is obtained. The result is based on some fundamental theorems on random variables:

(a)   The variance of a random variable can be written as the square of the expected value of the variable minus the square of the expectation.
(b)   If two random variables are statistically independent the expected value of their product is equal to the product of their expectations.
(c)   The variance of the sum or difference of two random variables is equal to the sum of their variances.

From (a),

$$\begin{aligned} \text{var}(Z) &= E[(Z - E(Z))^2] \\ &= E(Z)^2 - [E(Z)]^2 \end{aligned} \qquad 5.12$$

If $Z = QC$ (ignoring for the moment the fixed costs F), var(Z) = $E(Q^2C^2 - E(QC)^2$. Now making use of result (b), if Q and C are statistically independent,

$$\text{var}(Z) = E(Q)^2E(C)^2 - [E(Q)]^2 [E(C)]^2. \qquad 5.13$$

From Equation 5.12,

$$E(Z)^2 = \text{var}(Z) + [E(Z)]^2.$$

Using this result in Equation 5.13 we can write

$$\text{var}(Z) = \{\text{var}(Q) + [E(Q)]^2\} \cdot \{\text{var}(C) + [E(C)]^2\} - \{[E(Q)]^2 \cdot [E(C)]^2\}$$

Multiplying out,

$$\text{var}(Z) = \text{var}(Q)\,\text{var}(C) + \text{var}(C)\,[E(Q)]^2 + \text{var}(Q)\,[E(C)]^2$$
$$+ [E(Q)]^2\,[E(C)]^2 - [E(Q)]^2\,[E(C)]^2$$
$$= \text{var}(Q)\,\text{var}(C) + [E(Q)]^2\,\text{var}(C) + [E(C)]^2\text{var}(Q),$$

which, by theorem (b), is equivalent to Equation 5.10.

To obtain the expression for var(Z) given by Jaedicke and Robichek (1964), (i) add var(F) to the right-hand side of Equation 5.10; (ii) wherever var(C) occurs write var(P) + var(V), allowed by theorem (c); and (iii) wherever $E(C)$ occurs write ($E(P)$ - $E(V)$), allowed by theorem (c).

Jaedicke and Robichek assume that all the random variables in the break-even model are normally distributed. Their above results imply that the product of normally distributed random variables (Q and [P - V]) is normally distributed. This is not in general true; only the sums of normally distributed random variables are normally distributed (Ferrara et al. 1972; Kaplan 1977, 1982: chapter 6). Simulation probably offers the best means of generating the (approximate) distribution of net income, whatever the distribution forms of the random variables (Liao 1975).

Other developments have been concerned with the formal representation of uncertainty. Kottas et al. (1978) proposed using the first four moments of the distributions of random variables (rather than just the second) to model uncertainty more precisely, whatever the form of these distributions. Magee (1975) extended to break-even analysis a result from finance, specifically from the capital asset pricing model (which is based on the assumptions of both portfolio theory and the weak form of the efficient [capital] market hypothesis). This says that it is not total risk (usually represented by variance) that we should be concerned with, but systematic or market-related risk, which cannot be eliminated or reduced by combining this product with a number of others.

NOTES

1. For further discussion of this point see Dillon and Nash (1978), Vedder (1978), and Ekern and Bøhren (1979). The last-named show that the incremental and total approaches are both valid (a) under an expected monetary value criterion, if the incremental amounts are constant within states and may differ only between states, and (b) under an expected utility criterion, if the utility function is exponential and the shared (constant) and incremental amounts are statistically independent.

2. Kornbluth (1974) has pointed out two limitations of the Ruefli model, that (i) as with standard goal programming the interpretation of the dual variables (π_k) in the optimal solution is of little use, as they do not have the connotation of opportunity costs, and (ii) each division applies its own predetermined weights (w_k^+, w_k^-) to deviations from goals (g_k) set by central management, and the ultimate choice of program is very dependent on these predetermined divisional weights.

3. On this point see Leontief et al. (1953: chapter 3); Dorfman et al. (1958: chapters 11–12); and Baumol (1965: chapter 20). The theory underlying the input-output model is discussed in these references and in Hadley (1962: chapter 13); Allen (1965: chapter 11); and Mattessich (1961).

4. That this assumption is not necessarily as restrictive as it seems has been shown by Samuelson in his substitution theorem. See Koopmans 1951: chapters 7–9.

5. As it stands, if Equation 5.3 is solved for given levels of final demand, it may yield negative solutions for the outputs of some industries. A final demand b will only be economically meaningful (Hadley 1962 uses the term "producible") if there exists an $x \geq 0$ satisfying Equation 5.3. To avoid the possibility of negative outputs the input-output equations must meet the Hawkins-Simon conditions. See Hawkins and Simon 1949.

REFERENCES

Ackoff, R.L. 1969. "Institutional Functions and Societal Needs." In *Perspectives of Planning,* pp. 495–500. *See* Jantsch 1969.

_____. 1969. "Beering and Branching through Corporate Planning." In *OR 69,* proceedings of the Fifth International Conference on Operational Research, edited by J. Lawrence, pp. 21–29. London: Tavistock.

_____. 1970. *A Concept of Corporate Planning.* New York: Wiley-Interscience.

_____. 1974. *Redesigning the Future.* New York: Wiley-Interscience.

Allen, R.G.D. 1965. *Mathematical Economics,* 2d ed. London: Macmillan.

Amey, L.R. 1969. *The Efficiency of Business Enterprises,* chapter 9. London: Allen & Unwin.

_____. 1979. *Budget Planning and Control Systems,* pp. 33–36. London: Pitman.

_____. 1980. "Interest on Equity Capital as an Ex Post Cost." *Journal of Business Finance and Accounting* 7: 347–64.

Amey, L.R. and D.A. Egginton. 1973. *Management Accounting: A Conceptual Approach.* London: Longman.

Anthony, R.N. 1965. *Planning and Control Systems: A Framework for Analysis.* Boston, MA: Division of Research, Harvard Graduate School of Business Administration.

Baumol, W.J. 1965. *Economic Theory and Operations Analysis,* 2d ed. Englewood Cliffs, NJ: Prentice-Hall.

Beer, S. 1969a. "The Aborting Corporate Plan." In *Perspectives of Planning,* pp. 395–422. *See* Jantsch 1969.

_____. 1969b. "Planning as a Process of Adaptation." In *OR 69. See* Lawrence 1969.

_____. 1972. *Brain of the Firm.* London: Allen Lane (Penguin Press).

Bierman, H. Jr. 1963. *Topics in Cost Accounting and Decision,* pp. 36–46. New York: McGraw-Hill.

Branch, M.C. 1962. *The Corporate Planning Process.* New York: American Management Association.

_____. 1966. *Planning: Aspects and Applications.* New York: Wiley.

_____. 1969. "Goals and Objectives in Comprehensive Planning." In *OR 69. See* Lawrence 1969.

Butterworth, J.E. and B.S. Sigloch. 1971. "A Generalized Input-Output Model and Some Derived Equivalent Forms." *Accounting Review* 46 (October): 700–16.

Charnes, A. and W.W. Cooper. 1967. "Some Network Characterizations for Mathematical Programming and Accounting Approaches to Planning and Control." *Accounting Review* 42 (January): 24–52.

Charnes, A., W.W. Cooper, and Y. Ijiri. 1963. "Breakeven Budgeting and Programming to Goals." *Journal of Accounting Research* 1 (Spring): 16–43.

Cohen, K.J. and R.M. Cyert. 1965. *Theory of the Firm.* Englewood Cliffs, NJ: Prentice-Hall.

Colantoni, C.S., R.P. Manes, and A. Whinston. 1969. "Programming, Profit Rates and Pricing Decisions." *Accounting Review* 44 (July): 467–81.

Cyert, R.M. and J.G. March. 1963. *A Behavioral Theory of the Firm,* 2d ed., chapter 3. Englewood Cliffs, NJ: Prentice-Hall.

Dantzig, G.B. and P. Wolfe. 1960. "Decomposition Principles for Linear Programs." *Operations Research* 8 (February): 101–11.

Demski, J.S. 1967. "An Accounting System Structured on a Linear Programming Model." *Accounting Review* 42 (October): 701–12.

Dillon, R.F. and J.F. Nash. 1978. "The True Relevance of Relevant Costs." *Accounting Review* 53 (January): 11–17.

Dorfman, R., P.A. Samuelson, and R.M. Solow. 1958. *Linear Programming and Economic Analysis.* New York: McGraw-Hill.

Ekern, S. and O. Bøhren. 1979. "Consistent Rankings on Total and Differential Amounts under Uncertainty." *Decision Sciences* 10: 519–26.

Emery, J.C. 1969. *Organizational Planning and Control Systems: Theory and Technology,* chapter 5. New York: Macmillan.

Farag, S.M. 1968. "A Planning Model for the Divisionalized Enterprise." *Accounting Review* (April): 312–20.

Feltham, G.A. 1970. "Some Quantitative Approaches to Planning for Multiproduct Systems." *Accounting Review* 45 (January): 11–26.

Ferrara, W.L., J.C. Hayya, and D.A. Nachman. 1972. "Normalcy of Profit in the Jaedicke-Robichek Model." *Accounting Review* 47 (April): 299–307.

Forrester, J.W. 1961. *Industrial Dynamics.* New York: Wiley; Cambridge, MA: MIT Press.

_____. 1969. "Planning under the Dynamic Influences of Complex Social Systems. In *Perspectives of Planning. See* Jantsch 1969: 235–54.

Gilmore, F. and R.G. Brandenberg. 1962. "Anatomy of Corporate Planning." *Harvard Business Review* 40 (November–December): 61–69.

Hadley, G. 1962. *Linear Programming.* Reading, MA: Addison-Wesley.

Hawkins, D. and H.A. Simon. 1949. "Some Conditions of Macro Economic Stability." *Econometrica* 17 (July–October): 245–48.

Hedberg, B. and S. Jönsson. 1978. "Designing Semi-Confusing Information Systems for Organizations in Changing Environments." *Accounting, Organizations and Society* 3: 47–64.

Hicks, J.R. 1946. *Value and Capital,* 2d ed. London: Oxford University Press.

Hitch, C.J. and R.N. McKean. 1960. *The Economics of Defense in the Nuclear Age.* Cambridge, MA: Harvard University Press.

Holt, C.C., F. Modigliani, J.F. Muth, and H.A. Simon. 1960. *Planning Production, Inventories, and Work Force.* Englewood Cliffs, NJ: Prentice-Hall.

Ijiri, Y. 1965. *Management Goals and Accounting for Control.* Amsterdam: North-Holland.

Ijiri, Y., F.K. Levy, and R.C. Lyon. 1963. "A Linear Programming Model for Budgeting and Financial Planning." *Journal of Accounting Research* 1 (Autumn): 198–212.

Itami, H. 1977. *Adaptive Behavior: Management Control and Information Analysis.* Sarasota, FL: American Accounting Association, Studies in Accounting Research no. 15.

Jaedicke, R.K. and A.A. Robichek. 1964. "Cost-Volume-Profit Analysis under Conditions of Uncertainty." *Accounting Review* 39 (October): 917–26.

Jantsch, E. 1969. *Perspectives of Planning.* Paris: OECD.

Kaplan, R.S. 1982. *Advanced Management Accounting.* Englewood Cliffs, NJ: Prentice-Hall.

———. 1977. "Application of Quantitative Models in Managerial Accounting: A State of the Art Survey," Beyer Lecture. Pittsburgh, PA: Carnegie-Mellon University.

Kornbluth, J.S.H. 1974. "Accounting in Multiple Objective Linear Programming." *Accounting Review* 49 (April): 284–95.

Kottas, J.F., A. Lau, and H-S Lau. 1978. "A General Approach to Stochastic Management Planning Models: An Overview." *Accounting Review* 53 (April): 389–401.

Lawrence, J. ed. 1969. *OR 69.* London: Tavistock.

Leontief, W.W. et al. 1953. *Studies in the Structure of the American Economy.* New York: Oxford University Press.

Liao, M. 1975. "Model Sampling: A Stochastic CVP Analysis." *Accounting Review* 50 (October): 780–90.

Livingstone, J. Leslie. 1969. "Input-Output Analysis for Cost Accounting, Planning and Control." *Accounting Review* 44 (January): 48–64.

Magee, J.F. and D.M. Boodman. 1967. *Production Planning and Inventory Control,* 2d ed. New York: McGraw-Hill.

Magee, R.P. 1975. "Cost-Volume-Profit Analysis, Uncertainty and Capital Market Equilibrium." *Journal of Accounting Research* 13 (Autumn): 257–66.

Mattessich, R. 1961. "Budgeting Models and System Simulation." *Accounting Review* 36 (July): 384–97.

Modigliani, F. and K.J. Cohen. 1961. "The Role of Anticipations and Plans in Economic Behavior and Their Use in Economic Analysis and Forecasting." *Studies in Business Expectations and Planning,* no. 4. Bureau of Economic and Business Research, University of Illinois.

Morton, M.S.S. 1967. "Interactive Visual Display Systems and Management Problem Solving." *Industrial Management Review* 9 (Fall): 69–81.

Naylor, T.H. 1976a. "Corporate Planning Models." *California Management Review* 18 (Summer): 69–78.

_____. 1976b. "The Conceptual Framework for Corporate Modelling and the Results of a Survey of Current Practice." *Operational Research Quarterly* 27: 671–82.

_____. 1976c. "The Future of Corporate Planning Models." *Managerial Planning* 24 (March–April): 1–13.

Naylor, T.H. and M.J. Mansfield. 1976. "Corporate Planning Models: A Survey." *Planning Review* 4 (May): 8–12.

Naylor, T.H. and H. Schauland. 1976a. "A Survey of Users of Corporate Simulation Models." *Management Science* 22 (May): 927–37.

_____. 1976b. "Experience with Corporate Simulation Models: A Survey." *Long-Range Planning* (April): 94–100.

Naylor, T.H. and T.G. Seaks. 1979. *Corporate Planning Models.* Reading, MA: Addison-Wesley.

Novick, D. 1954. "Efficiency and Economy in Government through New Budgeting and Accounting Procedures." The RAND Corporation, report R-254, February.

_____. 1956. "Weapon-System Cost Methodology." The RAND Corporation, report R-287, February.

Ozbekhan, H. 1969. "Toward a General Theory of Planning." In *Perspectives of Planning,* pp. 45–155. *See* Jantsch 1969.

Ruefli, T.W. 1971. "PPBS: An Analytical Approach." In *Studies in Budgeting,* edited by R.F. Byrne, A. Charnes, W.W. Cooper, O.A. Davis, and D. Gilford. Amsterdam: North-Holland: 161–209.

Samuelson, P.A. 1951. "Abstract of a Theorem Concerning Substitutability in Open Leontief Models." In *Activity Analysis of Production and Allocation,* edited by T.C. Koopmans, chapter 7. New York: Wiley.

Schneider, E. 1966. *Pricing and Equilibrium.* English translation by E. Bennathan. London: Unwin.

Shank, J.K. 1972. *Matrix Methods in Accounting.* Reading, MA: Addison-Wesley.

Stedry, A.C. 1960. *Budget Control and Cost Behavior.* Englewood Cliffs, NJ: Prentice-Hall.

Steiner, G.A. 1969. *Top Management Planning.* New York: Macmillan.

Stewart, R.F. 1963. "A Framework for Business Planning," report no. 162, Long Range Planning Service. Menlo Park, CA: Stanford Research Institute.

Thompson, J.D. et al., 1959. *Comparative Studies in Administration.* Pittsburgh, PA: University of Pittsburgh Press.

Vedder, J.N. 1978. "Treatment of Differential Costs and Benefits under Risk." *Decision Sciences* 9 (April): 336–40.

6
Planning Based on a Systems Model of the Firm

The planning models surveyed in the preceding chapter are all nonsystemic in some degree. That is, they fail to take full account of the fact that a business enterprise is a system, within a three-tiered hierarchy of systems, a hierarchy consisting of the system itself, its subsystems, and the suprasystem. Beer's cybernetic firm comes closest to being a system, but as already noted this model suffers from regarding neither the parts of the business nor the business as a whole as purposeful. In so doing the model avoids all the troublesome problems of goal incongruence and motivation. Furthermore, the model is too general to be of much use, for the single type of structure that Beer finds characteristic of all organizations explains little of the workings of particular organizations. Broadly put, therefore, the purpose of this chapter is to construct a planning model that is both systemic and sufficiently detailed to be of some use. While the focus will be on business enterprises, the discussion may be extended to governmental and other types of organizations with only slight changes in terminology. Business enterprises are first of all sociotechnical systems, in the sense of Emery and Trist (1965) and others, having a technical subsystem (the production process) and a social subsystem (composed of the various human contributors to that process). Moreover, all business enterprises are open systems in Bertalanffy's sense of being able to import negative entropy (Bertalanffy 1962). They in fact do so, and are therefore called negentropic.

The main development of the systems model of the firm presented here began in Amey and Whitmore (1981).

Business enterprises are also highly complex (level 8 on Boulding's 9-point scale of system complexity; Boulding 1956) and adaptive. Their environment consists largely of other organizations. Finally, business enterprises are purposeful (or goal directed), displaying choice of ends as well as means; they are usually organized hierarchically and their parts (individual employees, functions, departments, divisions) are also purposeful.

In this chapter an attempt is made to bring together a number of ideas found in the systems literature, to introduce some new ones and to formalize these. These ideas center on the variety of objectives that influence a firm's behavior and on the nature of the firm's own objective. We shall formalize these ideas in a systems model of the firm that provides a basis for planning.

Concerning the variety of objectives influencing a firm's behavior, the first idea we adopt is Ackoff's (1974) distinction between the system's own objective, the objectives of its "parts," which he seems to equate with those of management and workers, and the purposes or demands of its environment. The same distinction is implicit in J. Kenneth Galbraith's "principle of consistency" (1967). All three tiers of objectives are included in our model, but we diverge from Ackoff and follow Cyert and March (1963) in specifying the "parts" of the system. The organization is seen as essentially a coalition of many stakeholders, including employees, management, stockholders, suppliers and customers, labor unions and governments, all of which have separate, and usually different, preference orderings. All members of the coalition strive to maintain a feasible solution, one that meets the minimal demands of all stakeholders and of the environment. In this way the system is formalized as a part of a three-tiered hierarchy of systems. Thus the system is placed in the middle of a three-tiered hierarchy of systems consisting of subsystems, the system itself, and the suprasystem.

As to the nature of the firm's own objective, we adopt the principle that the overriding objective of any open (in particular negentropic) system must be survival through more or less continuous selective adaptation to a changing environment. There is general agreement on this point, for Ackoff (1970), Ashby (1952), Beer (1969), Buckley (1967), Drucker (1958), Forrester (1969, 1975), and Simon (1957) all say in effect that the goal of an organization is survival through adaptation. Moreover, such survival would be best assured by planning that is long-range. Indeed, Forrester's extensive research (reported in Jantsch 1969) lends strong support to the proposition that it is long-term survival that should be the objective, on the grounds that complex systems have strong long-range cause–effect relationships that are ignored in short-term planning.

A SYSTEMS MODEL OF THE FIRM, WHOSE BEHAVIOR SATISFIES A VARIETY OF GOALS

Basic Concepts in the Model

Before discussing planning it is necessary to develop a model of the system whose activities are being planned. The model presented below, it may be noted, subsumes Simon's (1957) model as a special case. References to the correspondences between the two will be given as we proceed. The following are the main elements of the systems model:

σ The business system under study. As indicated in the Appendix ("A System as an Ordered Composition-Structure-Environment Triple") this may be described by the ordered triple ‹ composition, environment, structure ›, where N will here denote composition, $R \in_{(} \Sigma - \sigma)$ the relevant environment (Σ being the universe), and structure comprises the couplings of members of set N with each other and with R.

v State vector

x Action vector

ϕ A transformation that determines new state v', given initial state v and action x.

R The relevant environment, or suprasystem within which σ operates

Y The set of stakeholders or purposeful subsystems of σ , representing various interest groups.[1] $Y = G \cup N$, where

G $\{ 1, 2, \ldots, g \}$ is the subset of external stakeholders (stockholders, lenders, suppliers, customers, labor unions, governments, etc.), and

N $\{ g+1, g+2 \}$ is the subset of internal stakeholders (management, workers).

D_i Demand set, a schedule revealed by interest group i at each time point, showing what it is prepared to accept and provide under any given terms. It is the subset of all actions x acceptable to interest group i, $i \in Y$, when the system is in state v

F The intersection of the demand sets of all interest groups:
$$F = \bigcap D_i, i \in Y$$

E The set of actions x that are environmentally feasible[2] when the system is in state v

S Action choice set, representing the set of feasible actions when the system is in state v. By definition $S = F \cap E$. D, F, and hence S depend on E and v, that is $S = S(E, v)$. Selection of $x \in S$ ensures that the minimum demands of all stakeholders and of the environment are satisfied. S empty $(S = \emptyset)$ defines system "failure."

Let us now discuss these elements of the model in more detail. The vector of variables v, or *state vector,* describes the state of the system, monitored at equally spaced time points. Since a business is a dynamic system, time is imbedded in v by an index or clock where appropriate, that is, $v = (\ldots, t, \ldots)$ for time point t. In ways to be described presently, the system acts to modify the state vector in some desired manner. The *action vector,* x, denotes the decisions taken at a time point to alter state vector v. *Transformation* ϕ determines how state v will be transformed to new state v' by action x, and is written:

$$\phi\,(v, x) = v' \qquad\qquad\qquad\qquad 6.1$$

S, the action choice set, is the set from which x must be selected. S will depend on the current state v of the system, and hence action x will be feasible, given current state v, only if $x \in S$. If components of v are random variables, transformation ϕ will represent a mapping from one space of random variables to another. For example, the remaining operating life L of a machine in a plant may be a random element of v. Transformation ϕ would alter L to a new random variable L' in the span of an operating period.

The First Central Concept. The Firm's Action Choice Set: Multi-Element, and Constrained by the Demand Sets of Interest Groups

An artifact such as an ordinary machine has components that adjust at each time point so that only one element x is found in its set S for any given v; the system's behavior is predetermined, there is no freedom of action. Action x is uniquely determined by v, and the system simply unfolds according to the rule $v' = \phi\,(v,s)$, where s is the single element contained in S. By contrast, a business system and any other purposeful system with some freedom of choice or willpower generally has a choice set with many elements x. Should a business system ever find itself in a state v where S is empty, the system ceases to function. Should S contain only one element, the business system is reduced to a simple mechanical system. For example, in classical economic theory the business system is reduced to an artifact where action x is uniquely determined for the system by the economic principles of perfect competition.

That a business system will generally have a multielement choice set follows from our assumption that the system is imbedded in an Ackoff hierarchy of systems. It functions within a larger environmental system that places many natural limitations on its behavior, while leaving open a set of options. Besides these natural limitations emanating from R, the system's behavior is constrained by the demands of set G. It also has many purposeful subsystems representing various internal interest groups or stakeholders, each of which in turn usually comprises subgroups representing further purposeful subsystems—for example, the employee group consisting of management and worker subgroups.

Each interest group reveals a demand set at each time point, a schedule describing the goods and services it is prepared to accept and deliver under any given terms. By selecting action $x \in S$, the minimum demands of all interest groups are, by definition, satisfied. Use of this demand-set concept translates the decision-making power of an interest group into the form of a (weak) constraint that defines the choice set S. (In this approach there is an intentionally artificial separation of the decision-making process from the reward process.)

The demand sets largely reflect the opportunities available to interest groups elsewhere, that is, outside the system. For any given interest group, set D is the set of actions that are more attractive than any *opportunities* the group has for participation in other organizations or for no participation at all.[3] The demand set for workers, for example, will reflect labor market and industrial relations practices. It is mainly a function of R, only weakly of v. To illustrate, the demand set of a consumer in an imperfect market is the shaded region and boundaries in Fig. 6.1.

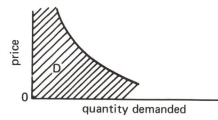

Fig. 6.1. Demand set of a consumer.

The demand set D also incorporates whatever monopoly power the interest group possesses in the socioeconomic and political environment in which the business system operates. For instance, a union or a management group may be able to narrow its demand set unilaterally to such an extent that S is thereby smaller (and, hence, system survival chances are lower) than would be the case if these groups had no monopoly powers. In other words, if D is reduced to $D' \subset D$, S will be reduced to $S \cap D'$.

To formalize this way of looking at organizational choice, we define D_i as the set of all actions x acceptable to interest group i when the system is in state v, with all interest groups taken together giving the total demand set F. In addition, E is defined as the set of actions x that are environmentally feasible when the system is in state v, that is, actions that fall within the constraints imposed by the environmental system within which business is conducted. E and F then jointly determine the set of feasible actions for the system. We shall see later in this chapter ("By Implanting an Idealized Information Structure" and "By Appropriate Organizational Design") that while E and F jointly determine the set of *feasible* actions, two other important elements enter into the selection of a particular action x.

The Second Central Concept: The Demand Sets of Interest Groups

Let us illustrate the components and structure of the demand sets of two types of interest groups. Consider first the set of all workers. (Actually, we need not refer to workers only as a group, for the demand set approach allows us to consider each worker individually; and, in reality, this is how a system deals with workers in the absence of collective bargaining.) While acceptable terms of work are very complicated to describe, including as they do issues of pay, hours, safety, work environment, fringe benefits, and so on, suppose that total wages w and hours of work q for the period are the key factors of interest. Then the demand set D will be some set of points (w, q), any one of which the workers would be prepared to accept, and some of which are just marginally or minimally acceptable in a sense we will define shortly.

A von Neumann-Morgenstern utility function $u(w, q)$ would order the points (w, q) in set D in utility terms from most to least preferred. D is, by definition, the set of all acceptable pairs (w, q). Thus no external opportunities are available to the group of workers that are more attractive than *any* of the elements of D.

Actually w and q are the only components of action vector x that are constrained by the set D. Therefore $(w, q) \in D$ is really shorthand for claiming that $x = (. . ., w, q, . . .) \in D$. Likewise in actuality the utility function u will have x as its argument (rather than $[w, q]$ alone) in order to accommodate the possibility that elements of x other than total wages and hours of work (such as purchases of unsafe equipment, for instance) may affect worker preferences.

Let us now look at the other type of demand set, namely, that of the group of owners. In a traditional business system, this group has the final decision-making power, which flows from the group's residual claim on the assets of the business. In their demand set, owners may be viewed as making a complicated tradeoff among current dividend payout, anticipated future dividend payouts, anticipated future requests for equity capital, and a willingness to retain the current senior management group (in virtue of the power of shareholders to elect board members). This complicated demand set, although lacking precise definition and intangible in many ways, operates nonetheless in every business system. Thus, for example, action x is in an owners' demand set D (i.e., is acceptable to the owners) if it contains some specified current dividend d and if the state ϕ (x, v) resulting from action x will be contained in some acceptable set K. In other words, D for owners is the set of all $x = (. . ., d, . . .)$ such that ϕ $(x, v) \in K$.

We can now make three observations about demand sets. First, in general only a few components of action vector x will be constrained by the demand set of any one interest group. If any interest group is partitioned into subgroups, say groups 1 and 2, then the combined demand set is the intersection of the individual demand sets (i.e., $D = D_1 \cap D_2$). For example, if q_1 and q_2 are amounts of labor to be provided by two workers for wages w_1 and w_2, respectively, then total labor q will be provided by them jointly for total wages w only if

$$x = (. . ., w_1, q_1, w_2, q_2, . . .) \in D_1 \cap D_2 \qquad 6.2$$

for some w_1, q_1, w_2, q_2, for which $q_1 + q_2 = q$ and $w_1 + w_2 = w$. The set D_1 constrains only the components (w_1, q_1) of x while D_2 constrains only (w_2, q_2).

SURVIVAL AS THE GOAL OF A FIRM MODELED AS A SYSTEM

Survival as a Prescribed Criterion for Assessing Decision-Making Performance and as a Minimal Goal in an Organization

What set of preferences will guide the choice of an action in S? The answer, in brief, is both nobody's and everybody's. Decision making in a business system is dispersed throughout the entire organization, with some elements of action x being fixed by high-level decision makers in the organization, and others by low-level decision makers. In other words, the decision-making process is hierarchical and complex, varying from one organization to another, and from one point or period of time to another. What does not vary is the fact that action x must meet the minimal demands of any given person or group involved with the business system. If it fails to do so, action x in essence excludes a particular individual or subgroup from the system. For example, if $(w, q) \in D$ only if $q = 0$, this worker or subgroup is, in effect, not employed by the organization. But any influence that a person has on selecting x, over and above setting these minimal conditions, depends on his/her organizational role, which in turn depends on a given firm's internal structure. Therefore, instead of proposing an optimal structure for a business system, we shall only prescribe a criterion for judging decision-making performance, namely the criterion of survival.

Survival prospects are the paramount concern in assessing the performance of the business system modeled here. In other words, we hold that survival should be a concern common to all business systems, and this because it meets the minimal demands of all stakeholders and the environment. The survival criterion for judging decision-making performance is Pareto-superior in the sense that if the business system does not survive, *all* stakeholders are forced to accept second-best choices, that is, choices outside their respective demand sets.[4] In other words, the longer the business system survives, the longer the interest groups can postpone acceptance of second-best choices.

Problems in Considering Survival as an Organizational Goal

Survival as an organizational goal is more easily prescribed than adopted, and this for the following reasons.

Organizations May Not Naturally Maximize
Their Survival Prospects

Since system survival is only a prescribed standard against which to measure decision-making performance, it is quite possible that systems in fact operate in quite a different manner, that they judge decision-making performance against some other standard. In other words, there is nothing in nature that causes decision makers in an organization to converge on that unique action x among all those available in S that maximizes survival prospects.

There May Be No Consensus on the Precise Survival Goal

Moreover, as we shall show shortly, the survival goal itself has not been well defined. In fact, since different interest groups have different preferences for alternative survival distributions, there turns out to be a built-in conflict over the precise survival goal. Thus an employee near retiring age would prefer actions that give a very high probability of survival for at least a short time; what happens after that does not matter. On the other hand, a young person who has just joined the organization often has a long horizon, and wishes to maximize the probability of long-term survival.

Consensus on a Goal May Not Even Be Measurable

There is the resulting problem of trying to reconcile the differing preference patterns (utilities) of different individuals. This problem is encountered in any group decision-making situation, and as yet there is no satisfactory way of comparing utility values between individuals in any group decision-making context.

A Large Firm's Survival May Be Due to Intervention
by External Forces

Survival is sometimes determined as much by the legal framework within which the firm operates as by its economic viability. Thus if the firm is a large one, governments and the courts are prone to do everything possible to avert its failure, and it may operate for years in an insolvent (failed) condition (Penrose 1959: 23). When a government intervenes to postpone failure, its demand set undergoes adjustment (or was not accurately defined in the first place).

A Firm May Appear Not to Survive by Giving Up Its Identity

A firm may find it advantageous to merge with or be acquired by another firm, thus losing its identity. Such loss of identity does not constitute failure, however, since $S \neq \emptyset$ before the merger or acquisition occurs. All that has happened is a reduction in the population of firms.

Some Firms' Failure May Be Desirable, to Make Way for New, More Economically Viable Firms

From a social point of view, it may be less costly to allow business systems to fail in order to make way for new systems that are more suited to survive. In this context adaptation occurs, not within a single organization, but over several generations of organizations that are mutating slowly, entering and exiting the business sector in an orderly progression. Failure of a particular business system may not violate the optimality of our survival criterion for judging organizational decision-making performance: It need not force interest groups to accept second-best choices if there is the simultaneous creation of a new business system offering better prospects. Moreover, the creation of new business systems that offer better prospects to interest groups may tighten their demands on existing business enterprises, to the extent, in some cases, of sufficiently shrinking the action set S as to cause failure.

Poor Quality Personnel May Render a Firm's Adaptive Decisions Dysfunctional

A further consideration that may offset the desirability of an adaptive organization is the quality of its personnel. If the adapting feature is badly conceived or implemented it may be destabilizing to the point where the organization disintegrates.

Survivability Not to be Confused with Security

A final problem arises in determining the optimal *degree* of survival. Continuous adaptation for long-term survival should imply a "lean beast," as Hedberg et al. (1976: 58–59) note:

> While a small buffer of flexible resources is an asset . . . excessive affluence can be as serious a liability as is poverty. . . . Discontent generally

decreases as an organization gains affluence. Slack resources build up. . . . Everyone can receive a little more, mutual self-satisfaction grows, and self-confident complacency sets in. Insensitivity toward environmental and organizational happenings accumulates and spreads. Since the usual organization is seeking as much affluence as possible, it can be charged with striving to maximize its unawareness of reality.

In other words maximizing survival prospects must be defined in such a way that it does not mean maximizing security.

What this means in terms of the systems model of the firm is that within S there is some subset $S_0 \subset S$ for which survival prospects for the long term are uniformly high. "Lean beast" management and organization effectively constrain the choice of some $x \in S_0$. The set S could be thought of as containing subsets of action vectors corresponding to different survival probabilities, as illustrated by the probability contours in the Venn diagram in Figure 6.2.

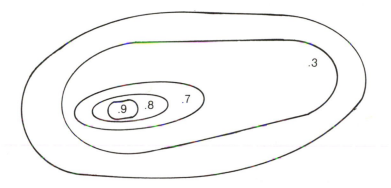

Fig. 6.2. The set S, showing subsets of action vectors corresponding to different survival probabilities.

The innermost contour contains all the actions on which 0.9 survival probability is placed. "Lean beast" management and organization would then mean artificially constraining the action choice set S, reducing the degrees of freedom of the system. Figure 6.3 illustrates the effects over time on set S of a "lean beast" action x' corresponding to survival probability 0.9 and an alternative action x that yields poorer survival prospects, say 0.7. This problem bears a certain similarity to a problem in price theory, namely that of determining the appropriate objectives of firms in different market situations. There we have the desire for maximum profits in perfect and imperfect competition, versus the desire for secure profits in oligopoly

(Rothschild 1947). Translating this problem into our context, we find that, in some cases, actions by a firm aimed at maximum security are identical to actions aimed at long-term survival. For example, entering into collusive agreements with competitors might serve both of these ends. In other cases, however, the two motives lead to conflicting patterns of behavior. Thus continuous adaptation for long-term survival may demand that the firm alter its prices with every change in revenue and cost conditions, whereas security maximization may demand stable prices (oligopoly). Or a firm wrongly interpreting "survival" as excessive security might engage in backward integration to safeguard its sources of supply (material or financial), thereby losing flexibility and becoming potentially less adaptive, especially if demand turns sour. Again, for security reasons the firm might desire size for its own sake, regardless of technical considerations, and thus build up its financial strength by reinvesting profits in the firm heedless of the yields obtainable elsewhere. As the earlier quotation observed, increased size frequently brings with it more conservative attitudes and policies, besides making the firm bigger than the optimal size in terms of costs.

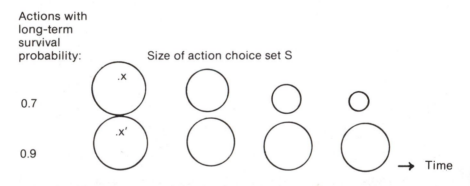

Fig. 6.3. The set S over time with more or less successful adaptation.

A way around this problem is indicated. We need only place upper bounds on the values of certain of the system's state variables (some of the subset which we later call the essential variables) to ensure that long-term survival does not include an excessive security element. Lower bounds would ensure that the system survived, not merely in a nominal sense, but with a reasonable degree of efficiency. For example, a small amount of organizational slack (Cyert and March 1963: 36–38) is justified in that it provides a cushion against uncertainty and allows some flexibility of action. Excessive slack, however, fosters conservative attitudes and an unwillingness to take risks. Top management must constantly strike the right balance between no slack and excessive slack. This can be interpreted as meaning that the essential variables define the structure of the contours in set S (as illustrated in Figure 6.2), in the sense that keeping the essential variables within given bounds assures that the action vector is chosen from one of the higher probability contours of set S.

PLANNING TO ENSURE ADAPTABILITY OF THE FIRM MODELED AS A SYSTEM

Survival is to be sought through selective adaptation, "selective" to the extent that the firm maintains its own identity and pursues its own objective, and is not simply cloned from the environment.

Ambiguous Meaning of Adaptation

Adaptation is itself not a clear term, for it can be interpreted in a number of different ways, some of which seem more appropriate to certain types of systems than to others. Bunge (1979), for example, concluded that it is an ambiguous term when applied to biological systems, where adaptation can mean (i) suitable performance of a function by a subsystem, (ii) adjustment of a species to its environment over several generations, or (iii) natural growth of a population (a surplus of births over deaths). In the biological case, survival means (iii), while (ii) is merely an indicator of (iii) in the Darwinian sense of "survival of the fittest." Logically, (iii) implies (ii) which in turn implies (i).

Let us now look at the relative importance of these different meanings, and their practical implications. Barring radical changes in our sociopolitical system, business enterprises seem in no danger of failing to provide for their own succession, and thus fertility meaning (iii) would seem to be trivial with respect to them. On the other hand adaptation in senses (i) and (ii) is necessary for long-term survival of a business system. This kind of adaptation is achieved by keeping the organization flexible at all times, by treating organization design as a variable; by the system learning how to adjust to its environment successfully, selectively matching its orientation to that of the environment in both direction and speed of change; and by motivating individuals working in the organization to act in ways that are congruent with the organizational goal of survival.

In sum, adaptation means enhancing the system's survival prospects by preserving the system's flexibility. We can measure the degree of such adaptation in terms of our notation as follows. If we measure flexibility by the number of members of the choice set $S(E, v)$, then we can say that state v is more flexible than state v' if $S(E, v') \subset S(E, v)$. Here greater flexibility is associated with better survival prospects, for any action available with v' is also available with v, and more. The only drawback to this measure is that two choice sets that cannot be ordered by set inclusion cannot be ordered in terms of flexibility. Still, this measure is a valuable one in identifying system changes that enhance its survival prospects.

Adaptation Through Planning

Let us now look at planning as a means of adapting. If T is some selected planning horizon, $\langle x_i \rangle = \langle x_1, x_2, \ldots \rangle$ a sequence of feasible future actions, and v the current state of the system, $P(T \mid \langle x_i \rangle, v)$ is the probability that the firm will survive beyond T periods, given the plan $\langle x_i \rangle$ and current state v.

Business planning entails the selection of an action sequence $\langle x_1, x_2, \ldots \rangle$, the first stage of which is set into effect and the others implemented in future periods. Plans are revised continuously in light of experience and changing expectations. If system survival beyond time T is the goal, the objective function for selecting the current plan, given that v_1 is the current state, is

$$\max_{\langle x_i \rangle} P(T \mid \langle x_i \rangle, v_1), \qquad\qquad 6.3$$

where the sequence of system states is given by v_1, $v_2 = \phi(v_1, x_1)$, $v_3 = \phi(v_2, x_2), \ldots$. Here $x_1 \in S(E, v_1)$, $x_2 \in S(E, v_2)$, and so on. The action x_1^* in the optimal sequence $\langle x_i^* \rangle$ is implemented in the current period and the resulting new state is $v_2^* = \phi(v_1, x_1^*)$. Implementing plan x_1^* is not without difficulties, as has already been noted. For one thing, it must be done jointly within the organization by one or more of the interest groups whose goals for system survival may not coincide with the plan, and may conflict with each other. Moreover, future actions in the sequence $\langle x_i \rangle$ may have random components because they are conditional on outcomes of random events in intervening periods.

ADAPTING FOR SURVIVAL

Assuming that long-term survival is the system objective, it is instructive to ask whether, and if so how, a business system has, or can be provided with, an adaptive instinct that leads it to select actions from S that will ensure survival, much as living species adapt and survive, over generations, by mutation.

By Encouraging Active System Planning

In the systems view planning is the major adaptive function. The reasoning behind this was given in Chapter 1. The organization is not passive in the face of environmental (and internal) change; rather, it is a purposeful system. However, the desired future state it hopes to achieve will generally not come about on its own. At the same time the organization believes that, if it takes appropriate action, it can increase the likelihood of achieving this desired state. Planning (conceived of as a continuous process), more than any other activity within the organization, is the obvious place for taking this action because achievement of the desired state involves solving a set of interrelated decisions spanning the entire system, and planning is the only place where this system of problems can be tackled as a whole. Therefore the main burden of adapting the system falls on the planning process, while all other adaptations are only partial adaptations, confined to some subset of the entire set of interrelated decisions.

Ackoff's "adaptivizing" organization (1974), here equated with one seeking long-term survival, approaches planning by viewing its future environment as essentially controllable, not controlling as in conventional planning. It formulates its planning problem with all but the inescapable constraints relaxed and all self-imposed constraints removed, thus making the set S as large as possible, offering the maximum flexibility of action. The organization consciously seeks to design or redesign its own future by creating as well as predicting future opportunities, and preventing future threats from developing, not merely predicting them—all of this over a fairly long horizon. Part of the redesign may come about by management exploiting an expanded set E due to technological advances.

By Creating a Participative, Minimally Constraining Working Environment

Such a continuous adaptive planning process should keep all involved in it in an adaptive mode. In other words, adaptation will also be promoted if this outlook is extended to all parts of the working environment. This is done provided the latter stimulates curiosity, experimentation, innovation, and creativity. Too often, however, the opposite is found in existing business practice, where the accounting system, standard operating rules, and other programmed behaviors act as stabilizers, introducing rigidity into the decision-making process when flexibility is what is required.

Allowing a Healthy Amount of Tension, By Countenancing a Range of Alternative Actions

Buckley (1967) has observed that a certain degree of tension between its elements is a normal state of affairs in any social organization, as necessary for its viability as free energy is to the operation of a machine. Another way of stating this requirement is to hold that the level of satisfaction of individuals' needs must not be raised beyond a certain point, for beyond that point there is too much security and welfare, which lead to inertia and loss of flexibility. In terms of the systems model of the firm presented here, maintenance of a certain degree of tension within the system would mean that actions x should be chosen close to the boundary of each interest group's demand set, with the result that the utility difference $u_i(x) - u_i^0$, where $x \in S$ and u_i^0 denotes the maximum external alternative utility level attainable by interest group i, should be kept small. This links up with Simon's (1957) notion of "surplus" for a *firm* (rather than for an industry, as in Marshallian economics). Whereas under a profit maximization objective the "surpluses" of all participants (stakeholders) disappear when all relevant markets (e.g., product market, labor market) are perfectly competitive, if the objective relates to adaptation for long-term survival the corresponding requirement is that the maximum total "surplus" of utility, described above, should be kept small in any single period, but over time should not be allowed to drop below a certain minimum level (slightly above u_i^0), for any interest group i.

A certain amount of uncertainty, ambiguity, and conflict should also be allowed to remain, leaving a range of permitted alternatives in subjects' actions.

Thus, as regards ambiguity, fuzzy controllers (based on the theory of fuzzy sets) can control urban traffic in large cities more effectively (result in a smaller average delay of vehicles) than a conventional effective vehicle-actuated controller (Pappis and Mamdani 1977). Since tensions are spread through an organization by communication networks and information flows in the form of social pressures or interpersonal influences, we should now examine the problem of determining the information structure appropriate for maintaining selected levels of tension.

By Implanting an Idealized Information Structure

Predictive Information on the Environment

The role of information in the business system model bears close scrutiny. Recall that our preliminary definition merely said that the state vector v described the system at a moment of time. In fact it does more than that. The state vector, *properly constituted,* contains the minimum amount of information required to determine both the system's outputs and future states if the "inputs" (meaning the decision variables x) are known. In other words the state vector provides a sufficient description of the system at a point in time if no knowledge of the system's past history is necessary to determine all future states, providing we know the decision variables. It would be idle to suppose, however, that an open system's behavior is entirely state determined. In all our references to "redesigning the future" it should be realized that this redesigning takes place only within limits permitted by the environment. Consequently predictive information on the environment plays an important, probably dominant, role in determining the system's future states. This is located in the firm's information structure, which *ideally* would include all the information represented in the state vector, forecasts of the environment underlying the system's plans, the accounting record, and so on. All would be part of an ideal information structure.

The Information Structure Evolves Like the State Vector of the System

Let I_0 denote the actual information structure of the system at a time point. Like the state vector v, this structure undergoes a transformation, ω, in each period:

$$\omega\,(I_0,\,x) = \; I_o'$$ 6.4

Transformation ω captures all of the dynamics of an information structure: recording outcomes of random events, updating probability distributions for future events, and maintaining a historical record of environmental and interest-group variables. It also encompasses the accounting process, in which aspects of state vector v are measured and recorded.

Accounting Records are Contained in the Information Structure

This measurement and recording process as we shall now show is not an exact one in real accounting systems. In fact it is relatively coarse. If vector a denotes the accounting record of v, there is a mapping, M, from v to a:

$$a = M(v)$$ 6.5

If this mapping is one to one, the accounting process produces an exact record of the real state of the system, although the record itself requires interpretation. In real accounting systems the mapping is many to one, and thus a is an aggregated, incomplete record of v.

Accounting Records Evolve Like the State Vector

A sequence of accounting records $\langle\, a_i\, \rangle = \langle\, a_1,\, a_2,\, \ldots \,\rangle$ provides a rough dynamic view of a business system. Changes between temporally adjacent records are due partly to the bookkeeping principles of accounting, which provide a rough approximation to transformation ϕ. Denoting this approximating transformation by α, the accounting records for consecutive years are given by

$$a' = \alpha\,(a,\,x)$$ 6.6

Here $\alpha\,(a,\,x)$ is congruent, and thus an approximation, to $\phi\,(v,x)$.

Accounting Records are Often a Proxy for the State Vector and Determine the Action-Choice Set

Frequently it is the accounting records of a business system that are examined when a judgment is to be made about its health. Such a judgment conventionally is based on tests on the accounting record a (or on a sequence of records $\langle a_i \rangle$) that involve (1) establishing whether certain essential elements of vector a lie within specified limits or (2) computing certain ratios of these elements and comparing them with specified limits (for example, checking the value of the current ratio). One might symbolically describe the judgment as a check to see if $a \in J$, where J is some set of acceptable records. With the mapping M, we may define a set K of state vectors v such that $M(K) = J$, that is K is the set of all state vectors v that map into acceptable accounting records. A business system may then be perceived as healthy in accounting terms if $v \in K$ or, equivalently, if $M(v) \in J$. In reality, owners may still base their judgment on whether $a \in J$ rather than on whether $v \in K$, because the latter may not be observable, whereas the accounting record a is.

The State Vector Plus an Idealized Information Structure Should Determine the Action-Choice Set

An important issue in accounting is the adequacy of the mapping M from v to a, in particular the accuracy and completeness of the record that M provides of v, as already noted. To illustrate the problem, let us denote by $S(I, v)$ the action choice set we would like to have, where v denotes the state of the system and I an *idealized* information structure. What we get in practice is not this set but a smaller one, $S(I_0, a)$, where the accounting record a replaces v, and a narrow information structure I_0 replaces I. The accounting record provides information about the historical values of assets and claims on assets, but little about the attributes of assets (e.g., their physical state). Thus, a is no more than a shadow of v. Moreover, although the actual information structure I_0 covers both formal and informal information elements, it is only a fraction of the ideal structure I, differing substantially from the latter in terms of both information technology and the depth and breadth of information content. To make matters worse, in many organizations attention is paid exclusively to the formal elements of I_0. For instance, accounting control systems such as budgetary control recognize only the formal aspects of organization and neglect the very important informal aspects.

Probably I_0 is quite inadequate in most firms today, and some move is needed toward the ideal information structure I to make adaptation more effective. Of course I_0 can be made to approach I only at some cost, a cost that must be balanced against the corresponding gains.

This raises the question of how one should value "information" in a system in which the criterion is maximizing the probability of long-term survival. Evidently, this will lead to a different valuation principle. In information economics the value of information is usually measured in terms of the expected increase in payoff (profit, or more generally utility, relying on the von Neumann-Morgenstern axioms of consistent behavior under uncertainty). More precisely, the value of perfect information is measured by expected payoff, the value of imperfect information by the conditional expectation, the conditionality pertaining to the reliability of the information structure (information sources). Under a survival criterion, "payoff" takes the form of a conditional *probability*—at least in our view. The distinction between perfect and imperfect information becomes more obscure. The value of information in making the system more survival-worthy depends much more broadly than in the traditional case on what is done with the information: whether, in fact, it leads to decisions that are adaptive, whether these decisions are *long-run* adaptive, whether the organization is appropriately structured to carry out such decisions, whether the information leads to learning, whether it is received in time to allow successful adaptation to be made, and whether the information structure is sufficiently flexible.

Some accounting theorists (e.g., Ijiri 1965: 85ff; Ijiri and Kelly 1980) have envisaged something approaching the idealized information system we have in mind in proposing an accounting system in which transactions are represented by vectors of characteristics of assets and claims. But of course a full state description would very likely include semi-accounting and non-accounting information (e.g., price/earnings ratio, product market share, respectively).

The Idealized Information Structure Should Provide Timely and Relevant Information, and Should Cause New Behavioral Issues to be Addressed

Another important question relating to the information structure concerns the extent and frequency of monitoring of the environment, and the frequency of observing outputs and determining states. In practice the environment is usually not monitored closely enough, and forecasts are not long enough, to meet the requirements of successful adaptation. In accounting, the time interval between measurements is usually constant and determined by administrative considerations and conventions rather than by the needs of the situation. Moreover, computerized structures tend to increase programmed behaviors and freeze the organization design (Mowshowitz 1976). In sum, existing information structures often have dysfunctional effects (Hedberg and Jönsson 1978). Therefore, to satisfy the heavy demands that adaptation for long-term survival puts on the firm's information structure, new kinds of information systems need to be designed that enable the system to learn rapidly and to cope with variety in its environment.

It should also be borne in mind that an information structure has very different implications for the behavior of decision makers than for behavior that is being reported on: A whole different set of issues is relevant for the former. Moreover, different types of people may occupy these roles, while the roles themselves may offer different kinds of satisfaction. People also differ in their information-processing ability and problem-solving styles (Lawler and Rhode 1976; Hopwood 1976).

By Appropriate Organizational Design

The First Way Organizational Design Influences Adaptability: By Selectively Matching the System with Its Environment

There are two ways in which organizational design may have a powerful influence on the system's success in adapting. First, besides changing the environment, changing the organizational structure may be the only way of selectively matching the system to the environment. "Taking the organization's structure for granted," as Ackoff notes (1970: 87) "may deprive the planner of his most powerful means of improving its performance. [On the other hand] if he designs an organization that is foresightful, innovative, and rational, part of the need for planning will be removed." Beer (1969: 398–99) expresses the same sentiments:

> Adaptation is the crux of planning [as] corporate planning becomes a machine for sequentially aborting incompetent plans. [In fact] the planning process . . . is founded in organizational structure, because this structure alone is that which adapts. [Indeed] if the structure of the organization is not adaptive, the organization cannot effectively change its plans. [Thus] a new sort of structure is required to exploit these capabilities . . . [which at present] are not understood.

Hierarchy is perhaps the only feature such an organizational structure would have in common with familiar structures, Beer believes. Two final opinions along these lines can be recalled from Chapter 2, namely Buckley's (1968) view that adaptation implies a willingness to change organizational structure as required by external events, and the prescription of Hedberg et al. (1976) for a "self-designing" organization which they believed would ensure adaptation and long-term survival. Keep in mind, finally, that an adaptive organizational structure, and decision modes that leave some discretion to decision makers and thus enable the system to learn from its mistakes and to be self-correcting, would in turn put heavy demands on the system's information structure.

The Second Way: By Selecting the Action to be Implemented

Organizational structure also has a bearing on the purposiveness of the parts as well as the whole, a purposiveness which, besides matching system with environment, is another factor in adaptability. Organizational design has an influence on which action $x \in S$ is selected for implementation and on how that action is implemented. In other words, organizational structure determines what and how work gets done.

Mixed Blessings of One Kind of Organizational Design: Decentralization

One type of organizational design is the decentralized one characteristic of many firms nowadays. Such a design has mixed results, however, for while a decentralized organization adapts faster than a unitary one (Mesarovic et al. 1970), decentralization raises problems of coordination of the subunits. They must be led to take actions consistent with achieving the system objective (of long-term survival through adaptation) while being left with maximum apparent autonomy.

Resolving the goal congruence problem through iteration. To illustrate the problem of decision making in a divisionalized firm, examine goal-setting in the two-division firm shown schematically in Figure 6.4. (In a section below—"By Motivation"—we examine a way of bringing about goal congruence other than by setting divisional performance targets.) When head office chooses an action x, it decomposes x into two components, x_1 and x_2, each associated with a division, that is, $x = (x_1, x_2)$. At instant 1 head office informs division 1 that it should choose x_1, assuming that $x_2 = b_1$ and that the choice set is C_1. Similarly, division 2 is informed that it should choose x_2 assuming that $x_1 = a_1$ and that the choice set is C_2. The choices of the divisions, therefore, are elements $(x_1, b_1) \in C_1$ and $(a_1, x_2) \in C_2$. If the resulting action choices are $x_1 = a^2$ and $x_2 = b_2$, then these are communicated at instant 2 to head office which in turn feeds them back to the respective divisions. The decision-making process is repeated in each division until there is convergence to an action pair (a, b) where

$$a = \lim_{n \to \infty} a_n \qquad b = \lim_{n \to \infty} b_n \qquad\qquad 6.7$$

and subscripts denote time or the iteration number. If C_1 and C_2 were made identical to S and other suitable conditions were imposed, the preceding convergence would be guaranteed to occur, and the action pair (a, b) would be feasible for the firm as a whole in the sense that $(a, b) \in S$.

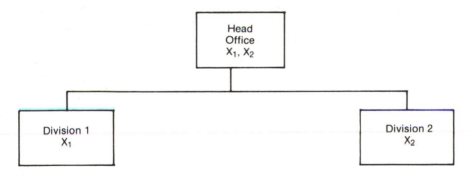

Fig. 6.4. Goal decomposition (or decentralized action-choice) in a two-division business system.

The action-choice sets of divisions should each overlap with, but not contain, the action-choice set of the firm. For reasons of both motivation and control it may be desirable to intentionally make the action-choice sets of divisions different from S. More generally, C_1 and C_2 might also be indexed by the iteration number. In any case, the final action (a, b) must be an element of S, and this implies that both C_1 and C_2 must overlap with S. For example, because of persistent cost overruns in past capital projects, C_1 and C_2 may constrain divisional capital budgets to artificially low levels. This gives the final investment actions embodied in vector (a, b) a reasonable chance of staying within the target budget for the whole firm, this target having been set with the survival prospects of the system in mind. Here C_1 and C_2 are proper subsets of S.

The goal decomposition approach works well when goals are set before the organization comes into existence.   In the decision-making process described above decomposition techniques are applied that are the same as those used in solving large-scale mathematical programs. Using such techniques to elicit subunit behavior consistent with achieving the system objective can usually be done only before the organization comes into existence. That is, the model of a firm yet to be established can be decomposed into parts, each with its own goal and measure of performance, in such a way that if each part is optimized the performance of the whole will be optimized. In other words subunits first are set up such that each has a goal (performance measure) whose individual optimization coincides with joint optimization of all subunit goals, which in turn coincides with optimization of the performance of the whole.

In already existing organizations it works only if the organization structure is changed to match the goal structure, or if some translation mechanism maps the goal structure onto the organization structure.   It is a more difficult matter for firms already in existence. These might not have been structured so as to make appropriate multilevel decomposition of the overall task and goal possible. Usually we find that they are structured along administrative lines (departments, divisions, or more generally "responsibility centers") that allow only for nonoptimal decomposition of the overall system objective. Hence goals and performance measures applied to such subunits are likely to be dysfunctional since the subunits will seek to optimize them. The problem results, of course, from the fact that the means of achieving the overall objective are not likely to be strictly separable by existing organizational subunits, some of which are involved in *interdependent* activities. The solution is either to change the organizational structure to enable attainment of the system objective—which, for a complex organization, is generally infeasible due to economic, technical, and human constraints—or to superimpose on the existing organization structure an objective- or decision-oriented information structure, by providing a translation mechanism to map from one structure onto the other (Ackoff 1970: 105; Mesarovic et al. 1970). PPBS in the public sector is an example of the latter approach. This approach is followed in the Ruefli model (shown in Chapter 5) in which in a three-tiered organization the highest level sets goals for the second level, which are oriented toward the system objective. Using these goals, the second level develops shadow prices to be assumed by the third level within the existing administrative framework. Goal congruence is then brought about iteratively, along lines similar to the iterative process described above for decentralized divisional decision making.

By Interest Groups Adjusting Their Demand Sets

The choice of an action x from choice set S also depends, of course, on the demand sets of the interest groups, since these sets partly determine the composition of S. Even if management and workers are persuaded of the overriding need to adapt, for example, the goals of other interest groups in the organizational coalition (e.g., a major supplier) may conflict with this objective.

To see how the demand sets of interest groups can affect the character of the choice set S and, hence, the survival prospects of the business system, consider the Venn diagrams in Figures 6.5 and 6.6. The diagrams presuppose, for simplicity, that the system consists of two interest groups (1 and 2). In Figure 6.5, we have two Venn diagrams that give different characterizations of the choice set S depending on whether one of the interest groups in the system has a dominant decision-making role.[5] In Figure 6.5a, neither group is dominant and the mechanism whereby action x is chosen from S is unclear. Essentially, x is a compromise of choices determined in the decision-making hierarchy of the system and may appear to be determined randomly. In Figure 6.5b, we have a more traditional construction (although not necessarily more realistic). In it, Group 1 (management, say) is the dominant group. The action choice set S for Group 1 is defined by the demand sets D_2 and E alone (i.e., $S = D_2 \cap E$). Group 1's utility function, which might be denoted by $u_1(x)$, then determines the choice of an action from S.

No group is dominant   Group 1 is dominant

(a)   (b)

Figure 6.5. The construction of action choice set S, (a) where there is not, and (b) where there is a dominant group. In (a) action $x \in S$ is not explicitly selected by any interest group. In (b) action $x \in D_2 \cap E$ is chosen according to the utility function $u_1(x)$ of Group 1, the dominant group.

In particular, that action is chosen that solves the following optimization problem:

$$\max_{x \in D_1 \cap D_2 \cap E} [u_1(x)] \qquad\qquad 6.8$$

Note that only x vectors in set D_1 *and* in set $D_2 \cap E$ will be considered by the dominant interest group—in the former set because it wants to, and in the latter set because it has to.

In Figure 6.6, the two Venn diagrams illustrate how demands of interest groups can adjust to prevent system failure. In Figure 6.6a, the demands of the two interest groups and the constraints of the environment do not all overlap anywhere. Any environmentally feasible action chosen·in this situation would lie outside at least one of the demand sets D_1 and D_2 and would therefore be second-best for at least one of them. To prevent system failure, either D_1, D_2, or both must be expanded or shifted to provide a non-empty intersection $S = D_1 \cap D_2 \cap E$. Figure 6.6b illustrates the former adjustment by the first interest group. Such an adjustment will occur only if the options open elsewhere to Group 1 decrease in attractiveness. That is, D_1 expands only if actions that were previously second-best become best for some reason. Such expansion of demand sets is precisely what occurs in corporate reorganizations and in compromise settlements in labor–management negotiations.

System eventually fails   System survives because Group 1 relaxes demands

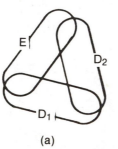

(a)

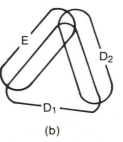

(b)

Figure 6.6. Relaxation of the demands (i.e., expansion of the demand set) of an interest group permits system survival.

By Motivation

As stated earlier (see Chapter 1, "Measurement of Performance," and Chapter 4, "Should Planning Budgets and Control Budgets Be Formally Distinct?"), management, workers, and all other interest groups represented in the organizational coalition must be motivated to contribute to the organization's adaptation. All must have a positive attitude toward adaptation, and not obstruct the adaptive efforts of other member groups. Of course, such a state of affairs is ideal and thus not likely to always obtain for three reasons. First, even if management and workers, who are the employee groups in the coalition, are persuaded of the overriding need to be adaptive, some other interest group may act in conflict with this objective. Such a situation may create "internal" disturbances over and above the "external" (i.e., environmental) disturbances to which the organization must selectively adapt. Second, the role of the owners of capital, the stockholders, in adaptation appears to be neutral in many cases. This is because a board of directors who are mainly stockholders with financial interests that are diversified across the securities of many firms will not have much concern with a particular firm. An organization with such a board therefore will not "seem endowed with good survival properties" (Fama 1980: 293). This factor will be partly offset, however, in cases where there are stockholders with large holdings (and, hence, owners' surplus in Simon's [1957] terms). These would dominate the board and inject a survival impetus.

Finally, recall from Chapter 4 that at the tactical level of planning the type of budgets best suited to planning and decision making are not the best for motivational purposes. In sum, the problem of where and how to induce motivation (to adapt) into an organization is a large and complex one, and not yet sufficiently understood for a position to be taken here.

ALTERNATIVE BUSINESS SURVIVAL NEEDS

Another view of what a business enterprise should do to survive that has many points in common with the foregoing, and which we came across only after drafting this chapter, is contained in a perceptive 1958 paper by Peter Drucker.

Drucker recounts how, 40 years earlier, the management of the Bell Telephone System was the first large firm to reject the idea that "the objective of a business is to make a profit," and to ask instead "on what will our survival as a privately owned business depend?" The survival of privately owned telecommunications in the United States and Canada, unique in developed countries, is said to be the result of the survival objective set by the Bell management at that time, an objective of "public satisfaction with our service." Although vindicated in practice, the Bell decision remained isolated and otherwise unjustified until biologists, within the last generation, laid a theoretical basis for understanding all biological systems, by defining "essential survival functions."

In extending these functions to the business firm, we stipulate that survival objectives (as we now call them) must be at once general and particular to a given business. They must have the same conceptual content in every business, but they must stipulate in different firms (a) different levels of performance in each objective area crucial to survival, and (b) each firm's particular required balance among survival objectives at any given time. The concept of "survival objectives" thus fulfills, says Drucker, the first requirement of a genuine "theory": that it be both formal (general) and yet empirical (particular, concrete, applicable or practical). Moreover, the particular survival objectives must be based on objective knowledge, not opinion or hunch. They cannot, on the other hand, "determine" business decisions but only guide or constrain decision and judgment.

Drucker believes there are five "survival objectives" of business enterprise against which each business, to survive, must reach a standard of performance set at some minimum level. These objectives are:

1. Having a human organization capable of joint performance of a common result, and of perpetuating itself.

2. Correct anticipation of its social and economic environment. The firm exists in society and economy; in fact it exists on sufferance, since society and/or economy can put any business out of existence at will. It follows that anticipation of social climate and economic policy, and organizational behavior to create what the business needs to survive in respect to both, are genuine survival needs of every business at all times.

3. To supply an economic good or service. This is the main reason why firms exist. Given uncertainty, we have not found any better way of supplying economic goods and services efficiently. Fulfilling this purpose is the only justification for the existence of business enterprises.

4. Not only adaptation to change, but also *innovation*. This is because business operates in a *changing* economy, technology, and society. Indeed the business enterprise was the first institution designed to *produce* change, according to Drucker; this novel characteristic of business enterprises was one of the main explanations of their complexity. All previous human institutions (the family, government, church, army) were designed to prevent change, since change has always been seen as a threat to human security.

5. Profitability. This is an absolute requirement of survival for it is the purpose, nature, and necessity of a business enterprise to take and to create risks, and "risks are genuine costs." Profit *maximization* is the wrong concept, however. The real question is "What is the survival minimum?" and Drucker believes that the minimum profit needed to ensure long-term survival may, in many cases, exceed present short-term maxima.

SOME REMAINING PROBLEMS

While the model of the firm presented here, and the type of planning it enables, would seem to be in the spirit of the systems approach to understanding reality, some difficult problems would confront any attempt to implement it. For one thing, long-term "survival" as the system objective is not formally well defined, and the problem of measuring group preferences, here expressed in terms of probabilities, has so far proved intractable—hardly an encouraging beginning. The ideal relation between the planning and survival horizons is another interesting consideration. Further problems concern devising organizational structures and information structures that facilitate and promote adaptability and survivability, properties that most existing structures singularly lack. Finally come the questions of whether motivation is one of the purposes of planning or should be induced from elsewhere; what kind of incentives should be used to motivate extrinsically, on what incentive payments should be based, and how risk should be shared within the organization.

SUMMARY

None of the models surveyed in the previous chapter took account of the firm's system properties; they were nonsystemic. Consequently they gave an incomplete picture of the firm's planning problem. In this chapter an attempt has been made to rectify this omission by developing a model of the firm in the setting of a three-tiered hierarchy of systems. The objective of the business system, following what has become a fairly well-established view in the systems literature and elsewhere (Ashby, Beer, Ackoff, Buckley, Forrester, Simon), was taken to be survival under a fairly long horizon, after the demands of its stakeholders and the environment are at least minimally met, with "survival" prospects measured in terms of a probability. Within this framework planning was presented as a dynamic process that bore the brunt of selectively adapting the firm to its environment for long-term survival. At the same time it was recognized that the aim of continuous adaptation would make heavy demands on the firm's organizational structure, information structure, and control system, and depend heavily on uniting all the interest groups in pursuit of the aim. This last matter, which involves motivation, is one stage in the implementation of plans that needs to be explored further because of the mismatch at the tactical level between the requirements of planning and the requirements for motivation. Since the motivation question may have ramifications extending beyond planning, and because research on this question has not yet produced results commanding widespread acceptance, it was decided that it was inappropriate and premature to discuss it further here.

APPENDIX: AN ORGANIZATIONAL STRUCTURE FOR LONG-TERM SURVIVAL

One of the most intriguing questions prompted by the foregoing discussion (in particular under "By Appropriate Organizational Design") is: What characteristics would be possessed by the organizational structure offering the greatest chance of long-term survival?

At a given time a business system has a given internal (organizational) structure K. Matsuno (1981) believes that this structure, made up of a network of relations between system elements, can be reduced to a set of elementary relations, and that the latter constitutes a more fundamental category than that of the system elements themselves. He tries to determine the conditions on these elementary relations that will make one among several different organizational structures most likely to survive in the long term. We will now describe and assess his analysis.

An organizational structure K existing at a given time consists of a network of relations (inner couplings) that can be reduced to a set of elementary relations. Matsuno calls the latter set the system's *microstructure*. An elementary relation is defined by two conditions:

(i)   The relation remains constant over some short interval of time with nonzero probability when the system is isolated from its environment;

(ii) So long as it remains unchanged an elementary relation does not affect other elementary relations that are operating simultaneously, that is, all elementary relations are independent except when they change.

Formally, if A is an elementary relation in organizational structure K, the (conditional) probability that it will remain constant over an arbitrary time interval (t, t_0), where $t_0 < t$, when open system σ is isolated from its environment E is $P(t, t_0 : A) \neq 0$. If system σ is isolated from its environment, neither the system itself nor structure K nor any of the constituent elementary relations can survive indefinitely. Consequently

$$\lim_{t - t_0 \to \infty} P(t, t_0; A) = 0$$

for all elementary relations. Assuming structure K is stationary over time interval (t_0, t) with probability P, that probability will be invariant whenever that interval is shifted along the time axis by an arbitrary increment t', that is, $P(t + t', t_0 + t'; A) = P(t, t_0; A)$.

The set of elementary relations operating at a given time will be denoted $\{A_j\}$. These relations are linked sequentially—they change over time, and hence, over time, the microstructure has the trajectory

$$\{A_j^1\} \to \{A_j^2\} \to \ldots \to \{A_j^n\}, \qquad 6.9$$

where $j = 1, 2, \ldots$ denotes an elementary relation, superscripts denote time instants, and arrows mean "is followed by." Matsuno represents the fact that σ is an open system by extending this sequence to

$$E \to \{A_j^1\} \to \ldots \to \{A_j^n\} \to E, \qquad 6.10$$

where E denotes, in the first instance, an input from the environment and, in the second, an output to the environment, and A_j^n is the set of end relations in the sequence. He interprets sequence 6.10 to mean that, while sequence 6.9 is a decay or weakening of the relations $\{A_j\}$, the system can survive, and structure K can remain viable, through interactions of the microstructure with the environment $(E \to \ldots \to E)$ compensating for the decay in any of the elementary relations. In other words, K maintains itself by changing its microstructure. (Actually, in an open system the elementary relations also change autonomously, without benefit of interaction with the environment, as a result of internal system dynamics missing in Matsuno's model.)

Looking at the sequence (6.9) of connected relations $\{A_j\}$, Matsuno then states that the probability that open system σ, when shut off from its environment over some short interval (t_0, t), can maintain that trajectory for $(1, \ldots, n)$, that is, can maintain the whole organizational structure K, is the double product of probabilities over all elementary relations j and time instants k:

$$P(t, t_0; K) = \prod_{k=1}^{n} \prod_{j} P(t, t_0; A_j^k) \qquad\qquad 6.11$$

The fact that each of the probabilities $P = P(\ldots; A_j^k)$ in Equation 6.11 can be written as

$$P = \exp(\ln P) = \exp[-(t - t_0)\left(\frac{-1}{(t-t_0)}\ln P\right)]$$

is then used in a limiting sense to study the behavior of $P(t, t_0; K)$ as the interval (t, t_0) is made very large, and to compare this with the behavior of some alternative structure, K'.

Reexpressing all of the probabilities in Equation 6.11 in exponential form as above gives

$$P(t, t_0; K) = \exp\left\{-(t - t_0)[\sum_k \sum_j \left(\frac{-1}{(t-t_0)}\ln P(t, t_0; A_j^k)\right)]\right\}$$

The double sum in brackets in the exponent, denoted by $W(K)$, measures the rate of decay of the connected relations. It is the sum of the decay rates of all the individual relations, that is, $-[\ln P(t, t_0; A_j^k)]/(t-t_0)$ for each $\{A_j^k\}$.

Now, says Matsuno, suppose open system σ with organizational structure K at a given time t_0 could alternatively maintain structure K', comprising the elementary relations $\{C_j^k\}, j = 1, 2, \ldots; k = 1, \ldots, m$. Which of these structures is "most likely to appear" as the time interval is made larger and larger, which effectively means "which structure is likely to adapt most effectively?"

To answer this question we compare the probabilities $P(\ldots; K')$ and $P(\ldots; K)$ and look at their limiting behavior; specifically, we consider the *survival* probability ratio as $(t - t_0)$ becomes large:

$$\lim_{(t-t_0) \to \infty} \frac{P(\ldots; K')}{P(\ldots; K)}.$$

The ratio

$$\frac{P(t, t_0; K')}{P(t, t_0; K)}$$

equals

$$\frac{\exp\left[-(t - t_0)\, W(K')\right]}{\exp\left[-(t - t_0)\, W(K)\right].}$$

If $W(K') - W(K)$ remains positive as $(t - t_0)$ becomes large, then $\exp\ -(t - t_0)\,[W(K') - W(K)]\ $ is driven to zero. In other words, the probability ratio approaches zero if $W(K) < W(K')$.

Hence, Matsuno concludes, the most likely structure K is the one that, over a long interval of time, minimizes rate $W(K)$ of decay of the set of connected relations in that structure, relative to the rates $W(K')$ of decay in the sets of connected relations in all alternative structures K'. That is, for an open system to remain stable against perturbations the rate of decay of the set of connected relations in it should be made as small as possible.

Remarks

1. Matsuno's paper is an interesting attempt to conceptualize, in system terms, just what is required to make an organizational structure survive in the long term, especially as the paper attempts to do so quantitatively.

2. At the same time his description of an open system in terms of "elementary relations" is of dubious validity. He states that these elementary relations "turn out to be . . . more fundamental . . . than [system] elements" in explaining system behavior, presumably because of his conclusion that it is the differing rates of decay of these connected relations in alternative organizational structures that determine which structure will maintain itself in the long run. But of course the network of relations constituting the organizational structure, which are to be reduced to elementary relations, cannot even be defined without first introducing the concept of system elements.

3. Matsuno says the relations that constitute the organizational structure can be "reduced" to elementary relations. But what would be examples of elementary relations in a business system? After reading his paper one is not clear. He states:

> Open systems comprising elementary relations and their sequential con-
> nections can autonomously evolve in a unidirectional manner if each
> elementary relation has room to adjust its own microstructure. Each
> elementary relation represents the intersection of various [individual]
> flows and their interlinks passing through it.

In the example he gives of a macroeconomic system the elementary relations are simply types of flows of goods and services per unit of time between economic units, measured in money. "Interlinks" do not appear
explicitly.

4. Matsuno states that the probability $P(t, t_0; K)$ does not depend on
whether the system interacts with its environment. It does seem intuitively
reasonable to say that if certain internal relations in an open system can be
maintained without interaction with the environment they can certainly be
maintained when the system is opened to the environment. It is less evident, however, that the probability $P(K)$ will be the same in both instances,
for the following reasons. First, environmental interactions may make it
easier to maintain the relations (hence increasing the value of P[K]), say by
providing information that confirms the system's earlier expectations. Second, if the environment is turbulent it may take longer than the interval $(t,
t_0)$ for the system to adjust its elementary relations (hence P[K] decreases).

5. A more general comment is that we need to put the process of adaptation in perspective. To have superior adaptive properties a firm must
selectively map the relevant environment into itself, which means into its
information or organizational structure. (As an open system, a firm's organizational and information structures are largely determined by the environment, although both must serve internal needs as well.) In the short run
this is probably for the most part a mapping of the environment into the information structure. In the long run, however, the firm's success in adapting critically depends on its ability to map the environment into its organizational structure. Matsuno's model does not take this into account. In control terms, where "variety" means the number of distinct elements in a set,
the above remark translates into saying that the law of requisite variety (for
a system to achieve a goal against a set of disturbances it must have at least
as great a variety as the variety in its environment) is limited to the short
run. Long-run regulation depends critically for its success on transforming
environmental variety into structure (Sahal 1982).

NOTES

1. Cyert and March (1963: 30), partition Y into subsets of "active" and
"passive" stakeholders. Membership of these sets will vary with the type of deci-

sion under consideration, the state of the system at the time, and over time. For example, many stockholders of system σ devote considerably less time to its affairs than do others. However, this "passive" group may become "active" if the payment demands they make on the system are resisted or postponed, or if the exogenous environment R becomes more turbulent. At any given time the set of "active" stakeholders may contain members drawn from both sets G and N; so may the "passive" set. The active–passive dichotomy simply means that, at a given time and state of the system, the latter group does not raise its demands on the system while the former does.

2. By "environmentally feasible" is meant actions that are consonant with the laws of nature and of society, and with the existing state of technology. E corresponds in Simon (1957: 175) to the constraint $H_j(x, y) = 0, j = 1, \ldots, k$, where x is a vector of contributions made by participants in the organization and y a vector of inducements received by these participants. See notes 3 and 5 for further details of Simon's scheme.

3. In Simon (1957: 175), D corresponds to the set of actions for which satisfaction function $S = S_i(x, y)$, for all i, is positive or zero. The following two notes describe more fully the similarities and differences between Simon's model and the one presented here.

4. One set of actions is said to be Pareto-superior to another if the utility of at least one individual (or interest group) is higher and the utility of none is lower. Thus if a set of actions x yields utility $u = (u_1, \ldots, u_{g+2})$ for the interest groups, and another set of actions x' yields utility $u' = (u'_1, \ldots, u'_{g+2})$, actions x are Pareto-superior to actions x' if

$$u_i \begin{cases} \geq u'_i \text{ for all } i, \text{ and} \\ > u'_i \text{ for at least one } i \end{cases}$$

A Pareto-superior set of actions may not be Pareto-optimal (see Chapter 7, "The Conditions For Pareto-Optimality").

5. The idea of a dominant interest group has its counterpart in Simon's model (1957: 173–74). Simon observes that "Theories of organization [0-theories], perhaps to a greater extent than the theory of the firm [F-theory], have been concerned not only with optimal solutions, but with the whole set of *viable* solutions— that is, solutions that permit the survival of the organization, e.g., in the theory of the firm, outputs that yield a positive profit." Consider an organization with an entrepreneur, one employee, and one customer. In F-theory the entrepreneur treats the other participants only as passive conditions to which he must adjust in finding the solution that is optimal to him. In 0-theory the participants are treated more symmetrically. Each participant is seen as receiving an *inducement* for his or her *contribution* to the organization (these are, respectively, sales revenue and costs of production for the entrepreneur, wages and labor services for the employee, goods and purchase price for the customer). It is postulated by Simon that each participant will remain in the organization so long as the satisfaction she obtains from her

inducements minus contributions, measured in terms of their utility to her, exceeds the satisfaction she could obtain elsewhere. "The zero point in such a 'satisfaction function' is defined, therefore, in terms of the opportunity cost of participation." Simon notes that the survival criterion will not, in general, yield a unique solution to the values of inducements and contributions (i.e., a unique set of viable solutions). Imposing the weak optimality condition that a viable solution is regarded as optimal if no further increase could be made in the net satisfaction of any participant without decreasing the net satisfaction of at least one other participant (the criterion of welfare economics referred to in Chapter 7) still does not guarantee a unique solution, in general. Simon therefore proposes imposing a stronger optimality condition, that is, to select the particular optimal (or rather viable) solution that maximizes the net satisfaction of one of the participants while leaving the net satisfactions of other participants equal to zero. The participant whose net satisfaction is maximized captures the entire "surplus" of satisfactions. In the traditional F-theory this is the entrepreneur. The idea of a dominant interest group in the systems model is closely analogous to Simon's idea of one interest group capturing the entire "surplus" of satisfactions.

REFERENCES

Ackoff, R.L. 1970. *A Concept of Corporate Planning.* New York: Wiley-Interscience.

_____. 1974. *Redesigning the Future.* New York: Wiley-Interscience.

Amey, L.R. and G.A. Whitmore. 1981. "Performance Measures for Sociotechnical Systems." In *Proceedings of International Congress on Applied Systems Research and Cybernetics,* pp. 1102–08, Acapulco, Mexico, December 1980. Oxford: Pergamon.

Ashby, W.R. 1952. *Design for a Brain.* London: Chapman & Hall.

Beer, S. 1969. "The Aborting Corporate Plan." *Perspectives of Planning* 395–422. See Jantsch 1969.

Bertalanffy, L. von. 1962. "General System Theory—a Critical Review." *General Systems* 7: 1–20.

Boulding, K.E. 1956. "General Systems Theory—the Skeleton of Science." *Management Science* 2: 197–208.

Buckley, W. 1967. *Sociology and Modern Systems Theory.* Englewood Cliffs, NJ: Prentice-Hall.

Buckley, W. 1968. "Society As a Complex Adaptive System." In *Modern Systems Research for the Behavioral Scientist,* edited by W. Buckley, pp. 490–513. Chicago: Aldine.

Bunge, M. 1979. *Treatise on Basic Philosophy,* vol. 4. Dordrecht, Holland: Reidel.

Cyert, R.M. and J.G. March. 1963. *A Behavioral Theory of the Firm.* Englewood Cliffs, NJ: Prentice-Hall.

Drucker, Peter F. 1958. "Business Objectives and Survival Needs: Notes on a Discipline of Business Enterprise." *Journal of Business* 31 (April): 81–90.

Emery, F.E. and E.L. Trist. 1965. "The Causal Texture of Organizational Environments." *Human Relations* 18: 21–32; reprinted in *Systems Thinking,* edited by F.E. Emery. Harmondsworth, England: Penguin, 1969.

Fama, E.F. 1980. "Agency Problems and the Theory of the Firm." *Journal of Political Economy* 88 (March): 288–307.

Forrester, J. 1969. "Planning under the Dynamic Influences of Complex Social Systems." In *Perspectives of Planning.* 235–54. See Jantsch 1969.

_____. 1975. "Counterintuitive Behavior of Social Systems." In *Collected Papers of J.W. Forrester,* chapter 14. Cambridge, MA: Wright-Allen Press.

Galbraith, J.K. 1967. *The New Industrial State.* London: Hamish Hamilton.

Hedberg, B. and S. Jönsson. 1978. "Designing Semi-Confusing Information Systems for Organizations in Changing Environments." *Accounting, Organizations and Society* 3: 47–64.

Hedberg, B., P.C. Nystrom, and W.H. Starbuck. 1976. "Camping on Seesaws: Prescriptions for a Self-Designing Organization." *Administrative Science Quarterly* (March): 41–65.

Hopwood, A.G. 1976. *Accounting and Human Behavior.* Englewood Cliffs, NJ: Prentice-Hall.

Ijiri, Y. 1965. *Management Goals and Accounting for Control.* Amsterdam: North-Holland.

Ijiri, Y. and E.C. Kelly. 1980. "Multidimensional Accounting and Distributed Data Bases: Their Implications for Organizations and Society." *Accounting, Organizations and Society* 5: 115–23.

Jantsch, E. 1969. *Perspectives of Planning.* Paris: OECD.

Lawler, E.E., III and J.G. Rhode. 1976. *Information and Control in Organizations.* Pacific Palisades, CA: Goodyear.

Matsuno, K. 1981. "Dynamics of Relations, Sequential Connectedness, and Feedback Loops in Open Systems." *I.E.E.E. Transactions on Systems, Man, and Cybernetics* SMC-11 (April): 310–12.

Mesarovic, M.D., D. Macko, and Y. Takahara. 1970. *Theory of Hierarchical Multilevel Systems.* New York: Academic Press.

Mowshowitz, A. 1976. *The Conquest of Will: Information Processing in Human Affairs.* Reading, MA: Addison-Wesley.

Pappis, C.P. and E.H. Mamdani. 1977. "A Fuzzy Logic Controller for a Traffic Junction." *I.E.E.E. Transactions on Systems, Man, and Cybernetics* SMC-7 (October): 707–17.

Penrose, Edith T. 1959. *The Theory of the Growth of the Firm.* Oxford: Blackwell.

Rothschild, K.W. 1947. "Price Theory and Oligopoly." *Economic Journal* 57: 299–320.

Sahal, D. 1982. "Structure and Self-Organization." *Behavioral Science* 27: 249–58.

Simon, H.A. 1957. "A Comparison of Organisation Theories." In *Models of Man,* edited by H.A. Simon, chapter 10. New York: Wiley.

7
Optimality and the Systems Approach

In the spirit of scientific inquiry, the next two chapters will be devoted to trying to refute the case that has been presented for the necessity of adopting a systems approach—to planning in particular, and to business problems in general. More specifically, we have noted earlier that not all things are systems: There are aggregates whose parts do not interact, and we cannot dismiss the possible existence of small elementary objects that do not contain at least two different connected things. For all the remaining cases where the object of study is a system we ask the question "Is the systems approach universally *necessary*, or are there cases where the first two aspects of systems referred to in the Appendix, namely the interrelatedness of components, and more generally *structure*, can be taken into account without the necessity of dealing with problems holistically?"

In this chapter we examine the question of economic efficiency and optimality from a general equilibrium point of view, to see whether there are any circumstances in which a systems approach is unnecessary or redundant. The discussion will accordingly be theoretical and methodological.[1]

In the following chapter we examine a number of the main criticisms leveled against planning as a worthwhile activity. That is, we try to answer the critics, the anti-planners. As we stated in Chapter 1 (under "Correcting Past Mistakes") this is necessary in view of the widespread lack of acceptance of planning.

GENERAL EQUILIBRIUM OF AN ECONOMIC SYSTEM

Consider the field of economic theory from a systems point of view, particularly from the point of view of those aspects of systems referred to in the Appendix (sections "What a Symptom Is" and "Structure: the Second Aspect of Systems") namely interrelatedness of components and structure. An economy is a system, composed of many interacting economic agents. In a market (free enterprise, capitalist) or mixed economy the price system performs the function of coordinating many individual decisions, for example, it takes into account the interactions between all the buyers and sellers in a single market caused by scarcity. This aspect of systems is performed by an "invisible hand," or at least it would be if all economic agents were price takers. We also know that in some (but not all) circumstances accounting or shadow prices can perform the task of allocating resources within a single decentralized firm in such a way that all interactions between components of the firm are duly taken into account.

Economic theory develops conditions for resource allocation and price determination throughout an economy on the assumption that all economic agents (consumers, producers) are optimizers. The analysis assumes that the optimal position is also the equilibrium position, that is, that any departure from the optimum will naturally bring forth forces tending to reestablish an optimal position. The price system plays the central role in solving this system of problems, and under certain conditions can lead to an optimal allocation of resources throughout the economy. There are, however, exceptions: it will do so only if (i) there are no interdependencies, leading to external economies and/or diseconomies between consumers or producers; (ii) there are no increasing returns to scale among producers; (iii) there are no market imperfections; and (iv) there are no significant indivisibilities in resource inputs.

Partial Equilibrium Analysis

The equilibrium analysis of economics is performed at different levels of generality: for the individual consumer or producer (i.e., firm), for a single market, and finally the simultaneous equilibrium of all markets, including the market for money.

The individual consumer allocates his expenditures on products (i.e., goods and services) to maximize his utility, subject to his budget constraint. The data (givens) of this problem are the consumer's utility function, his income or more precisely his initial endowment of resources, including time, and the prices of all products. The variables are the quantities purchased. The individual producer seeks to maximize profit, given the technology (production function), any input limitations, and the prices of all inputs and outputs.[2] The variables here are the quantities of inputs purchased and of outputs produced and sold.

At the level of a single market a single equilibrium price is determined by assuming optimizing behavior on the part of all consumers and producers, with the further condition that the market must be cleared—that aggregate demand must equal aggregate supply. The data here are those described above for every consumer and producer, including all prices except that of the output (product) under consideration. The variables are the price of this product and purchases and sales of the product by every consumer and producer. In the case of a market for a factor of production, incomes of consumers, determined by the productive services they sell, are an additional variable.

Note that in determining the equilibrium of a consumer or producer all prices are treated as parameters (i.e., givens), while in determining the equilibria of single markets every factor or product price is treated as a variable in analyzing its own market and as a given in the analysis of all other markets.

But of course this *partial equilibrium* analysis of one economic unit or one market at a time ignores all interdependencies—and all the pieces we have been talking about are interrelated. Thus the incomes of consumers that constrain the demand for products are earned by the sale of labour and other services to producers, and hence depend on the prices of these factors. Under perfect competition the latter are determined by supply and demand in factor markets. But producers' demands for the productive services supplied by factors depend on the prices at which they can sell their outputs. The latter depend on supply and demand conditions in product markets, and demand for products depends on consumers' incomes, hence on factor prices and partly also on profits, which are determined only after both input and output prices are determined. Different factor markets and product markets are also interrelated; in fact in the final analysis all markets are interrelated. Thus, in factor markets the demand for labor depends on production levels and also on the quantities of capital and other factors combining with labor, while in the product markets the demand for one product depends on the prices of other products.

Hence the piecemeal solutions offered by partial equilibrium analysis fail to take account of the system properties of the economy, specifically the interrelatedness of its components with each other and with the rest of the world; in a word, they ignore the system's structure, which comprises these two sets of relations. If we want to determine a real equilibrium of an economic system it must be a *general equilibrium,* in which all prices and quantities are determined simultaneously. Partial analysis is only justified if it can be shown, as a matter of fact, that the effects of interactions between a single economic unit and the rest of the economy (the rest of the world outside of the particular economic unit or market in a full general equilibrium analysis) are relatively small, such as when there is very weak substitutability or complementarity between a pair of products or a pair of factors, that is, when they are not strongly coupled.

General Equilibrium Analysis

In economic theory general equilibrium analysis provides a link between microeconomics, concerned with the behavior of single economic units within an economy (individual consumers, firms, or industries), and macroeconomics, which studies the behavior of the economy as a whole. That is to say, general equilibrium theory studies the behavior of an economy as a whole (aggregate level of output and employment, price level, and so on) but using microeconomic tools, that is, in terms not of aggregates but of individual decision makers, markets, and resources (inputs and outputs). In its fullest development the analysis seeks to determine not only the equilibrium behavior of a multimarket economy, including the money market, but includes also a government sector (federal, state, and local governments and all public and private agencies that set the rules by which consumers, producers, and markets must operate) and a foreign sector representing transactions with the rest of the world. It would also allow for the fact that some products are sold, not to final consumers directly, but to other producers to be incorporated in final products.

There are several points to be noted about the above discussion. A static long-run general equilibrium of an economy as described need not be *unique*; there may be other prices and quantities that also constitute an equilibrium state of the economy. Second, such an equilibrium *exists*, in the sense that it is possible and can be guaranteed, for a perfectly competitive economy in which there are no increasing returns to scale or indivisibilities, for most initial distributions of wealth. It *may* exist, but cannot be guaranteed to do so, for the exceptions mentioned. Finally, we are still ignoring the fact that an economy is a dynamic system. A dynamic general equilibrium model would have to include saving, inventories of various kinds, and exogenous disturbances, and would show the effects of these disturbances and the dynamic adjustment processes they set in motion, and hence the time paths of the prices and quantities in all markets.

To sum up, given economic agents (consumers, producers, and a coercive agent, government) and the environment of the economy, the availability of resources, markets (or a central planning agency performing the same functions), the choice criteria of the economic agents, and states of the economy (which could be represented by a matrix displaying the behavior of all economic agents[3]), it is possible, at least in theory, to take account of the economy's structure. This consists of all the interrelationships between its parts and between the economy and its environment. It is also possible to determine whether a simultaneous long-run equilibrium of all markets and economic agents in the economy exists (is possible), whether it will actually be attained automatically, and whether it will be maintained (is dynamically stable).

IS GENERAL EQUILIBRIUM ANALYSIS EQUIVALENT TO A SYSTEMS APPROACH?

General equilibrium analysis is the part of economics that tries to determine whether all the pieces (economic agents, markets, government) fit together in a way in which the behavior of every consumer is compatible with that of every other consumer and every producer, and compatible with every market being in a state of (long-run) equilibrium.[4] It attempts to take account of all the interactions, what we have called "structure" in the Appendix. We now ask whether this analysis is fully systemic.

Apart from the usual kind of statement about the unreality of much of the content of economic theory (perfectly competitive markets, the "invisible hand," economic agents as optimizers, the obsession with equilibrium states, untestability of so many economic hypotheses—in other words that general equilibrium theory is largely composed of mythical or defunct entities), we may still ask whether, as a deductive system, it satisfies all the requirements of the systems approach.

Taking the most generous view—a fully developed, dynamic general equilibrium model that includes government and a foreign sector, all of which is seldom seen in the literature—the answer is "not entirely." To begin with, the system (a particular economy) is not correctly specified, its boundaries not correctly drawn. As noted in the second section of the Appendix, this would require that any elements in the rest of the world (other economies, governments, or business enterprises) that interact strongly with the economy in question at a particular time should be regarded as part of the system at that time. In practice (i.e., in national economic planning) they are not; and this misspecification of sociotechnical systems such as economies and business enterprises is as widespread and serious a failure to meet the requirements of the systems approach as the failure to take full and explicit account of the remaining elements of structure (one-way couplings).

Second, in seeking to take account of all interactions within and between economies the general equilibrium model does not go far enough. There is imbalance in its representation of structure, for while internal couplings may be reasonably well represented and, subject to the point made above, so may couplings with other economic systems, the economy is not represented as a subsystem of society, strongly coupled with the politics, sociology, and culture of that society, and possibly with those of other societies (Bunge 1981). These couplings are missing.

Thus in seeking to solve simultaneously a set of interrelated problems the economists' general equilibrium analysis fails on at least two scores: The system is not correctly specified, and its structure, in the systems sense of the term, is only partially represented; outer couplings are confined to the economic realm, and a number of strong noneconomic couplings are ignored.

EFFICIENCY AND OPTIMALITY OF AN ECONOMIC SYSTEM

From this discussion of the general equilibrium model we go on now to discuss the only other part of economic theory in which the economy as a whole is modeled in detail rather than in terms of aggregates. This normative aspect of economics is called *welfare economics*.

Economists here try to evaluate the *social* desirability of alternative allocations of resources, asking in what circumstances one particular configuration of an economy may be considered "better" or "worse" than another, adopting a welfare criterion and establishing the conditions for achieving an efficient allocation of resources throughout the economy and an optimal configuration. The basic assumptions of this analysis are value judgments that one is free to accept or reject: There is no way of testing their truth or falsity.

The approach usually taken is to say that only individuals can judge their own welfare or "well-offness," which is measured in terms of utility, and whether they are better or worse off in one situation than in another. We will describe a change taking place in an economy, and the resulting state of the economy, as *efficient* if the change *could* make every individual better off, and will call a situation *optimal* if no one can *in fact* be made better off without making someone else worse off, that is, an optimal state is an efficient state that actually occurs. This is the welfare criterion called *Pareto-optimality*. It is a very weak criterion, because (i) many of the economic changes that take place make some people better off and some worse off, and (ii) so far no method has been devised for making interpersonal welfare comparisons in order to rank different states of the economy with respect to their social desirability. The Pareto criterion avoids making such interpersonal comparisons, but thereby becomes useless for evaluating type (i) situations.

The Conditions for Pareto-Optimality

For a state of the economy to be Pareto-optimal three conditions must be met. The first two relate to the allocation of products and resources (factors of production) among consumers and producers, respectively. The third relates to the composition of output. The latter can only be optimal if the first two are efficient. The conditions are: For a given distribution of wealth,

1. The allocation of products among consumers, to be efficient, should be such that the marginal rate of substitution in consumption between any two products, with leisure included as a product, should be the same for all consumers
2. To be efficient, the allocation of resources among producers (firms) should be such that the marginal rate of substitution in production between any two resources should be the same for all producers, whether they are producing the same or different products
3. If conditions 1 and 2 are met, the optimal composition of output will be such that the marginal rate of transformation between any pair of products is equal to the marginal rate of substitution between the same pair of products in consumption.[5]

These conditions are based on a number of assumptions: an absence of externalities in consumption (as would be introduced by interdependent utility functions and public goods) and in production (no external economies or diseconomies). Moreover, they are only necessary conditions; the second-order conditions must also be satisfied for all consumers and producers. Finally, these are the conditions for static efficiency and optimality. Resource allocation over time may introduce further complications (e.g., intertemporal externalities).

If an economy fails to meet any of these three conditions for one or more inputs or products, or fails to satisfy the underlying assumptions, it may still be possible for it to achieve Pareto-optimality through compensation, the imposition of appropriate unit and/or lump sum taxes and subsidies. Similarly, if the state of an economy is initially Pareto-optimal, and a change benefits some individuals but harms others, it would be possible to maintain efficiency and optimality if the gainers were to pay the losers exactly the amount by which they were worse off, and themselves remain better off (the Hicks–Kaldor compensation principle).[6]

. Economists have shown that, in general, perfect competition is the only market structure compatible with achieving economic efficiency and Pareto-optimality. The same result could in principle be attained in a centrally planned or a partly decentralized economy by the use of appropriate shadow prices, although it would be much more difficult (even impossible) administratively than by means of the price system in a market economy. Imperfection in any market generally precludes attainment of optimality. The effect of market imperfections, and of various distortions introduced by government (mainly through taxes), is that even if output is produced and allocated efficiently (conditions 1 and 2 are met), the composition of output (condition 3) will be suboptimal. An exception is provided by the market form known as bilateral monopoly *if* the monopolist and monopsonist jointly maximize their profits. Perfect competition in all markets is not, in itself, sufficient to guarantee efficiency and Pareto-optimality, however. There must, in addition, be no limitations on the availability of resources to individual producers, no resource indivisibilities, and no increasing returns to scale. Thus perfect competition, under suitable conditions, is one means of ensuring that the conditions are met. In principle, central planning or partial decentralization could achieve the same end using shadow prices.

The Systems Approach Partly Redundant

If conditions 1, 2 and 3 are met for all products and resources it would be possible to attain Pareto-optimality on a piecemeal basis, because of the simple proportionality of the efficiency and optimality conditions. That is, if the configuration of the economy is Pareto-optimal it is unnecessary to take account of all the interrelatedness by general equilibrium analysis. The Pareto conditions could be attained by considering economic agents and markets on a partial equilibrium, piecemeal basis. But the order of these piecemeal operations would have to be: 1 and 2, then condition 3. Hence the structure aspect of systems appears to be redundant here, subject to the qualifications mentioned in the previous section.

The findings earlier in this chapter ("Partial Equilibrium Analysis") and in this section can be summarized by saying that a piecemeal rather than a systems approach, while not valid in general, is valid if the effects of interrelationships are relatively weak, or if the state of the economy is Pareto-optimal. Bear in mind, however, that the assumptions underlying Pareto-optimality, by disallowing any kind of externality (including the intertemporal kind), eliminate much of the problem that the systems approach specifically addresses.

SECOND-BEST SITUATIONS

The case we have been discussing is, of course, mythical, as will readily be seen by considering the underlying assumptions of the Paretian conditions, the fact that there has never been a perfectly competitive economy, and the numerous distortions introduced by government policies. In the real world the Pareto conditions are violated in myriad ways, and a "second best" situation exists (it is so named because Pareto-optimality is considered the ideal state). If one or more of the Pareto conditions is violated, and cannot be fulfilled by means of compensation or other means as explained earlier, can a second-best position be attained by satisfying the remaining Pareto conditions? The theory of second best says no: If one or more of the Pareto conditions cannot be met, it is neither necessary nor desirable, *in general*, to satisfy the remaining conditions. One may not expect *any* of the Pareto conditions to be required for the attainment of a second best optimum (Lipsey and Lancaster 1956). This would suggest that in second best situations a piecemeal approach is no longer valid. Rather, we would adopt a general equilibrium approach in search of a second best optimum, with the violations included in the problem as additional constraints.

An Example of Second Best

A simple example will illustrate the point. Consider a closed economy with a single consumer, a single producer (and production function), n products, and a fixed supply x^0 of one resource not desired by the consumer. The necessary conditions for Pareto-optimality are derived by maximizing the consumer's utility, subject to the production function. Form the Lagrangean

$$L = F(q_1 \ldots \ldots q_n) - \lambda\, G(q_1 \ldots \ldots q_n, x^0),$$

where F is the consumer's utility function and G the production function. Setting the partial derivatives equal to zero we have

$$\frac{\partial L}{\partial q_i} = \frac{\partial F}{\partial q_i} - \lambda \frac{\partial G}{\partial q_i} = 0. \qquad i = 1 \ldots \ldots n \tag{1}$$

Writing F_i for the first partial derivative on the RHS, G_i for the second, and eliminating the multiplier, it follows that

$$\frac{F_i}{F_j} = \frac{G_i}{G_j} \qquad i, j = 1 \ldots \ldots n\text{-}1, \tag{2}$$

where the nth product is chosen as numéraire (usually money). If quantities (and prices) are such that (1) is satisfied for all i, the marginal rate of substitution in consumption for every pair of products will equal the marginal rate of transformation between the same pair of products, and the solution is Pareto-optimal.

Now suppose that something prevents attainment of one of the conditions represented in (1) for products 1 and n. We could represent this situation by assuming that

$$\frac{F_1}{F_n} = k \frac{G_1}{G_n} \qquad\qquad 7.3$$

where $k \neq 1$ is a positive constant differing from the optimal value of λ found by solving Equation 7.1. The necessary conditions for a second-best optimum would then be obtained by adding Equation 7.3 to the Langrangean as an additional constraint,[7] and re-solving. The expression becomes:

$$ L = F(\cdot) - \lambda \, G(\cdot) - \mu \left(\frac{F_1}{F_n} - k \, \frac{G_1}{G_n} \right) \qquad 7.4 $$

where μ is a second Lagrangean multiplier, and where the λ and μ in Equation 7.4 will usually both differ from the λ in Equation 7.1. Setting the partial derivatives equal to zero, the second-best solution (the necessary conditions for a maximum of L) corresponding to Equation 7.2 is

$$ F_i - \lambda \, G_i - \mu \left[\frac{F_n F_{1_i} - F_1 F_{n_i}}{F^2_n} - k \, \frac{G_n G_{1_i} - G_1 G_{n_i}}{G^2_n} \right] = 0 $$

$$ i = 1 \ldots n \qquad\qquad 7.5 $$

where

$$ F_{1_i} = \frac{\partial^2 F}{\partial x_1 \, \partial x_i} $$

and

$$ F^2_n = \frac{\partial^2 F}{\partial x^2_n} $$

The authors of the general theory of second best (Lipsey and Lancaster 1956) concluded from this that, since in general nothing is known *a priori* about the signs or the magnitudes of the cross partial derivatives F_{1i}, F_{ni}, G_{1i} and G_{ni}, nothing can be said in general about the direction or magnitude of the secondary departures from the Pareto conditions necessitated by non-fulfillment of one condition, and we should not expect any of the Pareto conditions to be required for the attainment of a second-best optimum.

Later work by Davis and Whinston (1965), however, has produced a counter-argument. These authors have shown that if the functions F and G are, by an appropriate numbering of products, both weakly separable[8] into those that violate a Pareto condition and those that do not, for example, if the violations relate to Q_i, $i \leq j$, in consumption and Q_i, $i \leq k$, in production:

$$F = F[F^A(q_1 \ldots \ldots .q_j), F^B(q_{j+1} \ldots \ldots .q_n)]$$

$$G = G[G^A(q_1 \ldots \ldots q_k), G^B(q_{k+1} \ldots \ldots q_n, x^0)] = 0$$

then the Pareto conditions still hold for all products numbered $i >$ max (j, k). This is because under the assumption of separability[9] of F and G

$$F_{ij} = G_{ij} = 0 \qquad i \neq j$$

(i.e., all the cross partial derivatives vanish), so that Equation 7.5 for a second-best optimum reduces to

$$F_i - \lambda G_i = 0 \qquad i = 2 \ldots \ldots n - 1. \qquad\qquad 7.6$$

Since Equation 7.6 has the same form as Equation 7.1, the Pareto conditions should be satisfied for products 2, ... , $n - 1$, and for a second-best solution a departure from the Pareto conditions is necessary only for the first and nth products.

Second-Best and the Systems Approach

Where does this discussion leave us with respect to the relevance of a piecemeal versus general equilibrium approach in second-best situations, assuming henceforth that a general equilibrium approach may be equated with a systems approach? Accepting the analysis of Davis and Whinston, in which the earlier "general" conclusion of Lipsey and Lancaster appears as a special case, we are concerned with situations in which one or more of the Pareto conditions is violated (and Pareto-optimality cannot be achieved by means of compensation), and where the utility functions (F) of consumers and production functions (G) of producers are (i) separable or (ii) nonseparable.

In the case where they are nonseparable the attainment of a second-best welfare optimum requires breaking all the remaining Pareto conditions. The problem, as we have shown, is to determine a new set of decision rules that will best compensate for the effects of the non-Pareto behavior. A piecemeal approach is no longer valid; a general equilibrium approach in search of a second-best optimum, with the violations added as additional constraints, is required. The entire set of functionally interrelated economic units must be considered as a whole. The Lipsey-Lancaster conclusion holds for this case, which supports the necessity of a systems approach.

If, on the other hand, the utility and production functions are separable, the analysis suggests that we can decompose the problem, and that a piecemeal approach remains valid (and a systems approach is redundant) for those products or economic units for which the Pareto conditions are satisfied, *provided* that none of these products ($Q_2 \ldots . Q_{n-1}$ in our example) is closely related[10] to the violators (products Q_1 and Q_n). This is because, as shown in Equation 7.6, the second-best problem has the same form as the model from which the Pareto conditions are derived, and hence the simple proportionality of the optimality conditions is retained for the conforming units (or products).

SUMMARY

In the Appendix and throughout earlier chapters we have repeatedly stressed the need for a systems approach—to planning by organizations, and more generally to problem-solving whenever the problem relates to a system. In this chapter we have focused particularly on those aspects of systems having to do with interrelatedness: of the parts, and of the system and its environment, all of which are captured in the term *system structure*. The systems approach, it will be recalled, involves a marriage of analysis and synthesis. In addition to studying the behavior of the parts it is necessary to see how the whole behaves, because the interaction of the parts has a synergistic effect. To this extent a piecemeal approach to problem solving, that is, analysis without synthesis, is the antithesis of the systems approach.

We turned to the field of economics to examine the manner of its problem solving, and more specifically to see to what extent it adopts a systems approach. Our particular purpose was to see whether there were any instances in which a systems approach, while not patently inappropriate, was redundant in solving the problems of economic organizations.

Our review noted, first, that in a market economy the price system performs the task of coordinating many individual decisions, taking account of all the relationships and interrelationships caused by scarcity. A centrally planned or only partly decentralized economy could achieve the same result by the use of appropriate shadow prices. But scarcity is only one of the causes of inter-connectedness; a systems approach must deal with all of them.

Considering an economy as a system, we were able to find only two cases in the whole of economic theory where the economy is treated holistically *and* at the same time in sufficient detail to permit analysis of the behavior of its basic units, individual consumers, firms, and markets. These are general equilibrium analysis and welfare economics. Disregarding the unrealistic assumptions and other abstractions on which these two normative theories are founded and regarding them simply as logico-deductive systems[11], we asked to what extent they succeeded in following a systems approach, and whether the latter was indeed necessary in all cases.

Ostensibly, full general equilibrium analysis takes into account all the interrelations between economic units, between the government and private sectors, and between the economy and the rest of the world in a simultaneous determination of long-run equilibrium prices and resource allocations. The analysis, which is static but could be made dynamic, is subject to a number of restrictive assumptions (an absence of external economies or diseconomies, increasing returns to scale, indivisibilities, market imperfections), in addition to which economists lack precise information on consumers' tastes and the technological possibilities open to producers. Economists do not, however, usually solve these decision problems (of consumers, producers, markets) simultaneously, but on a piecemeal basis, holding everything not under the particular economic unit's control constant, hence ignoring many of the economy's system properties. Such partial analyses are only justified if the effects of the interactions that are ignored are relatively small.

The economist's general equilibrium model is not free of shortcomings when judged from a systems point of view. For, apart from the fact that it is usually not made dynamic and is out of touch with reality in many of its underlying assumptions and concepts, it draws the boundaries of the system incorrectly by failing to treat as system components those external entities that *interact* with the system. Nor, strictly, does it represent structure completely by concentrating on the interrelationships between *economic* entities, because the economy is a subsystem of society, strongly linked with other subsystems of that society (its politics, sociology, and culture, for example) and possibly with those of other societies.[12] We cannot say, therefore, that the general equilibrium approach of economics is entirely equivalent to a systems approach.

Welfare economics is an attempt to discover whether one state of an economy is "better" or "worse" than another for any given initial distribution of wealth. An economy is regarded from a social point of view, and the analysis is used to answer questions about public economic policy alternatives, judged according to their effects on the welfare of the community, measured in terms of utility. Conditions are derived for achieving an efficient and optimal allocation of resources among consumers and producers and an optimal composition of output for the economy (the conditions for maximizing social welfare for a given distribution of wealth). The most commonly used criterion for establishing such conditions is the Pareto criterion, which says that a particular policy or state of the economy is optimal if no one can be made better off without making someone else worse off. Pareto-optimality cannot be attained unless the allocation of resources between consumers and producers is efficient. The conditions for Pareto-optimality are technical requirements that are ideology-free, being equally applicable to market, centrally planned, or partly decentralized economies, and that they make no judgment regarding the "ideal" distribution of wealth.

While not of particular interest practically because of its high level of abstraction, and the fact that the Pareto criterion cannot pronounce on the many changes that make some individuals better off and some worse off, the case of welfare economics is nevertheless interesting from a methodological point of view, for it shows that a systems approach is redundant if all the conditions for Pareto-optimality are satisfied. In this case the nature of the Pareto conditions permits the use of a piecemeal approach. As with general equilibrium analysis, however, the restrictive assumptions underlying the Pareto conditions qualify this last remark.

If one or more of the Pareto conditions (with their underlying assumptions) is not met we have a second-best situation. Second best is the typical situation in the real world. In such situations the necessity of a systems approach (with which we are now roughly equating a general equilibrium approach) depends on whether or not we can partition products into those that satisfy the Pareto consumption and production conditions and those that do not. In the former case a piecemeal approach remains valid for the Pareto-conforming products, and only the violating products need depart from the Pareto conditions. In the latter case, however, a second-best solution requires breaking all the Pareto conditions, and this solution must be sought simultaneously for all products.

Based on one discipline, economics, our review found no instances where a systems approach would be wrong, only some cases where, because of the structure of the problem, it is unnecessary. Obversely, a piecemeal approach, while not valid in general for dealing with problems of systems, can be valid in two situations that we mentioned.

The implications for national economic planning and policy making are at best suggestive rather than practically helpful, due to the abstract nature of the analysis, the weakness of the Pareto criterion, and the huge computation problem involved even for a wholly or largely decentralized economy. In our second-best world it might provide advice to governments in selecting second-best policies that introduce distortions designed to offset other distortions that they cannot or do not wish to eliminate (Lancaster 1969: 274).

NOTES

1. As Quirk and Saposnik (1968: 3) observe, "The highly abstract nature of economic theory is particularly evident in general equilibrium analysis, at least partially because . . . the number of variables . . . is arbitrarily large."

2. It is sometimes thought, with regard to the dual role of an individual as both consumer and producer, that the criteria of utility maximization for consumers and profit maximization for producers may involve an inconsistency when the same individual fulfills both roles. However, when properly interpreted, the two criteria are mutually consistent. See Quirk and Saposnik (1968: 34–36).

3. That is, the concept of state of the economy means a listing of the commodity (product) bundles chosen by each consumer and the input–output combinations chosen by each firm. If X is an $n \times s$ matrix describing the former and Y an $n \times r$ matrix describing the latter, a state of the economy would be represented by the $n \times (r + s)$ matrix $Z = [X, Y]$.

4. In the case of a centrally planned economy the corresponding statement would be whether it is *feasible* to fit all the pieces together, that is, whether the planned outputs are actually achievable with the given resources and technology.

5. The marginal rate of substitution (MRS) at a point between two products Q_1 and Q_2, in consumption, and utility function $U = f(q_1, q_2)$, is

$$-\frac{dq_2}{dq_1} = \frac{\partial f}{\partial q_1} \bigg/ \frac{\partial f}{\partial q_2},$$

that is, it is the ratio of the change in the quantity of one product to the consequent change in the other product necessary to remain on the same indifference curve, the slope of the indifference curve at a point. The marginal rate of substitution in production is defined similarly, with isoquant replacing consumer indifference curve. For the production function $q = f(x_1, x_2)$ for two variable inputs X_1 and X_2, the MRS in production at a point is

$$-\frac{dx_2}{dq_1} = \frac{\partial f}{\partial x_1} \Big/ \frac{\partial f}{\partial x_2}$$

The marginal rate of transformation (MRT) relates to the transformation, or production possibility, curve of a producer, and is the slope of this curve at a point. For the transformation curve $x^0 = h(q_1, q_2)$, x^0 being a given quantity of input X, the MRT at a point is

$$-\frac{dq_2}{dq_1} = \frac{\partial h}{\partial q_1} \Big/ \frac{\partial h}{\partial q_2}$$

6. The compensation principle, in any of its numerous versions, does not represent a logically consistent technique for extending the scope of the Pareto welfare ranking, however, since a ranking based on this principle is not necessarily transitive (Arrow 1951: 44–45).

7. Since the addition of a constraint cannot increase the value of the function to be maximized, the solution will necessarily be Pareto-inferior.

8. A function $F(q_1, \ldots, q_n)$ is separable if and only if $F(q_1, \ldots, q_n) = F_1(q_1) + F_2(q_2) + \ldots + F_n(q_n)$.

9. Davis and Whinston (1965) points out that, while separability is a sufficient condition for their result, the same result would be obtained even if the functions were nonseparable if the relevant cross partial derivatives happen to be zero at the optimum, or are nonzero but offsetting. The functions F and G will be separable if there are no externalities in consumption or production, respectively.

10. Consider the partial derivative for q_i, which appears in Equation 7.5. The term in square brackets shows the effect of the violated Pareto conditions. What Davis and Whinston say, in effect, is that if the value of this term is small relative to the first two terms, the violated conditions may safely be ignored in planning for products $Q_2, \ldots, Q_{n-1}$.

11. A theory is a system of propositions, hence a conceptual system, held together by the relation of deducibility and a common subject matter (Bunge 1981).

12. For example, participants in the OECD Conference on Social Policies in the 1980s (October 20–23, 1980) saw present societies facing formidable dilemmas: widespread loss of confidence in the capacity of the state to deliver either full employment or welfare services, tax revolts and anti-bureaucratic movements of both the right and the left, and some evidence of the emergence of new values in society seeking alternatives to the established pattern of state provision for welfare. Their diagnosis of the problem underlined the need to view economic and social problems together (*The Welfare State in Crisis*. Paris: OECD, September 1981).

REFERENCES

Arrow, K.J. 1951. *Social Choice and Individual Values.* New York: Wiley.

Bunge, M. 1981. "Some Methodological Problems of Economics." Paper presented to Conference on Mathematical Economics and Public Policy, University of Sussex, March.

Davis, O.A. and A.B. Whinston. 1965. "Welfare Economics and the Theory of Second Best." *Review of Economic Studies* 32: 1–14.

Henderson, J.M. and R.E. Quandt. 1980. *Micro-Economic Theory: A Mathematical Approach,* 3rd ed., chapters 9–11. New York: McGraw-Hill.

Lancaster, K. 1969. *Introduction to Modern Micro-Economics,* chapters 9–11. Chicago: Rand McNally.

Lipsey, R.G. and K. Lancaster. 1956. "The General Theory of Second Best." *Review of Economic Studies* 24 (December): 11–32.

Quirk, J. and R. Saposnik. 1968. *Introduction to General Equilibrium Theory and Welfare Economics.* New York: McGraw-Hill.

8
Answering the Critics
of Planning

Efficiency in the operation of firms ceases to be purely productive efficiency; it involves efficiency in prediction as well. . . . A rational production plan includes very importantly . . . plans about the future; and similarly with consumption plans.

(Arrow 1974)

INTRODUCTION

There is a considerable body of opinion among business management and some in the academic community that is strongly against planning. Much of the academic criticism is directed at planning for a whole society (national and regional social planning or national economic planning) and only to a lesser extent at corporate planning. We will consider all the arguments against planning, whether national or corporate. For the most part the reference point for these criticisms is present planning practice, although some attack even the systemic, adaptive, learning, and purposeful aspects of planning advocated in earlier chapters. Although most of the arguments are against planning altogether (Ackoff's inactivist or nihilist philosophy of planning), we will need to keep in mind other philosophies (reactivist: planning favored, but not systemic; preactivist: systemic planning favored, but the system not regarded as purposeful; interactivist: planning should be systemic, adaptive, learning, and purposeful, and short-term planning is justified, but not long-term). Since we have argued (a) that planning is a necessary and important part of the management process for an open system, and that (b) the particular features of business enterprise (sociotechnical) systems suggest that planning should be approached in a particular way, we need to consider these opposing views carefully.

It is hoped that the list of arguments presented against planning, wholly or in part, while not exhaustive, includes the most important ones. The order of presentation is somewhat random, and no attempt has been made to separate criticisms relating to plan preparation and revision from those relating to plan implementation, since many of the arguments cover both.

To keep matters in perspective, while there is evidence that many managers are not "sold" on the importance of planning, there is also some evidence that attitudes toward planning, at national and corporate levels, have been changing. As stated in Chapter 1 ("Acceptance of Planning"), planning is no longer held in disrepute at the national level in Western societies or associated with nonmarket economies (and a certain political ideology). Nor is it now so often assumed that planning carries with it the concomitant of strong central government or a highly centralized management style. Some of the recent changes in attitudes include elements of the systemic approach to planning: a relatively greater attachment to long-term planning and strategic planning (Ansoff 1976–77) and, in government, PPBS.

PATHOLOGIES OF PLANNING

We begin with two related arguments: "Planning fails everywhere it has been tried," and "Can it be rational to fail?" (Wildavsky 1973: 128). The failure of national economic planning, he claims, is most evident in the developing countries of the world, but the results are no different in the developed countries (e.g., France [Wildavsky 1971] and Japan [Miyazaki 1970]). "Nothing seems more reasonable than planning," says Wildavsky. "The reasonable man plans ahead . . . seeks to avoid future evils by anticipating them . . . tries to obtain a more desirable future by working toward it in the present." Nevertheless planning fails everywhere; and this surely is not rational. Everyone will agree that an organization may sometimes succeed without planning, and fail despite planning. "But suppose . . . the failures of planning . . . *as presently constituted* . . . are not peripheral or accidental, but integral to its very nature" (italics added).

Addressing first the argument that the very nature of planning, as currently practiced, guarantees that it will fail, we are bound to agree that there is a high probability that this will be so. The conventional ("old") approach to planning, at whatever level, is unlikely to be successful because:

(i) It does not treat the organization (whether economy or firm) as a system. Piecemeal planning runs grave risks if system components and different planning periods are strongly interrelated. There is also a high probability that such planning does not correctly define the system being planned for.

(ii) It does not give sufficient attention to the environment, and to the need to selectively map the environment into the system, as information or (organizational) structure.

(iii) It is not sufficiently long term, and there is now ample evidence that planning for social systems that is too short term often brings unfavorable long-term consequences (Forrester 1969: 237–54; 1975) and that social systems behave "deviously and diabolically."

(iv) It does not give sufficient recognition to the fact that the organization is an *open* system, with the result that objectives are too narrowly defined; specifically, it does not see the organization as part of a three-tiered hierarchy of systems, which must adapt to survive, and must satisfy the demands of its stakeholders at least minimally.

(v) *Economic* planning, particularly at the national level, usually fails to recognize that the economy is but one of the subsystems of society and is more or less strongly interrelated to the other subsystems (legal, political, social, and cultural). This probably accounts for many of the failures of economic planning for Third World countries by advanced industrialized countries and their institutions.

(vi) It does not put sufficient emphasis on the need for flexibility, in planning itself, in the design of the firm's information system and organization structure, and in its decision modes. In fact one can go further and say that all management systems must be interrelated with the formal planning system if planning is to be successful. If formal planning systems are too narrowly conceived and operated this will result in their isolation from the real needs of the organization (Stonich 1975).

PLANS CAN MISLEAD

Eilon (1980) argues that planning can lull management into a false sense of security, only to be rudely shattered when the unexpected suddenly happens.[1,2] Of course there is always the possibility of events occurring that are entirely unpredictable (such as natural disasters, major technological breakthroughs). But this argument implies that, once made, plans are adhered to come what may, or are seldom revised. This is an indictment of the conventional approach to planning. Even so, it may be doubted whether managements are fooled by their own plans to the extent suggested. As noted in Chapter 1 ("Correcting Past Mistakes") Modigliani and Cohen (1961) were frequently told by U.S. firms that plans were not binding on future decisions. This criticism of Eilon's is also contradicted by another, to be discussed later in this chapter ("Managers Are Not Committed to Planning"). But essentially it shows only that the existing approach to planning is weak and misconceived. It does not prove that planning should therefore be discarded rather than approached in a different way.

Eilon further argues that, while it may be claimed (Ackoff 1970; Ansoff 1980) that it is the process not the product of planning that matters, the fact remains that planning does have an end product, which people take too seriously and become overcommitted to. All this shows is that the transition to the "new" planning, directed toward the ongoing adaptation of the firm for long-term survival, will require the re-education of management and work force to produce the necessary change in attitudes. Admittedly, this will not be an easy task.

Eilon's argument that the interaction of managers through committees, seminars, ad hoc educational programs, business games, social functions, and job rotation can take the place of planning, and may be superior to planning, fails to do justice to the complexity and magnitude of the interrelated problems faced, and makes no concession to the fact that the firm is a nested system (part of a three-tiered hierarchy), with the consequent need for greater emphasis on the environment. It would be impossible for businessmen to deal with all these things "over lunch."

Blind Faith in Planning and the Failure to Learn from Experience

The argument here (Wildavsky 1973; Eilon 1980) is that planners embrace planning uncritically, and close their minds to criticism. Planning is good if it succeeds; society or the organization being planned for is bad if it fails. This is given as the reason why planners so often fail to learn from experience. To learn one must make mistakes, says Wildavsky, but in this view mistakes are never the fault of planning. If formal national planning fails in virtually all nations most of the time and continues to be practiced, this can only mean that blind faith triumphs over experience.

Wildavsky's arguments all refer to national planning, Eilon's to corporate planning. In either case, and whether or not the unsubstantiated statement that national planning mostly fails is true, no one should wish to defend the uncritical acceptance of planning without proof that its benefits outweigh its costs (see the section, "The benefits of planning may not justify the costs," below). If it were true that planning usually fails, the arguments listed earlier in this chapter ("Pathologies of Planning"), together with failure to forecast the future (extrapolation rather than prediction) or the use of poor forecasting techniques would between them go a long way toward accounting for it. At the same time one must recognize that, due to the often counterintuitive behavior of organizations and the unpredictability of certain events, even with the "new" planning there may be cases of failure despite planning and of success without planning, as Steiner (1969) acknowledged to be the case with the "old" planning.

"Learning from experience" is, in the above context, another way of saying "adapting." We have argued that the purpose of corporate planning should be constantly to adapt the firm in order to ensure long-term survival. We have also said (Chapter 2, section "Information System") that the information system must support this aim, by enabling the firm to learn from its mistakes, and be self-correcting (see below section "In Evaluating the Results of Planning"). The assertion that to learn one must make mistakes is a half-truth, of course. In learning a foreign language, for example, we learn through the errors we make in attempting to speak and write it but, if our memories serve us well, we also learn from books and/or from a teacher. In the first case the vehicle for learning is information on errors (mismatch information); in the second it is mapping the structured variety of written words or sounds from a book or teacher into our minds, there to be stored as structured variety, enabling us to recognize these words when we again see or hear them. As Ashby explains (1952: chapter 18), in actual experience learning from mistakes is considerably amplified by learning from one's environment (here a book and/or teacher).

MANAGERS ARE NOT COMMITTED TO PLANNING

The argument has often been made (e.g., Steiner 1969) that to be effective, planning needs strong commitment by top management. If this is lacking it is no surprise if other members of the organization fail to take it seriously. It is likely, as Eilon (1980) claims, that many managers are disenchanted with planning and have become rather cynical about its supposed benefits. Small wonder that it does not work, then. But is the fault in the entire notion of planning or in the particular way in which it has been customary to approach it?

THERE IS NO DIFFERENCE BETWEEN ADAPTIVE PLANNING AND AD HOC DECISION MAKING

Another argument put forward by Wildavsky (1973) is that while adaptation to changing circumstances is intelligent and reasonable, adaptive planning, involving continuous adjustment, smacks of ad hoc decision making and is hard to distinguish from any other decision process. By making planning reasonable "it becomes inseparable from the decision processes it was designed to supplant."

There are two responses to this argument. The first is that planning, however viewed, is not designed to supplant decision making. More particularly, it could never be equated with ad hoc decision making, of which it is the very antithesis. Planning is *anticipatory* decision making (see note 5, Chapter 1). But it is more than just a choice process: It involves selecting ends as well as means, appropriately integrating components, and coordinating activities across the entire system. Second, there is also a difference in scope with regard to adaptation. Properly conceived, planning bears the main burden of adapting the firm to its environment, by considering *all* decision problems and their interrelationships together, all components of the system and the part–whole relations, all relevant aspects of and relations with the environment. Decision making, because of its narrower focus, can only achieve partial adaptations, chiefly by building flexibility into decision rules, encouraging innovation, and so on.

A more serious misconception underlying Wildavsky's argument, however, is the implication that adaptation requires frequent changes in direction or pace which, once decided on, can be quickly implemented. Some adaptations can be made in this way, but they are usually only partial adaptations. Other adaptations, including those calling for a change in the basic purposes of the firm, may require very lengthy preparation.

PLANNING AND POWER

The argument here (Wildavsky 1973) may be paraphrased as follows. Planning requires causal knowledge; it takes place when managements are able to cause other people to act differently than they otherwise would. But power is a reciprocal relationship; it depends not only on what management can do, but on how those who are to carry out the plan respond. Planning may thus fail to achieve its objectives because top management lacks the necessary power, or because it exercises it ineffectively. This may manifest itself in an inability to hold to future objectives in the present, failure to sufficiently resolve conflicts over objectives, or failure to motivate people to achieve planned objectives.

These arguments are unexceptionable, but lose some of their force when applied to business enterprises rather than to national planning. As we saw in Chapter 3, conflicting aims are likely to be confined to objectives and goals. From a systems point of view we argued that such conflicts need not be completely resolved, that a certain amount of latent conflict, discontent, tension, and ambiguity has positive value, as one aspect of the flexibility needed in an open adaptive system. Wildavsky is right when he states that planning requires the power to maintain the primacy of future objectives in the present, if this is interpreted to mean that there must be no unresolved conflict over basic purposes and missions, and that management must maintain constancy of direction with respect to these despite changes in the environment or in the organization (Emery 1969: 10). In saying this we are assuming, of course, that objectives and goals will be revised whenever necessary as a result of changes in the environment or in the organization as part of the ongoing planning process, and that this may extend all the way up to missions and basic purposes if the magnitude of the changes demands it. (Wildavsky speaks of the "original goals" and "original objectives," leaving a presumption that in practice these are never changed: "What happens to the original objectives when behaviour changes in the light of new conditions?")

The other large question raised here by Wildavsky is how to motivate people to achieve corporate goals. Should motivation be built into plans or into formally separate controls, in each case in the form of performance targets, or should it be sought in other ways, for example, through internal prices or incentives, or through some combination of these? To what extent should it be intrinsic and to what extent extrinsic? These questions were raised, but not answered, in Chapter 1 (section "Measurement of Performance") and Chapter 4 (section "Should Planning Budgets and Control Budgets Be Formally Distinct?"). Wildavsky has here put his finger on a major problem; and when he wrote in 1973 that ". . . theories of society involving human motivation and incentive are barely alive" (p. 132), it must be admitted that, even in relation to business enterprises, we are still searching for answers a decade later. One could argue that, since motivation to work, more specifically to achieve some work objectives, is a psychological propensity, it should be left to the psychologists to determine how it is best achieved. The ideal solution would of course be to establish a business enterprise system in which cooperation replaced competition, in which the management–worker (or management–labor union) adversary roles were exchanged for cooperative endeavor. While not underestimating the difficulty of bringing about such a radical change, this suggestion is not as naive as it sounds. At least partial cooperation between owners, management, and workers in the administration of business enterprises already exists in some countries (e.g., West Germany, Japan). More fundamentally, one of the psychological presuppositions of microeconomic theories is that humans are competitive or aggressive rather than cooperative. Like most, if not all, of these psychological presuppositions, this one has never been tested. As Bunge (1981) points out,

> [To say] that man is competitive rather than cooperative . . . is simply false. We are all cooperative as well as competitive, and most of us more of the first than the second. Otherwise we would not be able to function as components of social systems, from family to international concern. Exaggerating competition at the expense of cooperation . . . makes it impossible to understand the very existence of social systems.

PLANNING IS CLAIMED TO BE "RATIONAL," BUT IS IT?

Wildavsky (1973) presents this argument in short and in extended, convoluted form. The short form of the argument, stated earlier, is that national planning fails wherever it has been tried, that it cannot be rational to fail, and that these failures of planning may be integral to its very nature. One can endorse Wildavsky's remark that to sanctify the perpetuation of mistakes is irrational, but still point out that the seeds of failure appear to lie in a misconception of the real nature of planning, whether by business or government.

The extended form of the argument (appearing under the heading "Planning Is Rationality") may be set out in the form of six propositions in support of planning (or certain attributes of planning), each followed by a refutation or qualification:

1. Planning is said to be desirable because it is *systematic*. "Systematic" means essentially "having the qualities of a system"; this implies that the planners have causal knowledge, which they do not.

2. Planning is said to be desirable because it is *rational*; but planners lack the necessary causal knowledge to make rational plans.

3. Rationality implies *efficiency*; but efficiency raises the prior question of *objectives*.

4. Efficiency requires *coordination*. Coordination in turn requires *redundancy* (to ensure that plans are achieved with a certain level of *reliability*); but redundancy is inefficient.

5. Planning is desirable because it is *consistent* (rather than contradictory); but consistency is not wholly compatible with *adaptation* (which is the primary aim of planning).

6. There are different *levels of rationality*. It is insufficient to consider the rationality of plans on one level in isolation, as is commonly done.

Although these arguments are directed against national planning, it is worth considering whether they are relevant to corporate planning also, bearing in mind that it is the conventional approach to planning that is under attack.

The first point requires no comment, except to remark that *systematic*, which means methodical (we could perhaps extend this to *logically consistent*), is not synonymous with *systemic*. The argument that those who try to plan for social systems do not possess the requisite knowledge of the system concerned will be examined below ("Planning Is Futile Because . . .").

As regards the second point, Wildavsky here uses "rational" to mean only "reasonable" (as in "the reasonable man plans ahead"). The precondition of formal national planning, says Wildavsky, is the existence of theory, with at least some evidence to support it, specifying causal relationships of the form "If we do X and Y, Z will result." "Planning takes place when people . . . are able to cause consequences they desire to occur." Here Wildavsky seems to be confusing the process with a successful outcome.

It would be evasive, however, to dodge the question of "rationality" altogether, for although Wildavsky interprets "rational" as meaning reasonable, his refutation links up with another meaning of "rationality" (or rational choice) encountered in economics and game theory. As Simon (1957) has pointed out, when discussing or theorizing about the behavior of business firms, whether normatively or positively, it is more realistic to replace the global rationality attributed to "economic man" in traditional economic theory by the principle of bounded rationality. (As an aside, it is interesting to note that Simon uses the terms "rational choice" and "rational adaptation" synonymously. In another paper in the same volume Simon discusses "the problem of behaving approximately rationally, or adaptively, in a particular environment," and the probability of survival).[3]

The assumptions underlying the notion of rationality attributed to "economic man" in traditional economics, it may be recalled, are that:

(i) He is completely informed about possible courses of action open to him at any time and their outcomes.

(ii) He has infinite sensitivity, implying that all functions represented in decision problems are continuous and differentiable (the general optimizing problem, by including nonnegativity constraints and inequalities, has removed many of the objections on this point).

(iii) He is rational, which was interpreted as meaning that he always sought to optimize something (e.g., minimize cost or maximize profit or utility).

Economists who held (or still hold) this view would allow that individual economic behavior is not uniformly rational in this sense, but would argue that, through interaction with the environment, individuals and firms learn the optimal decision rule over time, using further assumptions about efficiency and equilibrium (that the optimal position is also the equilibrium position) to support this (Einhorn 1976).

Simon would substitute for this "global rationality" of traditional economics "a kind of rational behavior that is compatible with the access to information and the computational capacities that are actually possessed" by firms in the kinds of environments in which they exist. In other words, he includes some of the properties of the decision maker(s) in defining rational behavior in specific situations—imperfect information, limited problem-solving skills, limited computational capacity leading to the use of simplified models of decision problems, and limited predictive ability. This leads Simon to postulate that the objectives of rational behavior will usually be of a "satisficing" rather than optimizing nature, where the former means behavior that is compatible with the information available to the firm, including information on cause–effect relationships, and so on, as described above (although the introduction of information on cause–effect relationships really enlarges the problem to encompass control systems and all means of making the controls effective, such as incentives).

To sum up, we agree with Simon that what constitutes "rationality" should pay some regard to certain characteristics of decision makers in their particular environments.[4] We can also accept Wildavsky's argument to the extent of saying that the current state of our knowledge is often insufficient to explain the behavior of social organizations, or to design the ideal organization, *directly,* without first doing some experimental modeling (Forrester 1975). But surely this is an advance on those (e.g., politicians) who believe they can do these things directly (by passing laws, initiating new social programs) based only on mental images, without benefit of any social systems understanding (see note 1, Chapter 4). Such understanding as we currently possess, if widely propagated, could lead to planning that is "approximately rational," in Simon's words (1957: 256).

Turning to the third point, Wildavsky's argument is that rationality implies that planning objectives should be achieved at least cost (see his previous point and assumption iii underlying the notion of "economic man"), but that the important question is "efficiency for whom and for what?" In other words efficiency raises the prior question of objectives. Like "rationality," the term "efficiency" has different meanings, even within economics, and Wildavsky's point involves two of them. Thus, from the point of view of a single firm we say that the most efficient way of producing is that which, at some given level of operation, requires the least expenditure of inputs, measured in money. Economists would say that, if it is rational, a firm would try to produce any output at minimum cost, whatever its objective happens to be. But in his remarks about objectives Wildavsky seems, at least in part, to be alluding to another kind of efficiency, which we discussed in the previous chapter. A state of the economy is described as *efficient* if it is impossible to make someone better off without making someone else worse off. This is the welfare definition of "efficient" known as Pareto-optimality. We can agree with Wildavsky that national objectives often tend to be vague, even contradictory, and sometimes undesirable for parts of the electorate. In the context of a business, it is important that it should have a clear idea of its basic purposes and missions, articulated in objectives and goals. Its planning should be guided by that principle of economy termed "efficiency" in the first sense, whatever its goals and objectives may be. According to our definition of Chapter 3 ("The Network of Aims; Selected Views"), attainment of optimal goals would require both efficiency in this sense and effectiveness (where the latter means the degree of success in completing some specified task on schedule).

The demands of efficiency as stated in the fourth point are more contentious. Wildavsky's argument here is that efficiency requires that plans (and decisions) should be coordinated, and be "mutually supportive rather than contradictory." Efficiency requires that objectives be achieved with the least input of resources. "When these resources are supplied by a number of different actors, hence the need for coordination, they must all contribute their proper share at the correct time. . . . Coordination, then, equals efficiency, which is . . . prized because achieving it means avoiding . . . duplication, overlapping and redundancy . . . (which) result in unnecessary effort." He also considers another criterion, "reliability," the probability that a particular function will be performed. Plans need to work at a certain level of reliability. To achieve this, redundancy is built into "most human enterprises." "Coordination of complex activities requires redundancy. . . . We ensure against failure by having adequate reserves and by creating several mechanisms to perform a single task in case one should fail . . . the more difficult the problem, the greater the need for redundancy." But redundancy is undesirable because it involves inefficiency.

Coordination in the systems sense refers to the harmonizing of relations, more specifically inner couplings, between system components. By couplings we mean, not merely relations, but that one part acts on another, influencing its behavior (see the Appendix, Couplings between Objects Versus Couplings between Qualities"). In Chapter 1 ("Integration, Coordination, and Orientation to the Environment") we concluded that survival of the firm entails coordinating related activities and not unrelated activities, and that planning was one of the principal means of achieving smooth coordination. It can be agreed at once that efficient use of resources is unlikely to be achieved if the interactions between related activities are ignored, with resulting disharmony in the functioning of components of the firm. Efficiency and coordination are not, as Wildavsky claims, synonymous, however, because efficient use of resources depends on within-component as well as between-component behavior and performance.

To be efficient, and hence rational, Wildavsky next argues that before (related) activities can be coordinated, we must first be fairly sure that they will in fact be performed. As he uses the term, reliability is thus concerned with effectiveness rather than efficiency, and hence with supervision, feedback control, and motivation. What he seems to be saying here is that planning must first of all be rational as regards the preparation of plans: Whatever is done should be done at least cost (consistent with quality and safety standards presumably), and planned activities should be coordinated (wherever they need to be coordinated). The remainder of his argument is concerned with the implementation of plans. Dated plans (goals, and perhaps medium-term programs) should be carried out with a high degree of effectiveness as well as efficiency. We might add that what he terms "reliability" also calls for an organizational structure capable of carrying out the plan.

   The argument that coordination requires redundancy, which he claims is inefficient and irrational, misses the point. First, Wildavsky fails to realize that what constitutes rational and efficient behavior in conditions of certainty may not be rational and efficient under *uncertainty*. In conditions of uncertainty it is not irrational to try to avoid uncertainty (e.g., by reserves of various kinds, organizational slack, multi-purpose machines, preventive maintenance programs, even contingency plans). In the same way, in designing its information system a firm will usually make some tradeoff between maximum efficiency in communication and ensuring that what is communicated is correctly interpreted, by building in some redundancy, in the information theory sense.[5] So, because of uncertainty, redundancy is not necessarily irrational and inefficient. Second, coordination, as distinct from uncertainty, does not require redundancy. The smooth functioning of interrelated parts of an organization is achieved mainly through planning (setting performance targets); the use of an internal price system as part of a decomposition technique to ensure that all components of the firm act consistently with each other and with the goals of the firm as a whole; and clear administrative rules, or some combination of these—in short, by some device that takes into account the interactions between components.

   Planning is also claimed to be desirable because it is consistent (the fifth point), by which we assume Wildavsky means that plans should be internally consistent. He distinguishes between what he calls "horizontal consistency" at a given time and "vertical consistency" over time. We agree that the open system and dynamic properties of business enterprises demand that plans should be consistent in both of these senses. Wildavsky seems to think that horizontal consistency and vertical consistency are contradictory, because the former requires "unusual flexibility" while the latter requires "extraordinary rigidity." The short answer to this is that flexibility, a prerequisite of survival for an open system, should apply to all aspects of a business organization: to plans of whatever duration, organizational structure, information system, decision modes, and so on. A firm that deliberately remains inflexible in the face of all changes will not adapt, and may not survive. We agree with Wildavsky that flexibility and adaptability are the attributes that social organizations should nurture and pursue. Under a systems approach to planning, consistency without rigidity would be ensured automatically, because systemic, adaptive planning takes into account the interconnectedness of decisions in a single time period, and of different time periods, constantly updating plans and building flexibility into all aspects of management.

Wildavsky's sixth point, about what he calls different levels of rationality, is well taken. Interpreted, this means, at the national level, that the economy is only one subsystem of society, and that in economic planning we may need to take into account the demands of (or constraints imposed by) other subsystems. The same applies, of course, to planning for any of these other subsystems, because they are all interrelated and part of the system we call society. Similarly in business planning, a firm with branch operations in the Third World or with a large export trade to that area would do well to consider the local culture, political system, legal system, and so on in its planning. In other words we must never forget that every system except the universe is part of a three-tiered hierarchy of systems.

What Constitutes Rational Choice?

The rational choice model of decision making assumes that firms have well-defined objectives. Given this premise, rational decision making by organizations or individuals means behavior that is consistent with achieving these objectives. This behavior is determined by means of a rational decision model, or rational analysis. The rational choice model underlies much of the current thinking in economics, management science, and the decision-making aspects of accounting and finance.

A more serious criticism of planning, on the grounds of its doubtful rationality, than the one made by Wildavsky is that what constitutes rational action for complex social organizations is not easy to identify (Hedberg et al. 1976: 63) and may not be (in fact almost certainly is not) correctly described by the rational choice model. The basis of this statement is a series of recent studies by psychologists and organization theorists, many of which are reviewed by Dyckman (1981).

To begin with, we now have a bewildering array of definitions of rationality, ranging from the economists' global rationality and Simon's bounded rationality already referred to, to "limited rationality" (March and Simon 1958), "process rationality" (March and Olsen 1976), "contextual rationality" (Sproul et al. 1978), and what we may call "*ex post* rationality" (Weick 1979; see also the references to Demski and Itami in the following section). This last interpretation would judge the rationality of behavior against goals that are determined *ex post*, not *ex ante* as in the rational choice model, and emphasizes the importance of adaptation (Day and Groves 1975).

March's (1978) study of the "engineering of choice" points out that observed behavior in forming tastes and preferences is not consistent with

the assumptions of the rational choice model, in which tastes are exogen-
ously determined. The evidence indicates, rather, that the assumed relationship may often be reversed: that preferences are often determined, at
least in part, by decisions, not the other way around. If this is the case,
"how do we act sensibly now to manage the development of preferences in
the future when we do not have now a criterion for evaluating future tastes
that will not itself be affected by our actions?" (March 1978). Certainly a
descriptive study of preferences presents challenges to the accepted theory
of rational choice.

Another factor influencing what we should regard as rational choice
concerns the role of organizational learning. Learned behavior is an important part of total behavior. But Einhorn and Hogarth (1978) note that the resulting behavior depends on how the learning takes place—on whether it is
inductive or deductive. The former kind of learning takes the form of a
trial-and-error process, which with repetition may over time become
codified into general rules or heuristics. Deductive learning is the kind that
results from formal training and education. We need to know more about
the relative importance of each of these processes in given organizations,
for they are likely to lead to different judgments as to what is rational behavior. While it is claimed on the basis of observation that most learning is
inductive, it can be argued that this could lead to counter-adaptive as well
as adaptive behavior, depending on the circumstances. "Learning by experience" and "experience is the best teacher" are likely to be inappropriate
guides in many cases, particularly in situations of rapid change and great
uncertainty, and no substitute for better systems understanding and a
thorough evaluation of performance against "*ex post* rational" goals. The
two kinds of learning process have important implications for the kind of
information provided to decision makers and the design of the information
system. Hogarth and Makridakis (1981) have shown, however, that access
to additional information tends to increase decision makers' confidence in
their judgments, but without a proportionate increase in their accuracy.

EVALUATING THE RESULTS OF PLANNING

Viewing planning as future control, Wildavsky states that "the determination of whether planning [*sic*] has taken place must rest on an assessment of whether and to what degree future control (i.e., achieving the desired future consequences of current actions) has been achieved . . .
achievement and not the plan must be the final arbiter of planning." Here

again, as in his second point, there is a confusion between the process of planning and the success or failure of that process.

But let us examine the main argument in more detail by first considering current practice. Firms commonly make the performance targets of their tactical plans (or at least of their short-term accounting budgets) serve the dual role of control targets as well. Performance is then measured as the relation between observed results in a given period and the common planning-control targets. This is done for parts of the system at more frequent intervals called *costing periods* (e.g., monthly or fortnightly). This is called *standard cost variance analysis* (and perhaps *contribution margin variance analysis*) and *budgetary control*. This is also done for the system as a whole for accounting-budget periods (typically one year). Differences between observed and target results are analyzed into price, quantity, and a number of subsidiary variances. The planning-control targets reflect the expectations held by management at the beginning of the accounting-budget period. These targets are not systematically revised every time expectations change.

An extension of this procedure has been proposed by Demski (1967) and Itami (1977). This involves preparing another set of targets at the end of the performance measurement period (costing period or budget period, as the case may be), representing what the firm would have done if it had had perfect information at the beginning of the period (Demski) or had acquired it during the period (Itami) and had acted optimally on this information. These targets are *ex post* targets, and the budgets embodying them could be thought of as retrospective *ex ante* plans. Denoting *ex post* planned results by I^p, observed results by I^o, and *ex ante* planned results (the result of acting optimally in the light of imperfect information) by I^a, performance in relation to plan can then be analyzed under the Demski scheme as follows: $I^a - I^o = (I^a - I^p) + (I^p - I^o)$, where the first term on the RHS is a rough indication of forecasting error[6] and the second measures the opportunity loss of failing to act optimally with perfect information throughout the period. Performance could, alternatively, be measured in terms of ratios: $I^o/I^a = I^p/I^a \cdot I^o/I^p$, where the first term on the RHS measures the reciprocal of the forecasting error (i.e., how much better performance could have been by acting optimally with perfect rather than imperfect information).

But even in relation to the conventional approach to planning, neither of these measures really isolates the effects of planning per se. Rather, they measure the combined effects of forecasting, controls, and any motivational devices used to make the controls effective. In short, they measure the success of forecasting and plan implementation.

In the systems view, what is important is the ongoing *process*, not any given plan. This process, it will be recalled, should comprise deciding on aims (basic purposes, missions, long-term objectives, short-term goals), revising these when necessary, forecasting the future, constantly monitoring the environment in considerably more detail than is customary in conventional planning, preparing to bring about future aims by present actions, selecting among alternative ways of achieving aims, where necessary setting schedules for their achievement, creating an organizational structure capable of achieving them, designing an information system, acquiring and using information in a way that is compatible with achieving the system's aims, appropriately integrating the system and its subsystems, perhaps also appropriately coordinating its activities. All this was to be directed toward adapting the system for long-term survival.

If this is agreed on, the success of planning should then be measured by how well the system adapts. But this requires a fairly long planning horizon, because major adaptations (e.g., those calling for a change in the firm's basic purposes or missions, or involving the research and development of advanced technology) may take years to complete, and because social organizations have been shown to have important long-term cause–effect relationships that would otherwise be ignored (see the references to Forrester in Chapter 4 "Short Versus Long"). How well the system adapts, then, can only be measured, retrospectively, in terms of whether and how well it survives over some past period, or better, in terms of its future survival prospects beyond some agreed, fairly distant, horizon. The firm's performance may be satisfactory in terms of how well it achieves its immediate tactical planning targets, although this does not tell us much because as we saw in Chapter 6 the accounting records give a very coarse and inaccurate representation of the firm's state vector. The system's survival prospects may still be poor. Even on a purely financial level, for example, the firm may have been quite profitable but be on the verge of bankruptcy. Yet this would appear as satisfactory performance, at least in relation to an *ex ante* plan, if the ultimate performance index is some measure of profitability. And even if the current period's tactical plans are systemic in the sense of ensuring that planned actions to achieve the firm's own goals will at least minimally satisfy the demands of its stakeholders and of the environment, long-term survival may not be ensured unless these short-term plans are consistent with long-term plans that are themselves survival-worthy.

To sum up, the success or failure of planning is not to be found in the way Wildavsky suggests, or as businesspeople currently judge it. It can only be judged over a long horizon, because long-term survival through adaptation should be the purpose and justification of planning. As we have indicated in Chapter 6, long-term survival as an organizational goal raises a number of difficult conceptual and measurement problems. The fact that part of the difference between observed results and planned results for a single period was due to inaccurate forecasting and part to "control loss" in implementing the plan tells us nothing about how well the firm is adapting or about its survival prospects *unless* planning is systemic and is seen as the main vehicle for the continuous adaptation of the firm toward long-term survival. Planning can be judged a success only if it matches the orientation of the firm to the state of its environment with reasonable accuracy on an ongoing basis over the long term.

PLANNING IS FUTILE IN LARGE CORPORATIONS

Recall Wildavsky's argument earlier in the chapter ("Planning Is Claimed to Be 'Rational' . . .") to the effect that planning cannot be systematic as often claimed because planners simply do not possess the necessary causal knowledge of social organizations. He adds ". . . planning is not the solution to any problem. It is just a way of restating in other language the problems we do not know how to solve" (1973: 149). This sort of argument receives support from de Greene (1981), who states that "limits to the complexity [of large human organizations] that can be effectively understood and managed" are possibly imminent. "It may be that the use of the cumulative experience of mankind and 'learning by doing' have reached points of diminishing returns." Conditions that could lead to such limits to complexity, says de Greene, are (a) the tight coupling among world subsystems and between a system and its environment; (b) the vast amount of indigestible and irretrievable information that exists; and (c) the growth of bureaucratic organizations of super-critical sizes.

As regards (a), de Greene says that whereas until recent centuries human systems consisted of associations of loosely coupled systems, in recent times the amount of coupling between human systems and between human systems and the natural environment has increased dramatically. At the same time the world and most of its constituent subsystems are moving into a state far from equilibrium, due to "explosive changes in sociotechnical systems," and growing disparities between subsystems and between the world socioeconomic system and the natural environment. States far from equilibrium are characterized by a number of critical points around which the system is hypersensitive to fluctuations. The world has become one vast turbulent *field* in which distinctions between system and environment become more and more arbitrary. When a system is forced farther and farther from equilibrium, instabilities develop, and a succession of instabilities leads to increasing levels of system complexity. In physical systems, at least, transitions to successively higher levels of complexity are marked by the emergence of new properties. We do not yet understand this far-from-equilibrium behavior of systems, how to deal with their increasing instability, or comprehend the emergent forms. De Greene concludes from this that the limits of "total system adaptability" are fast being reached. Concerning (c), de Greene mentions the recent failures associated with such sociotechnical systems as transportation, health, welfare, criminal justice, energy, and industrial production, which he believes can be attributed, to a considerable extent, to old management methods rationalized as still appropriate. He contends that many human organizations such as large social bureaucracies appear to have passed the critical size and complexity beyond which effective management is impossible.

De Greene bases these gloomy forecasts on two recent theoretical developments in natural science: the modern field theory of critical phenomena in physics (Wilson 1979) and the theory of fluctuations and self-organization of physico-chemical systems far from equilibrium (Nicolis and Prigogine 1977). He believes these offer a number of "major constructs, generalizable to both nonliving and living systems," although admitting that their "*direct* applicability . . . to complex living systems, however highly suggestive, is moot."

It is difficult to assess whether these new developments in science apply also to social systems, and if they do, the ways in which they need to be modified to allow for the greater complexity of the latter. The crop of recent failures of sociotechnical systems to which de Greene refers is certainly strong evidence that something is wrong, although whether these failures were due to the organizations concerned passing beyond a critical level of complexity is not proven. Some of the other things de Greene mentions, however, might have been important determinants: the fact that the world has become one vast turbulent field, and that managements try to use old remedies for new ailments. Failure to regard any of the subsystems mentioned (transportation, health, etc.) as interrelated to other subsystems of society, failure to plan systemically and, recalling Forrester's (1969) findings, failure to plan far enough ahead, might well explain a large part of these failures of planning. It will also be recalled (see note 1, Chapter 4) that Forrester (1975) believes we now *do* know enough to make useful (computer) models of business systems. High complexity, it should be remembered, has a positive as well as a negative side: A high degree of complexity means that the system has many degrees of freedom, hence a wide range of possible behaviors, and can survive a wider range of disturbances than less complex systems can.

PLANNING IS USELESS BECAUSE THE
WORLD HAS BECOME TOO UNCERTAIN

Arguments put forward on these grounds include the following:

Planning is just a waste of time nowadays—especially so-called strategic planning. In today's world there is no point looking further forward than a one- or two-year budget. Anything longer-term is just not worth the paper it is written on (attributed to a senior executive of a Dutch company, in Lorenz 1979).

. . . I am not opposed to planning as such, but I advocate a pragmatic approach: short-term planning, say up to a year or two, is obviously necessary, but planning for a more distant horizon has just not come up to scratch. The world has become too uncertain and our tools have remained lamentably crude. . . . (Eilon 1980, writing under the *nom de plume* S. Opal).

In order to rely on the planning mode [of strategy making], an organization must be large enough to afford the costs of formal analysis, it must have goals that are operational, and it must face an environment that is reasonably predictable and stable. (This last point inevitably raises the comment that planning is most necessary when the environment is difficult to understand. This may be true, but the costs of analyzing a complex environment may be prohibitive and the results . . . discouraging.) (Mintzberg 1973).

Even if the future were known with certainty some planning would still be needed, to adapt to a certain, although changed, future, or to prepare for a different desired future of the firm's own making.

Uncertainty is a pervasive characteristic of life, for individuals and organizations, and has been increasing at an increasing rate in recent years under the impact of technological change and the growing interdependence between the subsystems of society. Every indication is that uncertainty will continue to increase, and that there will be no return to the more placid conditions of the past. Yet this has not prevented individuals from planning ahead and making rather large commitments. And uncertainty is probably the main reason why firms come into existence (see the reference to Coase 1937 in the First part of Chapter 1); it avoids some of the uncertainty of coordinating production and exchange between masses of individual buyers and sellers. Even in conditions of great uncertainty forecasting and planning may enable the firm to anticipate some future opportunities and threats, and prepare for them.

Cyert and March (1963: 102, 110) state that firms facing uncertainty resort to a form of crisis management. They take essentially contingent decisions and rely on rapid feedback to learn whether the decisions were "right" or not, to minimize the need for predicting uncertain future events. They devote little time to *long-run* planning. This kind of behavior is undesirable on two scores. First, it ignores the firm's system properties and thus incurs the costs of making interrelated decisions piecemeal. (It is also a denial of the fact that, as a purposeful system, the firm is able *within limits* to determine its own ends, even in an uncertain world). Second, and this is perhaps the most important counter-argument to the views quoted at the beginning of this section, if we stop at short-term planning, over the long run it may be worse than no planning at all, because social organizations usually have important long-term cause–effect relationships that create "a fundamental conflict between the short-term and long-term consequences of a policy change" (Forrester 1975). Short-term measures taken as long as two or three decades ago are responsible for many of the problems we face today.

The trouble with the argument that a high level of uncertainty, leading to disruption of established institutions and organizations, is a negative judgment on the feasibility of long-term forecasting (and planning), and that the solution is to invent and develop institutions and organizations that are " 'learning systems,' . . . systems capable of bringing about their own continuing transformation" (Schon 1971: 30, 248) is, we believe, that it does not sufficiently consider the fact that adaptation must be rapid to be effective, and may have long lead times. For the organization that waits until it receives signals of incipient breakdown, it is often too late to act, as recent industrial and business history in North America attests. It does not survive, or is kept alive only by very costly life-support systems from outside whose justification may be questionable. Organizational learning, and public learning, are by all means to be encouraged. But why exclude learning about the uncertain future that can take place through systemic, adaptive planning?

A second counter-argument is that systemic, adaptive planning as we have described it recognizes uncertainty, instability, change, and impermanence as the *norms* rather than the exceptions in the life of organizations, because it is an open system approach to planning, unlike the conventional approach. Flexibility and uncertainty avoidance are prominent characteristics of actual organizational behavior. Firms engage in a variety of activities to avoid uncertainty. They try to learn more about the future by forecasting, planning, market and economic research, R & D. They try to eliminate or offset uncertainty by expanding the boundaries of the system to absorb some of it (by mergers, acquisitions, associations of firms, interlocking directorates). They establish buffers to cushion them against shocks (reserves of various kinds, organizational slack), and build flexibility into the system in various ways (keep excess plant capacity or larger inventories to meet peaks in demand, buy multi-purpose rather than single-purpose machines, and so on). The fact that components and subsystems are typically only loosely coupled adds a further element of flexibility. Forecasting and planning are here envisaged as more or less continuous processes.

The counter-arguments presented thus far are not by themselves sufficient, however, to justify planning when the level of uncertainty and change in the environment reaches giant proportions, constituting what Emery and Trist (1965) describe as a *turbulent field* (see also the remarks of de Greene 1981 in the previous section). By "turbulent field" they mean that, due to a build-up of forces (e.g., growth in size and increasing interdependence of business organizations, continuous technological change, and increasing interdependence between elements of society), the relevant environment of businesses widens and its causal texture becomes vastly more complex.[7] But more than this, autonomous changes occur in the environment quite independently of the interactions between its component business organizations. The relevant environment reaches such a level of complexity and degree of interconnectedness that newly emergent change processes appear. When this happens the outcomes of actions by the organization become increasingly unpredictable; uncertainty increases by a quantum jump. Emery and Trist (1965) provide an illustration of such a situation in the experiences of the National Farmers Union of Great Britain.

A number of writers have addressed the problem of how organizations should respond to turbulent fields, or to a permanent or semi-permanent quantum increase in uncertainty. The conclusion they all come to is that continued adaptation and survival require that they should behave as a resolute bloc, with cooperation, collaboration, and negotiation replacing competition and conflict over at least a limited area of their interactions.

Emery and Trist state that in turbulent environments individual organizations, however large, cannot expect to adapt successfully through their own direct actions. They should search for common values of overriding importance to them all. Commitment to these congruent values may succeed in transforming a richly coupled, turbulent environment into a more simplified and placid one, and this transformation will be adaptive to the extent that the shared values adequately represent the changed requirements of the environment. This adaptive role attributed to shared social values may be peculiar to human organizations, for Ashby (1952: 205) states that examples of natural environments that are both large and highly interconnected are rare.

All this has relevance to organizational objectives and structure. The organization that seeks to adapt and survive in a turbulent field will place more importance on setting objectives and goals that offer a high degree of convergence with the interests of other similar or dissimilar organizations in its environment (compare the systems model of the firm presented in the beginning of Chapter 6). In place of hierarchically structured forms of organization that may be appropriate in environments consisting primarily of like, competitive (and perhaps highly interdependent) organizations whose fates are to some extent negatively correlated, some kind of organizational structure that will maximize cooperation appears to be required in environments consisting of similar or dissimilar firms whose fates are positively correlated. Emery and Trist consider that professional associations provide one such model of what they call an organizational matrix type of structure, which has been well tried. This type of organizational structure, it may be noted, may approach our definition of *system* structure in the Appendix, in that it would incorporate some of the system's outer couplings. Note also that in what they call a disturbed-reactive environment, illustrated by an oligopolistic market, much of the "environment" (all the other interdependent firms) would move inside the system's boundaries (see the Appendix, "Correctly Circumscribing a System").

Mesarovic and Pestel (1974) examine a problem similar to the one above but arising *within* an organization, and come to a similar conclusion, that of vertical restructuring toward cooperative system goals and horizontal restructuring between system parts.

Others who have considered the problem of turbulent environmental fields include Rapoport (1970), Trist (1977), Schon (1971), and Susman (1981). After enumerating a number of illustrative changes that have taken place recently in organizational environments, the combined effect of which is to produce a turbulent field, Susman states that planning needs "to be supplemented by enabling conditions which are appropriate for prob-

lems which a single organization can seldom solve without cooperation
and/or negotiation with like or dissimilar organizations. . . . These enabling
conditions are (a) forums with representation sufficient to include all parties with an affected interest in the problems at issue, and (b) a problem-solving mode which searches for common values underlying different interests and encourages commitment to solving jointly defined problems."
He calls this search for common values "action research," and believes that
planning and action research are complementary approaches in dealing
with environments characterized by turbulence and a high degree of interdependence.

There is no suggestion by any of these writers that in the conditions of
great environmental uncertainty described as a turbulent field planning is
useless. The title of Susman's paper, for example, is "Planned Change."
But cooperative endeavor will only prove survival-worthy if it makes possible continued successful adaptation by each of the participants. If the
shared values and the united actions around common problems do not
adequately reflect environmental realities, no firm will be able to achieve
the approximate matching of its orientation to that of the environment, in
speed and direction, required for successful adaptation. The kind of cooperation between firms on common problems here envisaged would require
each of them to re-examine the value system of its top management, and its
objectives and goals (see the Steiner pyramid of aims in the beginning of
Chapter 3), change or revise priorities within its value system, and modify
its objectives, goals, and organizational structure as necessary. These
changes would all be part of the planning process.

THE BENEFITS OF PLANNING MAY NOT
JUSTIFY THE COSTS

Let it be said at once that no kind of planning should be undertaken unless the benefits outweigh the costs. The benefits and costs associated with
different approaches to planning can be specified. The problem is to measure them. There is also the fact that systemic, adaptive planning and the
variant of this to fit a turbulent environment have a long horizon. This, together with the fact that probably few if any firms are yet employing these
approaches to planning, means that it is impossible to establish empirically
whether they are justified on cost-benefit grounds. Mintzberg (see the previous section) therefore cannot prove that the costs of analyzing a complex
environment are prohibitive and the results discouraging, any more than we

can disprove his assertion. Evidence is simply not available yet. Only time will tell if sufficient organizations will eventually adopt the "new" planning. All that can be said at this stage is that, given the increased explanatory power offered by the systems approach, which can hardly be disputed, and the well-established findings of Forrester (1969 and elsewhere) and his colleagues that the consequences of planning for social organizations tend later to reverse themselves if the planning horizon is too short, there is a *presumption* that survival prospects will be greater with systemic, adaptive planning. They will be sufficiently greater to translate into positive net benefits compared with conventional planning or no planning at all.

Table 8.1 attempts to specify the costs and benefits associated with (a) no planning, (b) conventional planning (here interpreted generously as involving mainly prediction rather than extrapolation), (c) systemic, adaptive planning, and (d) planning in a turbulent environment, which is a fusion of (c) and cooperation based on shared values. Each successive column compares benefits and costs with the preceding column. The costs of failure to survive long-term would be measured as the present value, on an after-tax basis, of: The revenues foregone by ceasing operations

> *minus* the costs avoided by ceasing operations
> *minus* the proceeds of liquidation of the assets
> *plus* the payments made to creditors and stockholders
> *plus* the legal costs of bankruptcy.

EMPIRICAL EVIDENCE IN SUPPORT OF PLANNING

A sample of empirical studies indicating that planning does pay is provided by Ansoff et al. (1970), Thune and House (1970), Herold (1972), Karger and Malik (1975), Wood and LaForge (1979), and Forrester (1969). Ackoff (1970, 1974) cites evidence of various aspects of planning, but does not provide any complete case histories.

In their study of relationships between performance and methods of growth (mainly through acquisitions of other firms) of a large sample of U.S. manufacturing firms in the period 1947–1966, Ansoff et al. found that those firms that planned their acquisitions outperformed the nonplanners "on virtually all relevant criteria." Based on a sample of 36 U.S. firms, Thune and House reported that those in the drug, chemical, and machinery industries that engaged in formal long-range planning (defined as the determination of corporate strategy and goals for at least three years ahead, and

Table 8.1. A comparison of benefits and costs of four approaches to planning

	No planning	Conventional planning	Systemic, adaptive planning	Planning in a turbulent environment
Benefits	The costs of forecasting and planning avoided The short-term gains (if any) from making decisions (rather than forming expectations) and relying on rapid feedback to adapt	The value of increased long-term survival prospects	The value of further increased long-term survival prospects The gains from: Planning on an ongoing basis Solving all interrelated problems together Planning long-term Making adaptation the overriding aim Paying more attention to the environment Preparing for future opportunities and threats Creating future opportunities, preventing future threats from developing	In addition to the items in the previous column: The gain through the reduction in environmental uncertainty Any reduction in forecasting costs (at least some of which are now shared) Compared with *conventional* planning: The value of increased long-term survival prospects

Table 8.1. (Cont.)

	No planning	Conventional planning	Systemic, adaptive planning	Planning in a turbulent environment
Costs	The cost (in terms of reduced profits) of making interrelated decisions piecemeal The long-term cost of taking decisions that have favorable short-term consequences but unfavorable long-term consequences The cost of failing to prepare for potential opportunities and threats The cost of not creating future opportunities and not preventing future threats from developing The cost of failure to survive long-term	The costs of not planning systemically (not taking into account all interdependencies) The cost of not making adaptation the primary aim of planning The cost of not planning on an ongoing basis The cost of not comprehensively planning long-term The cost of not paying sufficient attention to the environment The cost of faulty expectations The cost of not trying to influence the environment in the firm's favor The cost of conventional planning and limited forecasting	The added cost of detailed and more frequent monitoring of the environment The cost of increased forecasting The cost of the continuous planning process The cost of comprehensive long-term planning The cost of organizational restructuring The cost of creating future opportunities and preventing future threats from developing The cost of designing and operating an information system that enables the firm to adapt and learn rapidly	Additional to the previous column: The costs of cooperation, negotiation, consultation with other firms The costs of revising value systems of top management or priorities within them, revising objectives and goals, modifying organizational structure

Source: Compiled by the author.

establishment of specific action programs, projects, and procedures to
achieve goals) consistently outperformed informal planners (those that did
not do these things), while no clear association could be established in the
food, oil, and steel industries. Over all six industries, the long-term planners significantly outperformed the others on three of five financial performance measures. The relationship between long-term planning and successful performance was strongest among medium-sized firms in rapidly
changing markets. Thune and House controlled for differences in size between responding firms. These writers speculated that it would probably be
naive to conclude that long-term formal planning was the sole cause of successful performance, and that it is more likely that such planning is a
characteristic of well-managed firms that "use more sophisticated methods
for organization design and analysis, managerial selection, development,
compensation, and . . . control."

Herold's study of firms in the U.S. drug and chemical industries vali-
dated the findings of Thune and House, but was based on a very small sample. Wood and LaForge, using the Guttman scaling technique, found from
a sample of 15 that U.S. banks that planned long-term had a competitive
advantage over banks that did not. This result was found to be statistically
significant. To Karger and Malik, long-range planning meant formal integrated planning with a horizon of at least five years. They collected ques-
tionnaire data from 38 firms in six industries for a period of ten years. The
response rate was 14 percent. They found that the long-term planners outperformed the others in 10 of 13 financial measures.

The results of Fulmer and Rue (1973) were mixed. They investigated
the relationship between financial performance and long-term planning
with a sample of 386 firms in three industry groups. The sample was partitioned into long-term planners and non–long-term planners, and performance was measured in terms of four different criteria. Their findings did not
show a systematic relation between long-term planning and successful financial performance; in one industry the long-term planners outperformed
the rest on all four measures, in another industry the results were reversed,
while in the third industry the results were mixed.

It is difficult to attach much importance to any of these empirical results in our context, for several reasons: first, that presumably all of the
firms studied employ conventional rather than systemic, adaptive planning; second, because none of the definitions of "long term" used in these
studies is long enough to capture the kind of relationships Forrester speaks
of;[8] and third, because in most cases the sample size is too small to
generalize from. The first point is, of course, crucial. Studies of conven-

tional planning, which we would *expect* to produce poor results, are of very limited value.

SUMMARY

We can discount the force of all of the arguments against planning here presented by first noting that they are criticisms of *conventional* planning. There seems to be a widespread belief that conventional planning, whether practiced by governments or corporations, is often a failure when judged by its results. Certainly this kind of planning is no match for the increasingly turbulent environments in which organizations must seek to survive. Implicit in this last statement is our belief that there is unlikely to be a permanent reversion to more placid environments. Nor is it designed to chart the "devious and diabolical" behavior of social systems. Some of the arguments (e.g., those presented in this chapter, "Blind Faith in Planning" and "Managers Are Not Committed to Planning"), can be agreed to at once.

The arguments of most substance have to do with the futility of trying to deal with increasing organizational and environmental complexity, and hence uncertainty, occasioned by a combination of recent trends including the increased interdependence between organizations and between the subsystems of society. Systemic, adaptive planning, which treats organizations as open systems, is founded on the recognition of interdependence and change as being of primary importance in dealing with organizational problems. It is hard to believe that an approach that unquestionably provides more explanatory power is inappropriate. We have also referred to certain ways of partially offsetting uncertainty, one of which would also reduce some of the interdependence that is one of the causes of that uncertainty. A lot could also be done by ridding organizations of all manner of existing rigidities that obstruct adaptation. On the cost-benefit question judgment must be reserved for lack of evidence.

NOTES

1. In an editorial entitled "A Challenge to Planning" in vol. 8, no. 2 of *Omega* (the international journal of management science, of which Eilon is the editor), an imaginary dialogue between "H.I. Rantoff" and "S. Opal" presents arguments for and against planning, respectively. Writing as "H.I. Rantoff," Eilon presents the views of H. Igor Ansoff (1965, 1980) and R.L. Ackoff (1970), both

advocates of planning. Writing as "S. Opal" (himself) he challenges the arguments by which they justify the need for planning.

2. Actually Eilon is here quoting a statement by Ansoff (1980) that long-range planning, which is only an extrapolation of the past, will, in conditions of uncertainty, put the future of the firm at risk. As the title of his paper indicates, Ansoff presents this picture of the conventional approach to planning only to expose its weaknesses, and goes on to say that the modern approach to planning emphasizes adaptiveness and the *process* of planning.

3. H.A. Simon 1957: chapter 15.

4. At the same time it could be argued that this need not lead to the conclusion that all objectives, whether of planning or decision making, need be of a "satisficing" nature, because it is possible to subsume the obstacles to complete rationality in a more general maximizing model in which learning is included as one of the objectives (Baumol and Quandt 1964), and other limitations are shown as constraints.

5. For a number of mutually exclusive events $x_1, x_2, \ldots, x_n$ with associated probabilities $p_1, p_2, \ldots, p_n$ the expected information content of a definite message saying that one of the events has occurred, *before* it arrives, is given by the entropy measure

$$H(p) = \sum_{i=1}^{n} p_i h(p_i) = - \sum_i p_i \log_2 p_i,$$

$$0 \leq H(p) \leq \log_2 n.$$

The redundancy (R) of the message is measured by

$$R = 1 - \left(\frac{H(p)}{H(p)_{max}} \right), 0 \leq R \leq 1,$$

that is, as the complement of the efficiency of the message (the expression in parentheses). $H(p)$ has a maximum value of $\log_2 n$ when the events are equiprobable.

6. Assuming that the firm equates its desired future state to that given by the forecast (i.e., does not act purposefully; see Chapter 2, "Prediction").

7. Whatever the state of the environment may be, Emery and Trist (1965) further propose that a proper understanding of organizational behavior cannot be obtained unless attention is paid to the causal texture of the environment, that is, it requires some knowledge of each of the following elements:

$$\begin{bmatrix} L_{11}, L_{12} \\ L_{21}, L_{22} \end{bmatrix}$$

where L denotes coupling, L_{12} exchanges from system to environment, L_{21} exchanges from environment to system, L_{11} the system's internal interdependencies (organization structure), and L_{22} denotes interdependencies in the environment. These are referred to as its *causal texture*. Naylor and Gattis (1976) report that, as part of the planning process, some firms are beginning to model the environment as well as having a corporate planning model. The modeling and monitoring of L_{22} (as well as the exogenous elements of L_{21}) might give early warning of incipient turbulence in the environment.

8. See note 1, Chapter 4. To Forrester, "long-term" means "beyond ten years."

REFERENCES

Arrow, K.J. 1974. "Limited Knowledge and Economic Analysis." *American Economic Review* 64 (March): 1–10.

Ackoff, R.L. 1970. *A Concept of Corporate Planning*. New York: Wiley-Interscience.

_____. 1974. *Redesigning the Future*. New York: Wiley-Interscience.

Ansoff, H.I. 1965. *Corporate Strategy*. New York: McGraw-Hill.

_____. 1976–77. "The State of Practice in Planning Systems." *Sloan Management Review* 18: 1–24.

_____. 1980. "So Much for Present-Day Practice—But What About the Future?" *Financial Times* (London), January 2.

Ansoff, H.I., J. Avner, R.G. Brandenburg, F.E. Portner, and R. Radosevich. 1970. "Does Planning Pay? The Effect of Planning on Success of Acquisitions in American Firms." *Long Range Planning* 3 (December): 2–7.

Ashby, W.R. 1952. *Design for a Brain*. London: Chapman and Hall.

Baumol, W.J. and R.E. Quandt. 1964. "Rules of Thumb and Optimally Imperfect Decisions." *American Economic Review* 54: 23–46.

Bunge, M. 1981. "Some Methodological Problems of Economics." Paper presented at Conference on Mathematical Economics and Public Policy, University of Essex, March.

Coase, R.H. 1937. "The Nature of the Firm." *Economica* 4 (November): 386–405.

Cyert, R.M. and J.G. March. 1963. *A Behavioral Theory of the Firm*. Englewood Cliffs, NJ: Prentice-Hall.

De Greene, K.B. 1981. "Limits to Societal Systems Adaptability." *Behavioral Science* 26: 103–13.

Day, R.H. and T. Groves, eds. 1975. *Adaptive Economic Models.* New York: Academic Press.

Demski, J.S. 1967. "An Accounting System Structured on a Linear Programming Model." *Accounting Review* 42 (October) 1967: 701–12.

Dyckman, T.R. 1981. "The Intelligence of Ambiguity." *Accounting, Organizations and Society* 6: 291–300.

Eilon, S. 1980. Editorial. "A Challenge to Planning." *Omega* 8: 127–36.

Einhorn, H.J. 1976. "A Synthesis: Accounting and Behavioral Science." *Journal of Accounting Research* 14 (supplement): 196–206.

Einhorn, H.J. and R.M. Hogarth. 1978. "Confidence in Judgement: Persistence of the Illusion of Validity." *Psychological Review* 85: 395–416.

Emery, F.E., ed. 1969. *Systems Thinking.* Harmondsworth, Middlesex: Penguin.

Emery, F.E. and E.L. Trist. 1965. "The Causal Texture of Organizational Environments." *Human Relations* 18: 21–32.

Forrester, J. 1969. "Planning under the Dynamic Influences of Complex Social Systems." In *Perspectives of Planning,* edited by E. Jantsch, pp. 237–54. Paris: OECD.

_____. 1975. "Counterintuitive Behavior of Social Systems." In *Collected Papers of J.W. Forrester,* chapter 14. Cambridge, MA: Wright-Allen Press.

Fulmer, R.M. and L.W. Rue. 1973. *The Practice and Profitability of Long-Range Planning.* Oxford, OH: The Planning Executives Institute.

Hedberg, B.L.T., P.C. Nystrom, and W.H. Starbuck. 1976. "Camping on Seesaws: Prescriptions for a Self-Designing Organization." *Administrative Science Quarterly* 21: 41–65.

Herold, D.M. 1972. "Long-Range Planning and Organizational Performance: A Cross-Valuation Study." *Academy of Management Journal* 15: 91–102.

Hogarth, R.M. and S. Makridakis. 1981. "Forecasting and Planning: An Evaluation." *Management Science* 27 (February): 115–38.

Itami, H. 1977. "Adaptive Behavior: Management Control and Information Analysis." *Studies in Accounting Research,* no. 15. Sarasota, FL: American Accounting Association.

Karger, D.W. and Z.A. Malik. 1975. "Long Range Planning and Organizational Performance." *Long Range Planning* 8 (December): 60–64.

Lorenz, C. 1979. "Corporate Strategy in an Age of Uncertainty." *Financial Times* (London): June 27.

March, J.G. 1978. "Bounded Rationality, Ambiguity, and the Engineering of Choice." *The Bell Journal of Economics* 9 (Autumn): 587–607.

March, J.G. and J.P. Olsen, eds. 1976. *Ambiguity and Choice in Organizations*. Bergen: Universitets forlaget.

March, J.G. and H.A. Simon. 1958. *Organizations*. New York: Wiley.

Mesarovic, M.D. and E. Pestel. 1974. *Mankind at the Turning Point*. New York: Dutton.

Mintzberg, H. 1973. "Strategy Making in Three Modes." *California Management Review* 16 (Winter): 44–53.

Miyazaki, I. 1970. "Economic Planning in Postwar Japan." *Journal of the Institute of Developing Economies* 8 (December): 369.

Modigliani, F. and K.J. Cohen. 1961. "The Role of Anticipations and Plans in Economic Behavior and Their Use in Economic Analysis and Forecasting." *Studies in Business Expectations and Planning*, no. 4. Bureau of Economic and Business Research, University of Illinois.

Naylor, T.H. and D.R. Gattis. 1976. "Corporate Planning Models." *California Management Review* 18: 69–78.

Nicolis, G. and I. Prigogine. 1977. *Self-Organization in Nonequilibrium Systems: From Dissipative Structures to Order Through Fluctuations*. New York: Wiley.

Rapoport, R.N. 1970. "Three Dilemmas in Action Research." *Human Relations* 23: 499–513.

Schon, D.A. 1971. *Beyond the Stable State*. New York: Random House.

Simon, H.A. 1957a. "A Behavioral Model of Rational Choice." In *Models of Man*, edited by H.A. Simon, chapter 14. New York: Wiley.

_____. 1957b. "Rational Choice and the Structure of the Environment." In *Models of Man*, chapter 15. See Simon 1957a.

Sproul, L., S. Weiner, and D. Wolf. 1978. *Organizations and Anarchy*. Chicago, IL: University of Chicago Press.

Steiner, G.A. 1969. *Top Management Planning*. New York: Macmillan.

Stonich, P.J. 1975. "Formal Planning Pitfalls and How to Avoid Them—Part 2." *Management Review* (July): 29–35.

Susman, G.I. 1981. "Planned Change: Prospects for the 1980s." *Management Science* 27 (February): 139–54.

Thune, S.S. and R.J. House. 1970. "Where Long-Range Planning Pays Off." *Business Horizons* 13: 81–87.

Trist, E.L. 1977. "A Concept of Organizational Ecology." *The Australian Journal of Management* 2: 171–75.

Weick, K. 1979. *The Social Psychology of Organizing,* 2d ed. Reading, MA: Addison-Wesley.

Wildavsky, A. 1971. "Does Planning Work?" *Public Interest* 19 (Summer): pp. 95–104.

_____. 1973. "If Planning is Everything, Maybe It's Nothing." *Policy Science* 4: 127–53.

Wilson, K.G. 1979. "Problems in Physics with Many Scales of Length." *Scientific American* 241: 158–79.

Wood, D.R., Jr. and R.L. La Forge. 1979. "The Impact of Comprehensive Planning on Financial Performance." *Academy of Management Journal* 22: 516–26.

Appendix: Systems and the "Systems Approach"

Although this book is about planning and not about systems per se, it contains many references to systems and systems ideas. Indeed, this book proposes a systems approach to the problem of planning. This Appendix therefore aims at providing readers with all the information they need to follow the discussion, a necessary service in view of the systems literature's vast, scattered, uneven, and somewhat bewildering state. Throughout the text this Appendix is identified with a capital A. The discussion follows very closely on Bunge (1979a).

WHAT A SYSTEM IS

Interacting Components: The First Aspect of Systems

No universally accepted definition of *system* exists as yet. We can, however, capture the essential aspects. First, a system is a complex conceptual or material entity whose components are interrelated rather than loose: at least one component acts on the others, thus modifying their behavior. As such, a system is to be distinguished from an aggregate, whose components do not interact. Thus the number 15, the sum of the integers one to five, is an aggregate but not a (conceptual) system, whereas the total of the assets side of a balance sheet is not merely an aggregate or whole but also a system (an information system), since the components, or at least some of them, interact in determining each other's value. The value of the plant and machinery is different, taken in isolation, from when it is regarded as part of a particular combination of assets. An aggregate is not held together by links of this kind. The behavior of each component is independent of the behavior of the others. The notion of *system* as distinct from *aggregate* is very old, but has only recently been exploited systematically.

Two things follow from this first property. One is that the whole is not just the sum of its parts because the latter are linked together and interact: the whole can behave in ways that none of the parts can. Performance of the whole "depends critically on how well the parts fit and work together, not merely on how well each performs when considered independently" (Ackoff 1974: 14–15). Concepts such as holism, synergy, and Gestalt place emphasis on performance of the whole as distinct from that of its parts. The second consequence of this interrelatedness is that a system cannot be broken down into isolated subsystems (components that happen to be systems). If a system could be thus broken down, the combination of all the subsystems would constitute an aggregate, not a system.

Concrete Versus Conceptual Systems

In the sequel we narrow the discussion to concrete systems, which are objects composed of at least two different connected things (objects). We distinguish these from abstract systems, whose components are conceptual rather than material (e.g., a theory is a conceptual system; so is the state space of a concrete system). All of the objects we shall be considering—human beings, business organizations, information systems—fall within the narrower category of concrete systems.

Structure: The Second Aspect of Systems

The second essential aspect of systems is that of structure and environment. By *structure* we mean something more than internal structure. We mean not only relations among the system's components but also those between system components and the environment. *System* structure is therefore not synonymous with organizational structure. Some of these relationships must be more or less stable at a given time for the system to be identifiable. In general, however, the relations (couplings, links, connections) may be more or less strong, permanent or temporary, disappearing and reappearing, static or dynamic. In fact the couplings of system components one with another and with the environment are not merely relations, but re-

lations by which one component alters the behavior of another. Before defining the environment let us say something about couplings and variables.

Couplings between Objects Versus Couplings between Qualities

Couplings in concrete systems are energy (including information) or
matter transfers, and any behavior-influencing relations that exist between
two objects or two physical qualities, that are representable by mathematical functions or operators. Dynamic connections (termed *flows*) are a special case of energy or matter transfers. (If a physical flow carries information, the entire system is called an *information system.*)

The reader should note that few mathematical representations of couplings are interpretable as relations between two objects; most are interpreted rather as relations between qualities. Let us look for a moment at
mathematical representations of couplings more closely to see how they
may be interpretable as relations between two objects. In mathematical
functions the variables (which are used to denote qualities, not objects) are
the arguments of a function and sometimes the function itself. For example, in the representation $y = f(x)$, x and perhaps y are variables. (Note
that it makes sense to speak of variables in a system only when they are representable mathematically.) A coupling is best represented mathematically
by the composition of two or more functions or else by a function of two or
more variables, that is, by either

$$F = f \circ g \qquad\qquad\qquad\qquad\qquad\text{A.1}$$

or

$$G = h(x, y) \qquad\qquad\qquad\qquad\qquad\text{A.2}$$

where G takes a constant value and $\circ$ or h represent couplings. To show
how two variables (e.g., x and y coupled as in Equation A.1) may be con-
strued as each belonging to a different (rather than the same) component, or
as one belonging to a system component and the other to the environment,
and $\circ$ as thus representing a coupling between two objects rather than between two qualities, we decompose Equation A.1 into $F = f(y)$ and
$y = g(x)$, and interpret y to be both an output variable of the component
represented by g and an input variable to the component represented by f. In

this sense a coupling becomes a common variable of two components or of a component and the environment.

Note also that while only *some* couplings between concrete objects are representable by formal (mathematical, in particular functional) notation, *all* couplings between conceptual objects are so representable (e.g., by logical connectives, if not by more sophisticated mathematical functions and operators). For example, in the conceptual system p consisting of propositions q and r and the logical operator of conjunction, $p = q \wedge r$, the operator $\wedge$ is a coupling.

We can now define the system's environment as the set of all things coupled with components of the system. This is the immediate or "relevant" environment, that part that exerts a significant influence on the system, not the total environment. A further important point about the definition of the environment is noted below ("Correctly Circumscribing a System").

A System as an Ordered Composition-Structure-Environment Triple

In sum we can say that a system has a definite composition (specific components), a definite environment, and a definite structure at any given time. (The more strongly coupled the system is to other systems, the more difficult it is to identify its composition, and hence its environment. In that case the boundaries of the system are unlikely to be rigid.) To be able to speak about a system at all we need to know at least these three things. Thus the minimal model of a system, σ, at time t is the ordered triple $\sigma = \langle C, E, S \rangle$, where C stands for composition, E for environment, and S for structure (Bunge 1979a). The ordering of C, E and S is a natural one in the discovery process: We must know the system's components before we can identify its environment and structure, and the environment must be known before the structure because the latter is the set of relations among the components and between the components and the environment. To complete the model, we should require C and E to be mutually disjoint subsets ($C \cap E = \emptyset$) and S a non-empty set of relations on the union of C and E.

These ideas may be illustrated by reference to a business school. The composition of this system is the combination of its staff and students; the environment is the exogenous natural environment and social milieu and the structure consists principally of the relation of teaching to learning.

Atomic Component and Universal System

To round off this section, note that not everything is a system. (We assume there are elementary things that have no parts, and we know there are aggregates of independent parts.) Moreover, since the environment of a system is the set of all things coupled with components of the system, every system is part of a larger system. Ultimately all systems are subsystems of the totality of systems, the universe, which we denote by Σ . Anticipating the later discussion, Σ is defined as being without environment, and is the only system that is closed at all times in the sense of having no exchanges with its environment: $E(\Sigma , t) = \emptyset$ for all t, where $E(\ ,\ )$ is the environment function.

CORRECTLY CIRCUMSCRIBING A SYSTEM

Although we now know what a system is in general, we still face a problem when it comes to specifying correctly what belongs to a specific system, that is, in drawing the boundaries of or locating a given system. Our definition of structure gives a clue to the solution of this problem, and can help us avoid adding to the many cases of system misspecification that appear in the literature. A common example of such misspecification is found in studies of business enterprises, where the error lies in regarding all variables excluded in the institutional or legal definition of the organization as necessarily exogenous (belonging to the system's environment). A variable should be regarded as "external" only if the coupling from the environment to the system is one-way. If the environment acts on the system in such a way that the "external" variable affects the system variables and is in turn significantly influenced by "internal" variables it should be classed as endogenous and the boundary of the system extended to include the relevant part of the environment (Fig. A.1). *Environment* can now be properly defined as the set of all things coupled *unidirectionally* with components of the system, the direction being from environment to system, the influence, if any, of system on environment being insignificant.

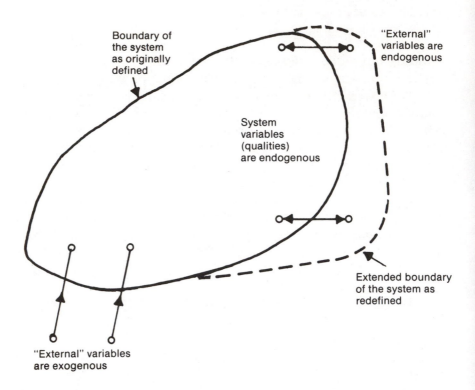

Fig. A.1. Correctly circumscribing a system.

THE "SYSTEMS APPROACH" TO RESEARCH

What It Is

The "systems approach" to research or "systems thinking," consists in recognizing that if we wish to understand the behavior of anything that possesses the properties of a system we need to study not only the relationships among the system's parts but also the system's relationship to one or more larger systems. This is based on the assumption that everything is part of some system, and every system except the universe is part of some larger system. In other words the new approach is characterized by the complementary use of synthesis and analysis, rather than just analysis, in research and problem solving. Analysis, the breaking down of a phenomenon, problem, or thing, into its parts, which is the traditional method employed by science to explain the behavior and properties of wholes, is augmented by synthesis, or the fitting of wholes into larger wholes. Thus a company may be composed of many parts (departments, divisions, or functions) and in turn operate in an environment (other organizations with which it has transactions, up to the economy and society of which it forms a part). To understand its behavior completely we must study the part/whole relations and the whole/larger whole relations.

Justification

We can now justify the systems approach to studying planning. The justification lies in the analytical power possessed by the "system" concept that is not shared by other methods of studying organizational phenomena. The utility of the "systems approach" to research lies in the greater explanatory power that results from combining the two orientations of part/whole and whole/larger whole, namely analysis and synthesis, when the thing we are studying is a system.

Motivation

The systems approach consists of putting analysis and synthesis together, an intellectual innovation described as a revolution by Ackoff (1974), who speaks about the Systems Age which, while it sounds simple enough, is profound, and leads to radically new thinking on a number of problems previously regarded as settled. This approach to research has been instrumental in solving problems that defied solution by more traditional methods in science. It has achieved this result partly by focusing on the structural characteristics of systems and thus crossing the artificial boundaries between disciplines standing in the way of extremely general theories.

The system concept and the systems approach to research were developed in response to two needs: the long-standing need in science to discover similarities between things with specific differences, in this case things made up of interrelated parts; and the need to comprehend very large wholes made up of a complex variety of components, calling for an interdisciplinary approach.

Misconceptions

Let us now dispel some popular misconceptions about the "systems approach" to research. They are exemplified by such claims as:

The systems approach to research is holistic: it focuses on wholes rather than parts.

The systems approach to research replaces the traditional analytical mode of thought in science by a new synthetic or systems mode of thought.

Analysis and reductionism (expressing the behavior of a whole in terms of the behavior of its parts) are incapable of explaining totalities.

These claims are either partially true or completely false. In the first and second the systems approach to research is viewed as something that replaces traditional methods in science rather than as something that augments and adapts them. The third claim is groundless because holism, which is the opposite of reductionism, is just as incapable of explaining any totalities precisely because it excludes from discussion the system components and the relations between them. What is true is our claim made in the beginning of this Appendix, namely that "the whole is not just the sum of its parts," for while every system is a whole, not every whole is a system. What makes the whole into a system is precisely the actions exerted by some parts on others. In view of these observations it is better to speak of the *systemic approach* to research and avoid the term *systems approach*, which has come to be associated with holism. We thereby capture the two features of analysis and synthesis.

Nor is the claim always true that the systemic approach consists of working from the top down (or from the outside in). Its truth depends on the circumstances, specifically the complexity of the system under study. In investigating some systems we may start with the totality and its environment and proceed to discover its composition and structure. With more complex systems (e.g., social systems) we may have to start with the components, and by studying their behavior try to discover the structure of the whole. What *is* quite true generally is the order of investigation, in which we must identify first the composition, then the environment, and finally the structure, and then recognize that the whole forms part of a larger whole or wholes.

Weaknesses

The systemic approach to research is new and the underlying systems theory is still developing and not without defects. The latter is not surprising, since one of the main objectives of the systemic approach is to discover similarities, in either concepts or structural characteristics, that hold for or occur among systems of many diverse kinds. After some 40 years systems theory has yet to produce precise definitions of its principal concepts (such as system, state, and steady state), or even a universally accepted terminology. Another weakness we will dwell on later is that in their zeal to achieve utmost generality, some people have freely extended principles developed by systems theorists for certain kinds of systems, particularly biological systems, to systems of much higher complexity (e.g., social systems) without making the necessary modifications or reinterpretations. But these weaknesses, which need only be temporary, do not cast doubt on the utility of the system concept and the systemic approach.

Another possible limitation on the use of the systemic approach requires lengthier explanation, and is the subject of Chapter 7.

WAYS OF CLASSIFYING SYSTEMS

Having explained what systems are, and how, by adopting the systemic approach in research, we increase our theories' explanatory power, we should now consider various ways of classifying systems. We will consider classification of systems by function, by how the system is represented, by degree of complexity, as entropic or negentropic, and by type of behavior, before noting an important difference between human and organizational behavior and that of other systems.

Natural or Artifact: Having a Goal or Having a Function

Whenever we deal with natural systems it is reasonable to think about the system's goal. But not all systems are natural. Some are explicitly constructed by another system to accomplish the constructing system's goals. We call such constructed systems *artifacts*, and say that they have a *func-*

tion. Churchman (1968: 12–13) cites some advantages of thinking about an artifact in terms of its function:

> The way to describe an automobile is first by thinking about what it is for, about its *function,* and not the list of items that make up its structure [by structure he means what we have called composition]. If you begin by thinking about what it is for . . . you will [say] . . . that an automobile is a mechanical means of transporting a few people from one place to another, at a certain prescribed cost. As soon as you begin to think in this manner, then your "description" of the automobile begins to take on new and often quite radical aspects. . . . [Is] a two-wheeled automobile a possibility? [Is] an automobile without any wheels whatsoever also a possibility?

Manner of Representation

We can classify systems according to the way we represent them. If we wish to represent only the composition, structure, and environment of a system we use a graph or matrix. However, since most systems of interest to us have dynamic properties, we represent them by change models such as the input–output or the state space models, with their corresponding mathematical expression in differential or difference equations. The state space representation of dynamic systems has so far proved the most versatile, having been used across the greatest variety of disciplines (e.g., engineering, biology, economics).

Degree of Complexity

We can also classify systems according to their complexity, as measured by the number of *conceivable* states the system may be in (the number of components of the state space of the system). *Complexity* thus refers to the number of different kinds of behavior a system may exhibit, which in turn is a function of the number of basic units of behavior (called *acts*) of which the system is capable and the number of different combinations (concatenations) of these acts.

Degree of Complexity as the Level in a Hierarchy of Systems

Various systems writers have attempted to construct a hierarchy of systems arrayed by degree of complexity. The most well known of these is probably that of Boulding (1956), who distinguished the following levels in increasing order of complexity:

1. Static structures (frameworks)
2. Simple dynamic systems (e.g., clockworks)
3. Cybernetic systems (systems with feedback)
4. The most elemental living system (the cell)
5. Plants
6. Animals
7. Humans
8. Social organizations
9. Transcendental systems (concerned with "the ultimate and absolutes and inescapable unknowables").

This hierarchy reveals a major shortcoming in current views and versions of planning and control. The hierarchy shows business enterprises, which have been characterized as sociotechnical systems, to be of level 8 complexity, whereas most of our present tools and theoretical procedures for describing, analyzing, and planning or controlling them are seen not to go beyond level 3 (exemplified, for example, by budgetary control techniques).

Degree of Complexity as Degrees of Freedom of a System's States

Complexity may also be expressed in terms of degrees of freedom, an aspect of system states common to all concrete systems and familiar to the reader from statistics (statistical estimation). We cannot proceed, however, without first introducing the concepts of state of a system, change of state, state function, and state space.

State, change of state, state function, state space.   Although the concept of *state* plays an important role in systems theory, decision theory, modern control theory, and so on, as yet we do not have a definition of "state" sufficiently general to be applicable to all (concrete) systems.[1] Consequently we must make do with the following: A *state* of system at any given time relative to some given frame of reference is the information needed to determine the behavior of the system from that time on (adapted from Żadeh, in Zadeh and Polak 1969). This information will comprise a number of variables called *state variables* or more precisely *state functions,* each representing a property possessed by the system, and together characterizing the system at a given instant relative to a set of reference frames. The *state space* of the system relative to this set of reference frames is the codomain of the total state function, formed as the Cartesian product of the codomains of the components of all the individual state functions. We can distinguish between this total or *conceivable* state space and the *possible or lawful* state space: Laws and constraints restrict the codomains to the ranges of the state variables. In the case of a system the state space is restricted in another way, as we will now explain by distinguishing between a thing, an aggregate, and a system. Note that for any concrete thing, aggregate, or system of things there is no unique state function but a large number of them, limited only by the frames of reference which we can conceive of. There is no such thing as an absolute state function for a given thing, aggregate, or system, and hence a statement such as "The state of the business (or of the economy) at a given time is so and so" is true only for a particular frame of reference.

We begin by considering a *thing,* defined as a single concrete object together with the properties it possesses, and distinguish it from a conceptual object (e.g., a proposition, a theory). Every thing is in some state at a given time relative to a given reference frame. In fact every concrete thing has at least two different states: At a given time it either possesses a particular property associated with a given reference frame or it does not. A conceptual object, on the other hand, does not have states. Hence if x is a thing and y a conceptual object, and denoting state space by $S(\cdot)$, the state space of x at a given time relative to a given reference frame is

$$\left| S(x) \right| \geq 2 \qquad\qquad\qquad\qquad \text{A.3}$$

while

$$\left| S(y) \right| = \emptyset \qquad\qquad\qquad\qquad \text{A.4}$$

An *aggregate* (a) is a set of independent or noninteracting components. These components may be things or conceptual objects. Suppose an aggregate is made up of r noninteracting components, the partial state spaces of which are $S(c_i)$, $i = 1, \ldots, r$. Then the state space of the aggregate is

$$S(a) = \bigcup_{i = 1}^{r} S(c_i), r \geq 2 \qquad\qquad\qquad A.5$$

Thus if there are three mutually independent things, each of which can be in two states denoted by 0 and 1, the state space of the aggregate of these things is

$$S(a) = \{0, 1\}^2$$
$$= \{\langle 0,0,0\rangle, \langle 1,0,0\rangle, \langle 0,1,0\rangle, \langle 0,0,1\rangle, \langle 1,1,0\rangle,$$
$$\langle 1,0,1\rangle, \langle 0,1,1\rangle, \langle 1,1,1\rangle\} \ .$$

Equivalent statements would be that the state space of the aggregate will have $n_1 \cdot n_2 \cdot n_3$ points, where n_i is the number of states of component i, $i = 1, 2, 3$, or that the state space will have 2^r points. Equation A.5 is not contradicted by the statement that the properties of an aggregate are not equal to the sum of the properties of the parts, as the reader will readily see from the fact that if two things u and v form an aggregate, the latter possesses the property of being composed of u and v, which neither of its parts does.

A *system* is a set of components, at least two of which are interacting at any given time ($r \geq 2$). The state space of system σ relative to a given reference frame is

$$S(\sigma) \neq \bigcup_{i = 1}^{r} S(c_i). \qquad\qquad\qquad A.6$$

For one thing some or all of the r components of the system are interrelated, so their values are mutually restricted: The states of some or all components are at least partly determined by the states other components are in. For another, the system possesses certain emergent properties that none of its components has (e.g., a human being may swim, a company become bankrupt). The state space of the system (relative to a given reference frame) cannot be constructed simply from the partial state spaces, as in the case of an aggregate, but must take these other things into account.

Finally, all (concrete) things, and hence systems, are changeable, quantitatively and/or qualitatively. This amounts to saying that for all choices of state function the state space has at least two points. An *event* is a change of state of a thing or system, which is represented as a trajectory in a state space. Although it changes, and hence becomes composed of different things with different relations, a given system is regarded as retaining its original identity unless and until it ceases to exist or is absorbed into another system. Thus the name Benjamin Franklin continued to identify the same system (although this system had undergone many changes) throughout his lifetime; the situation is similar with a company, even if it is reconstructed, but not if it is acquired or merged with another company.

Complexity as degrees of freedom. Picking up the discussion again from the previous section, suppose that a system has r components ($r \geq 2$), each of which could, if it were able to act independently of other components, take on two values associated with a given reference frame. If all the components were independent the state of the whole could range over 2^r different points in this state space. But of course the very essence of *system* is that the components are not independent. Unless at least two of the r components interact the whole is not a system. Suppose further that at a given time the components are all interacting but that only m actual behaviors related to this reference frame are observed, $m < 2^r$. That is, the actual variety of behavior in this respect is less than when the state of each component takes on its full range of values independently of the values taken on by the other component states. We then say that the system's behavior is constrained to the degrees of freedom, m, of the full set of behaviors. The possible (as distinct from conceivable) state space of the system associated with the given reference frame at a given time will contain the following number of different points:

$$2^r$$

- k_1 excluded by mutual restriction of values due to
  interrelatedness of components
+ k_2 representing emergent behaviors of the system (behaviors
  of which the system but not its parts is capable)
- k_3 excluded by constraints on the possible values of components
  of the state function other than those due to
  interrelatedness

$$= \overline{m}$$

The actual degree of complexity of the system could then be expressed as m. Since there are any number of conceivable reference frames, this measure is relative. To establish it as an absolute measure we would have to include all possible reference frames, it being understood that these frames should be independent of each other (mutually exclusive), not contain any linear combinations, and that reference frames and their associated system properties should not influence each other. (A further condition is that it must be possible to use the reference frame for parametrizing the states of the system property in question.)

Complexity measured in terms of degrees of freedom appears to vary directly with complexity understood as level in a hierarchy of systems, the first measure of complexity, a fact that has important practical implications for control, as Buckley (1968) has noted:

> On the biological level, the component parts of [the system] have relatively few degrees of freedom, and changes in the environment are relatively directly and inexorably reacted to by selective structural changes in the species. [Social] systems are capable of persisting within a wide range of degrees of freedom of the components, and are often able to "muddle through" environmental changes that are not too demanding.

A social system, in other words, is able to adapt to a wide variety of disturbances, environmental and internal, and survive: in terms of our example and an appropriate set of reference frames, $m \rightarrow (2^r - k_1 + k_2)$, or putting it another way, many of the k_3 constraints may be treated as weak constraints. The human body can also adapt to changes, but within somewhat narrower limits ($m \ll [2^r - k_1 + k_2]$), while an ordinary machine that can operate in only one fixed way cannot adapt at all; it either operates or ceases to operate (in relation to an appropriate reference frame for rate of activity, $m = 2$).

A "Thermodynamic" Property of Systems: Closed and Open Systems

Concrete systems may be classified according to a property analogous to a thermodynamic property of physical systems. The analogy should hold, since all concrete systems are physical (wholes composed of at least two connected things). While thermodynamics is concerned specifically with the study of the general laws governing heat-change processes, it provides a distinction that can be generalized to a wider range of processes in concrete things. This is the distinction between processes of increasing and decreasing entropy.

The second law of (classical) thermodynamics asserts that concrete systems increase in entropy monotonically until they reach an equilibrium state in which entropy is at a maximum. At this point the system becomes inert and ceases to exist. "Entropy" can be understood as the degree of disorder in a concrete system, the randomness of the states of the system's parts in relation to some reference frame, or as the probability of the state of the system (in relation to a set of reference frames) actually occurring. In its most general terms, the second law then states that concrete systems go from less probable to more probable states (from less entropic to more entropic states). The trouble is that there is a class of systems for which the second law does not hold (until, eventually, such systems cease to exist, an interval that may be measured in decades or even centuries). It so happens also that this class of systems spans most of the systems of interest to us, such as human beings and social organizations.

A General Mathematical Formulation of Entropy Change

Whether or not the second law holds over the life of a system determines whether or not the system is a closed entropic system or an open negentropic system ("Negentropic" meaning "in a state of negative entropy"). Denoting entropy by ϵ , the total change in entropy in a closed system such as an ordinary machine (meaning a machine without feedback) is

$$d\epsilon = d_i\epsilon > 0 \qquad\qquad\qquad A.7$$

where the subscript i denotes the production (increase) of entropy due to irreversible processes going on within the system (the process of wearing out). In the case of an open system the total change in entropy is

$$d\epsilon = d_i\epsilon + d_e\epsilon \qquad\qquad\qquad A.8$$

where the subscript e denotes the change in entropy *made possible by* matter-energy-information inflows from the environment. The first term on the right ($d_i\epsilon$) is always positive by the second law, and hence the entropy change in a closed system is always positive. The second law holds only when $d\epsilon > 0$. The second term on the right of Equation A.8 ($d_e\epsilon$) may be negative or positive, and consequently the total entropy change in an open system may be negative as well as positive. An open negentropic system is one in which

$$d\epsilon \ < 0, \text{ i.e., } \ \left| d_i \epsilon \right| < \left| d_e \epsilon \right| \ . \qquad\qquad\text{A.9}$$

Comparing equations A.7 and A.8, we note that only open systems can become negentropic. If they do they disobey the second law.

A closed system is exemplified by an ordinary machine. The general course of events (or evolution) of a machine is toward increasing entropy. Eventually it wears out and all work stops. It becomes inert. At this point it reaches its equilibrium state, and in this state is entropy is a maximum. Closed systems go from less entropic (less probable) to more entropic (more probable) states.

Human beings and social organizations are examples of open systems. These have the capability of becoming negentropic. A human being is subject to the same kind of irreversible processes that cause all concrete systems eventually to run down and become inert. But in this case the system imports certain things (matter, free energy, and/or information) from its environment in amounts that make it possible to more than offset the increase in entropy due to irreversible processes. The system is able to produce negative entropy in amounts sufficient to arrest and reverse the increase in entropy due to irreversible processes and become negentropic. In other words, the net import of materials makes possible a transfer of negative entropy from the system's environment. An open system "feeds" on negative entropy from its environment. This is referred to as "entropy transfer." The essential distinction between closed and open systems, first pointed out by von Bertalanffy (1950), is drawn in these terms. An open system is one that is open to entropy transfer, a closed system one that is not. Open systems go from more entropic (less improbable) to less entropic (more improbable) states.

We end this section by noting that the entropy change in systems is therefore incompletely specified by the second law of (classical) thermodynamics, that the distinction between closed and open systems in the sense of Bertalanffy is important because it tells us something about their respective typical behaviors, and that open systems are of primary interest to us, closed systems generally playing the role of tools used by open systems.

An Incomplete Specification of Closed and Open Systems, and a Qualification

In the literature it is not uncommon to find a closed system defined as one that does not exchange things (matter, energy, information) with its environment, one whose boundaries are impermeable by these things, one without an environment; and an open system as one that engages in exchanges with its environment, whose boundaries are permeable. If σ is a system with environment $E(\sigma, t)$, σ is closed at time t if and only if $E(\sigma, t) = \emptyset$, otherwise it is open. This is an insufficient definition for two reasons. First, adoption of this definition would allow us to convert an open system containing n components into a closed system with $(n + 1)$ components simply by regarding the environment as a component. Conditions A.7 and A.9 prevent us from playing around with the system's boundary. Second, and more important, such a definition tells us nothing about the behavior to be expected of a system. $E(\sigma, t) \neq \emptyset$ is sufficient to characterize an open system, but not the fact that an open system may become negentropic, for which we need the thermodynamic definition A.9. Accordingly, in the sequel and throughout the text whenever we refer to systems as being open or closed we will mean it in the sense of Bertalanffy, *open or closed to entropy transfer*. And since open systems typically do, *but may not,* become negentropic, we will use the term *negentropic* (rather than merely *open*) whenever it is appropriate to do so.

The qualification refers to the classification of all concrete systems as either open or closed. As we saw earlier in this Appendix ("Atomic Component and Universal System") everything except the universe, the totality of systems (Σ), interacts with some other things, and thus the universe is the only system that is closed at all times and in all respects. All other systems are only temporarily or relatively closed (or equivalently open) in this sense. For example, while all systems are gravitationally open, some may be closed to the exchange of matter, some to the exchange of energy (including information).

The Conditions Defining an Open Negentropic System

Most systems of interest are not only open but also negentropic. In stating that a system is (relatively) open (closed) to entropy transfer, something more is implied than that its boundaries are permeable (impermeable) by matter-energy-information flows. For a system to be open to entropy transfer three conditions must be met:

1. The boundaries of the system must be permeable by energy in some form (matter, free energy, or information)
2. The system must be a net importer from its environment, taking in more than it puts back, and

   3. *The system must possess the organizing ability to use the physical energy or information base to decrease entropy,* or in other words to achieve increased order and complexity.

Let us examine these conditions in more detail.

   To explain the first, consider an ordinary machine again. A machine receives inputs of matter, energy, and/or information and carries out some transformation on them, yielding matter, energy, or information of a different form. But the machine itself does not exchange matter, energy, or information with its environment; it does not absorb these things into itself. The composition of the machine is unaffected by the entire process, and the relationships between its components do not change. Sooner or later it wears out. It is incapable of using the things it imports to reverse this process.

   On the second point, unless the system is a net importer from its environment it lacks the physical base that is the *means* whereby the system may become negentropic.

   The third point states that there must be something inside the system capable of converting an inflow of energy or information into an import of negative entropy. If it is to become negentropic the system must have the organizing capacity to use the physical energy or information base to offset increasing entropy due to irreversible processes. The system must be able selectively to organize and utilize the inputs from the environment for its own maintenance and self-regulation. *Attempts by an open system to become negentropic will fail unless condition A.9 is met.* Simon (1969: 97–99) stresses this point:

> . . . complex systems will evolve from simple systems much more rapidly if there are stable intermediate forms [and information confirming these is provided by feedback from the environment] than if there are not. . . . It is this information about stable configurations, and not free energy or negentropy from the sun, that guides the process of evolution and provides the selectivity that is essential to account for its rapidity.

In effect, the rules for adaptation and survival are derived inductively from past experience. The following example given by Buckley (1967: 47) clearly illustrates the point at issue. When a person speaks to a companion in a language foreign to the companion, she is emitting only noise or vibrating energy so far as the companion is concerned. That is, there is no mapping of the structured variety of sounds or vocal energy to the repertoire of meaningful sounds in the mind of the companion. The companion lacks the ability to organize and utilize what he is hearing to convey meaning. We note, then, that what *causes* an import of energy or information to become an import of negative entropy is not the inputs themselves but rather something inside the system, its internal dynamics (the interplay between its parts). This activity is autonomous, spontaneous, not the result of an import of energy from the environment or of an outside stimulus.

Autonomous Interactions Convert Energy Inflows into Negative Entropy

These autonomous interactions between system components come about, very broadly, in two different ways: through the existence of flexibility and discretion in decision making, and as a result of tension between system components. These can be illustrated by reference to a business enterprise.

Members of the business organization are constantly interacting with one another and with the environment. The autonomous character of certain interactions arises because the aforementioned interactions are usually much too rich to be covered by standing operating rules and instructions. The discrepancy between the requirements of real situations and prescribed rules of behavior—the unmapped exigencies of actual situations encountered inside and outside the system—produces uncertainty, ambiguity, and conflict, which in turn give rise to a range of permitted alternatives in the actions taken by members of the organization. It is within this range of discretion that much of the system dynamics occurs. Autonomous interactions between components of the system also derive from the fact that open systems such as business enterprises are of a high level of complexity in the systems hierarchy referred to earlier in this Appendix ("Correctly Circumscribing a System"). The range of environmental interchanges that high-level systems engage in is wide and, as a result, so is the range of uncertainty, ambiguity, and incongruence that such systems are subject to. The last-named effect reminds us that it is not just interactions with the environment that produce discrepancies. A given internal (organizational) structure may also generate exigencies, in the form of conflicts of interest, ambiguous standards and instructions, and role discrepancies.

The second way in which autonomous interactions between system components are generated derives from the fact that a certain degree of tension between the parts of a system is a normal state of affairs. Some tension is as necessary for the viability of a human being or a social organization as free energy is to a machine. Communication networks and information flows spread tensions through a business organization in the form of social pressures of interpersonal influences. Tension may manifest itself in strain, striving, frustration, enthusiasm, aggression, deviant behavior, or creativity (Buckley 1967), and may be destructive or constructive relative to the goals of the organization. The optimal level of tension in the organization should be set relative to a level of attainment of system goals that allows at least minimal satisfaction of members' needs.

Summary

The main points in the discussion of this section on the "thermodynamic" distinction between closed and open systems will now be summarized.

1. In terms of the permeability of their boundaries by matter-energy-information flows, all systems except the universe are only relatively closed or open. The universe is the only system that is closed at all times and in all respects. But this is an incomplete definition of closed and open systems because it tells us nothing about their typical behaviors.

2. The feature that is a sharp dividing line between system behaviors is whether the total change in entropy in the system is positive or negative. In this sense (Bertalanffy) closed systems are those in which the change is always positive. In open systems it may be positive or negative and typically negative (the system can become negentropic). We may thus speak of entropic systems and negentropic systems. The terms *closed* and *open systems* are used throughout this book in the sense that a closed system is one that is not open to entropy transfer, an open system one that is open to entropy transfer and is capable of becoming negentropic. The term *negentropic* will be used in connection with open systems that have demonstrated the capability of reversing increasing entropy.

3. Entropic systems evolve toward greater uniformity (increasing entropy), negentropic systems have an inherent tendency to evolve toward greater complexity (entropy decreasing and becoming negative or more negative).

4. To become negentropic a system must be open to inflows of energy and/or information from its environment and import more than it exports to the environment. Open systems are not automatically negentropic systems, although they typically are. To become negentropic an open system must in addition have the ability to convert imported energy and/or information into negative entropy. This capability is expressed by saying that the system is open to entropy transfer. The system must be able to organize, selec-

tively structure, and utilize the inputs from the environment to achieve greater order and complexity. The process of conversion is carried out by the system's internal dynamics, a strictly autonomous activity not triggered from outside the system, and by feedback of information from the environment. In an organization such as a business enterprise the autonomous interactions take two main forms: built-in flexibility and discretion in decision making, and the existence of a certain degree of tension between components and members of the organization. Through feedback information the organization learns which adaptations are successful, and is thus enabled to be more selective in its future adaptations and achieve greater order and complexity more rapidly. Two further points not previously referred to are:

5. Closed systems only achieve a state of equilibrium as an end state when the systems become inert and incapable of performing work. Entropy is then a maximum. The characteristic state of an open system is a steady state (at least this is so in organismic systems[2]), a state in which the ratio between system components is constant, a stable stationary state distinct from the equilibrium state. In this state the system is working at its maximum potential and in certain conditions entropy is a minimum. As applied to systems, the term *steady state*, like *state*, is not yet well defined (Amey 1979: chapter 4).[3] All of this can be compressed into the statement that closed (indeed all entropic) systems tend toward the lowest energy level, while (open) negentropic systems tend toward a high energy level.

6. A further property of open systems not possessed by closed systems is that if they attain a steady state they can do so by different paths and from different starting points (true of organismic systems, at least). This property is called *equifinality*. The state attained by a closed system depends on the starting point and is reached by a fixed pathway (Amey 1979: chapter 4).

Type of Behavior

A Fourfold Classification

We can classify concrete systems according to how their behavior is determined (Ackoff 1971). We begin by making a broad distinction between anticipatory and nonanticipatory systems (between systems whose behavior does or does not depend on the expected outcome of their actions).

There are two kinds of nonanticipatory systems: state maintaining and goal seeking. An example of a *state-maintaining system* would be a heating system regulated by a thermostat. Such a system only reacts to changes or initiating events (stimuli), which completely determine its behavior. It is an adaptive, but not a learning system: It cannot choose its behavior or improve with experience. A *goal-seeking system,* unlike a state-maintaining system, has a choice of behaviors and, if it is equipped with a memory, can learn as well as adapt (it can become more efficient at adapting). An example would be an automatic pilot on an aircraft. Such a system can respond differently to a particular event in an unchanging environment until it produces the particular outcome that is its goal.

Anticipatory systems, on the other hand, are capable of expecting either reward or punishment when contemplating some future act or engaging in an activity, and of preparing to obtain the reward or avoid the punishment. A stimulus, or engaging in an act, leads the system to expect or foresee a future event, the outcome. Such foresight presupposes learning, the ability to pair a particular stimulus or act occurring while the system is in a particular state with a possible future event. Hence only learned behavior can be anticipatory, and learning in turn means that the system must have a memory. If behavior is learned, it is also motivated: The outcome of the action is expected to bring a reduction in motivation. Let us examine the two kinds of anticipatory system: purposive and purposeful.

A *purposive system* is able to form expectations and prepare for future events. For behavior to be purposive a system must be able to display choice of actions, form expectations, learn, and presumably it must also value (stick to) its purpose or goal. It must be tenacious. An example of a purposive system is an animal with salivary glands, which secrete saliva when the animal perceives food, in preparation for possible future digestion.

A *purposeful system* is a system that can choose its goals under constant conditions. It selects ends as well as means, and hence displays will. The system itself chooses the goal (the goal is not already wired in). It is also an expectation-forming and learning system. Human beings and social organizations are examples of purposeful systems. All purposeful systems are open and negentropic, but the converse is not necessarily true: Only the highest forms of open systems (human beings and social organizations) are purposeful. These ideas are summarized in the table below:

Table A.1. Classification of systems by type of behavior

Type of system	Behavior determined by	The system can	
		Adapt	Learn
Nonanticipatory			
State maintaining	Environment and system's previous state	X	
Goal seeking	Environment and previous state	X	X (If it has memory)
Anticipatory			
Purposive	Environment, previous state, and expectations	X	X
Purposeful	Environment, previous state, expectations, and will (whereby the system sets its own goals)	X	X

Source: Compiled by the author.

An Example of Purposeful Behavior

Purposeful behavior of a business is illustrated by a firm that, at time $t = 0$, is planning ahead to $t = 5$, and expects product prices to rise substantially between $t = 1$ and $t = 2$. To do the best it can over the whole planning period the firm may very well hold back sales and build inventories in the first period so that it can benefit more from the higher prices expected to rule in the second period.

A Frequent Error in Describing Purposeful Behavior

We should avoid making a mistake that is commonly made in explanations of purposeful behavior, which is to regard purposeful, if not all anticipatory, behavior as *determined* by the future (see Ackoff and Emery 1972). Bunge (1979b: 302ff) has pointed out the error by first agreeing that anticipatory behavior, be it conscious or unconscious, is not indifferent to the end (future) result, and occurs *as if* it were *somehow* directed by it. But *unconscious* (nonintentional) anticipatory behavior is actually determined by the immediately previous state, and the system's whole history of blind successes and failures and its environment. And what determines *conscious* (intentional) anticipatory behavior is not the future, but an idea of the future, thought in the present and the environment. (Those who do not like the idea of "ideas" determining future physical events can regard an idea of the future as a present neurophysiological process.)

Organismic or Social

We can now infer two differences between living organisms and organizations. From the section "Degree of Complexity" earlier in this Appendix we can conclude that organizations have a higher level of complexity than the organisms of which they are constituted. Their states characteristically have more degrees of freedom and they can survive a wider range and variety of shocks than organisms can. From the last section we can derive another difference, namely that the parts of an organization possess will, whereas in an organism only the whole does. We should take these differences into consideration whenever we are concerned with planning (and controlling) organizational behavior. And we should keep them in mind also whenever applying systems theories to the study of organizations, for much of the development of systems theories has hitherto had only organismic or mechanistic systems in mind, not organizations.

COMPLEX, ADAPTIVE SYSTEMS AS MODERATELY INTEGRATED

A final feature of systems we should examine is degree of integration (cohesion, wholeness, systemicity).

Complexity and Integration are Inversely Related. So are System Integration and Subsystem Integration

Recall from previous sections ("Structure: The Second Aspect of Systems" and "A System as an Ordered Composition-Structure-Environment Triple") that a system is modeled in terms of components, an environment, and a structure consisting of the relations between components (inner couplings) and relations between the latter and the environment (outer couplings). The system's degree of integration is then measured by the strength, quality, variety, and number of the inner *couplings* relative to the effect of disintegrating actions by the environment on the system. Thus a human community is stable as long as it is held together by shared values and interests, the strength of which is greater than that of internal rivalries and conflicts and environmental disturbances.

Bunge (1979a) notes that in the case of physical, chemical, and perhaps biological systems, what measures their degree of integration is their binding energy or equivalently their dissociation energy. For example, if two things, 1 and 2, form a linear system represented by the equations

$$\frac{dF_1}{dt} = a_{11}F_1 + a_{12}F_2$$

$$\frac{dF_2}{dt} = a_{21}F_1 + a_{22}F_2,$$

the degree of integration of the system can be defined as:

$$w = \frac{|a_{12}|}{|a_{11} + a_{12}|} + \frac{|a_{21}|}{|a_{21} + a_{22}|}$$

assuming the a_{ij} are time invariant. If $a_{12} = a_{21} = 0$, the components do not form a system; in every other case they do. If all the $a_{ij} = 1$, then $w = 1$, and the system is maximally cohesive.

But such a measure cannot be generalized to systems where information links play at least as important an integrating role as energy forces, as is the case with social systems. Hence, there is no universal measure available of the degree of integration of a system.

It can be postulated that, for any given kind of system in a given environment, there is a minimum *size* (number of components) below which the aggregate is not integrated, and a maximum size above which the system becomes unstable and breaks down. Indeed, it can be established empirically that the greater the complexity of a system the lower, in general, is its degree of integration. A further inverse relation can be established between the integration of subsystems and that of the system. That is, if the components of a system are themselves systems, the integration of the subsystems competes with that of the system.

Conditions Necessary for an Open Negentropic System to Adapt

All this has some relevance to the question of what conditions are necessary for an open negentropic system to adapt successfully. It turns out that, for the negentropic system to adapt, not all components should be as tightly coupled as possible, but rather that components whose activities are related should be well linked while those with unrelated activities should not be (Ashby 1952: 154–57). Some of the links between components may take place through the environment rather than directly. Adaptation thus demands independence (restriction of communication) as well as integration (communication). Care must be taken to avoid too much integration, which increases the time required for adaptation to occur.

Human Beings and Human Organizations Have Loosely Coupled Components

Human beings and human organizations are highly complex open negentropic systems that are not tightly knit throughout. While the number of couplings between components or subsystems may be very large, many of these may be temporary and conditional, one component or subsystem affecting another only under certain conditions, such as when a certain variable remains constant except when the disturbance coming to the system exceeds a certain threshold value. Many of the variables pertaining to the environment (at least the natural physical environment) may likewise be constant over appreciable intervals of time, a fact not of great help to us since the greater part of the environment of an organization, indeed of social systems generally, consists of other organizations that are less stable than the natural physical environment (see Chapter 8, "Planning is Futile in Large Organizations"). The whole thus typically comprises a set of subsystems within which components are highly coupled, but between which couplings (and hence communication) are more restricted. According to Ashby (1952: 208), this is commonly the case with almost all natural systems, a fortunate fact, for without it adaptation would take an unconscionably long time.

SUMMARY

We take a systems approach to discussing planning because it has the greatest explanatory power and represents an attempt at complete scientific explanation, wherein synthesis accompanies analysis whenever the thing to be explained is a "system." Recent interest in ecology has been one manifestation of awareness of the systemic character of the firm. We have seen that the minimal model of a system includes three things: composition, environment, and structure, where "structure" consists of the relations between the parts of the system, and between the latter and the environment (thus differing from the common notion of organizational structure, which includes only the first set of relations). We have also seen how systems may be classified in various ways: as natural or artifact, by how they are represented, by degree of complexity, as closed or open, as entropic or negentropic, by type of behavior and, finally as organismic or social. Human beings and social organizations were characterized as complex, adaptive, purposeful, negentropic systems. The idea that a system is "open" if certain things are exchanged across its boundaries was found to be trivial, since all systems except the universe are at some time "open" in this sense, and because such a definition tells us nothing about the behavior of the system. Bertalanffy was the first to view an open system as a system that is open to entropy transfer and that typically becomes negentropic. Such a system (open and negentropic) differs dramatically in its typical behavior from systems not having this capability: it can adapt and survive by maintaining a high energy level and increasing in complexity (changing its internal organizational structure, sometimes by changing the environment in its favor), and reach its goals from different starting points and by different paths. In its human forms (human beings and social organizations) it is also purposeful (capable of learning, forming expectations, and selecting its own goals), and its components and subsystems are typically loosely coupled.

The central theme of this book is that by continuing to discuss planning (and control) within a closed entropic system framework, as accounting does at present, we are missing important insights. Accordingly, readers are urged to gain a good grasp of the notion of a negentropic system and of a business enterprise as a purposeful system whose parts, if they are systems, are also purposeful systems.

NOTES

1. This section, and to a lesser extent other parts of this Appendix, draws on Bunge (1977, 1979a).

2. See Amey (1980) for further discussion of this point.

3. To understand what is meant by the term *steady state,* consider a model of the production of a firm with two inputs, K (capital) and L (labor), and a single output, Q. Rates of output and input per unit of time are related in the production function

$$Q = a \, L_1^\beta \, K_2^\beta \qquad\qquad\qquad \text{A.10}$$

If constant rates of input of L and K are yielding a constant rate of output Q this is formally expressed by setting the time derivatives of L, K, and Q equal to zero:

$$\frac{dL}{dt} = \frac{dK}{dt} = \frac{dQ}{dt} = 0. \qquad\qquad \text{A.11}$$

The system is then in a steady state with respect to all its input and output variables, *providing* that this stationary state is also stable in some sense (that any movements away from this state remain within certain bounds).

Since most of the variables with which we are concerned are *observed* to change only at discrete intervals of time it may be more appropriate to express the model in discrete form (in terms of a difference rather than a differential equation). Letting $q_t = \log Q_t$, $l_t = \log L_t$, $k_t = \log K_t$, and $\gamma = \log a$, the model represented by Equation A.10 may be linearized to give

$$q_t = \gamma + \beta_1 l_t + \beta_2 k_t \qquad\qquad\qquad \text{A.12}$$

Taking first differences we have, corresponding to Equation A.11′ in the continuous case:

$$\Delta q_t = \beta_1 \Delta l_t + \beta_2 \Delta k_t \qquad\qquad\qquad \text{A.13}$$

A steady state with respect to all system variables would then be described by the condition

$$\Delta q_t = \Delta l_t = \Delta k_t = 0 \qquad\qquad\qquad \text{A.14}$$

for all t in the steady-state interval, providing again that this state shows stability in some sense. An *equilibrium* state of this system occurs when $q_t = q_0$, $l_t = l_0$, and $k_t = k_0$, and is given by

$$q_0 = l_0 = k_0 = -\infty \qquad\qquad\qquad\text{A.15}$$

(corresponding to $Q^* = L^* = K^* = 0$ in terms of the original variables), where the zero subscript denotes the initial values of the variables. The precise meaning of *steady state* is not well defined, however, until the following particulars are specified:

(a) Which features of the system are being considered (e.g., all system variables or only some of them)
(b) How these features are measured, and
(c) With what frequency they are measured (e.g., "stationary" may imply, not constancy over time, but behavior that is periodically repetitive over time—one of the ways in which it is understood in economics).

REFERENCES

Ackoff, R.L. 1971. "Towards a System of Systems Concepts." *Management Science* 17: 661–71.

_____. 1974. *Redesigning the Future*. New York: Wiley-Interscience.

Ackoff, R.L. and F.E. Emery. 1972. *On Purposeful Systems*. Chicago, IL: Aldine-Atherton.

Amey, L.R. 1979. *Budget Planning and Control Systems*. London: Pitman.

_____. 1980. "System Objectives and Budgetary Control." *Behavioral Science* 25 (March): 130–39.

Ashby, W.R. 1952. *Design for a Brain*. London: Chapman & Hall.

Bertalanffy, L. von. 1950. "The Theory of Open Systems in Physics and Biology." *Science* 111: 23–29.

Boulding, K.E. 1956. "General Systems Theory—The Skeleton of Science." *Management Science* 2: 197–208.

Buckley, W. 1968. "Society as a Complex Adaptive System." In *Modern Systems Research for the Behavioral Scientist*, edited by W. Buckley, pp. 490–513. Chicago, IL: Aldine.

_____. 1967. *Sociology and Modern Systems Theory*. Englewood Cliffs, NJ: Prentice-Hall.

Bunge, M. 1977. *Ontology I: The Furniture of the World, Treatise on Basic Philosophy,* vol. 3. Dordrecht, Holland: Reidel.

_____. 1979. *Ontology II: A World of Systems, Treatise on Basic Philosophy,* vol. 4. Dordrecht, Holland: Reidel.

_____. 1979b. *Causality and Modern Science,* 3d rev. ed. New York: Dover.

Churchman, C.W. 1968. *The Systems Approach.* New York: Delta.

Simon, H.A. 1969. "The Architecture of Complexity." In *The Sciences of the Artificial,* edited by H.A. Simon, chapter 4. Cambridge, MA: MIT Press.

Zadeh, L.A. and E. Polak. 1969. *System Theory.* New York: McGraw-Hill.

Index

AUTHOR INDEX

267

SUBJECT INDEX

About the Author

Lloyd R. Amey is Professor and Head of Accounting at McGill University, Montreal. He received his Ph.D. in economics from the University of Nottingham, England, and is a CPA (Australia). He has taught in England, the United States, and Canada. In addition to *Corporate Planning*, Professor Amey is the author of *The Efficiency of Business Enterprises*, *Budget Planning and Control Systems*, and numerous journal articles. He is the coauthor, with D.A. Egginton, of *Management Accounting: A Conceptual Approach* and the editor of *Readings in Management Decision*.